DECISION ANALYSIS

Introductory Lectures on Choices under Uncertainty

DECISION ANALYSIS

Introductory Lectures on Choices under Uncertainty

HOWARD RAIFFA

Harvard University

ADDISON-WESLEY

Reading, Massachusetts

Menlo Park, California / *London* / *Don Mills, Ontario*

This book is in

the Addison-Wesley Series in

BEHAVIORAL SCIENCE: QUANTITATIVE METHODS

Frederick Mosteller, *Consulting Editor*

Second printing, July 1970

AL 1/73 06290

To Arthur H. Copeland, Sr.

PREFACE

More often than not, the decisions you make in your personal or professional life can be made without a lot of fuss. Either your best choice is clear to you without much analysis, or the decision is not important enough to warrant any great amount of attention. Occasionally, however, you probably find yourself in a situation where you feel it is worth your time and effort to think systematically and hard about the different courses of action you might pursue. You might even be willing to push a few numbers around, if you thought it would help you make a better decision. In these lectures I suggest a scheme you can use to organize and systematize your thinking when you encounter a situation in which you must make a difficult and important decision. As we unfold the organizational scheme I have in mind, we shall find ourselves particularly concerned with situations in which the consequences of any action you may take are not certain, because events may intervene that you cannot control or predict with certainty and whose outcomes will inevitably affect your final condition. Surely an atmosphere of such uncertainty overcasts many of the real situations in which you have to make a decision of lasting importance.

In very rough terms, the analysis of a decision problem under uncertainty requires that you

1) list the viable options available to you for gathering information, for experimentation, and for action;

2) list the events that may possibly occur;

3) arrange in chronological order the information you may acquire and the choices you may make as time goes on;

4) decide how well you like the consequences that result from the various courses of action open to you; and

5) judge what the chances are that any particular uncertain event will occur.

After you have taken these five steps—that is, after you have systematically described your problem and recorded your judgments and preferences—you can begin to synthesize information. You first make a series of calculations and then fix on a certain strategy that you believe you ought to follow in information gathering, experimentation, and action. You will select this strategy because it seems the best of the many that are available to you. I do not assert that the strategy you will choose is "best" in any universal sense. However, as compared with the body of strategies that you thought it worthwhile to consider as candidates in the first place, it is the best strategy *you* can choose for the situation at hand. Naturally, you have brought to bear on the whole analytical process your basic preferences for consequences, your judgments about uncertain quantities, and your personal understanding of the structure of your problem; in this important sense, you are yourself a part of the analytical process.

These lectures do not present a *descriptive* theory of actual behavior. Neither do they present a *positive* theory of behavior for a superintelligent, fictitious being; nowhere in our analysis shall we refer to the behavior of an "idealized, rational, and economic man", a man who always acts in a perfectly consistent manner as if somehow there were embedded in his nature a coherent set of evaluation patterns that cover any and all eventualities. Rather, the approach we take *prescribes* how an individual who is faced with a problem of choice under uncertainty should go about choosing a course of action that is consistent with his personal basic judgments and preferences. He must consciously police the consistency of his subjective inputs and *calculate* their implications for action. Such an approach is designed to help us reason and act a bit more systematically—when we choose to do so!

The methodology of these lectures requires that preferences for consequences be numerically scaled in terms of *utility values* and that judgments about uncertainties be numerically scaled in terms of *probabilities*. I dwell at length on the intertwining concepts of utility and subjective probability, and demonstrate that these concepts are logical concomitants of some very basic behavioral assumptions. These matters lie at the heart of a continuing controversy about the foundations of statistical decision theory and of statistical inference. I adopt the so-called Bayesian viewpoint, which uses both utilities and subjective probabilities; and after arguing the validity of this approach throughout most of the book I attempt to locate it in a broader perspective in the final chapter, which is devoted to a brief historical account of the theory of subjective probability and an overview of the different existing schools of statistical thought.

Chapters 0 and 1 are short, easy to read, and should give you a fairly detailed idea of what is in the first eight chapters of the book. I shall not repeat that material here. By the time you reach Chapter 9, the next-to-last chapter, I shall have introduced and illustrated all the main concepts of the book. Under the title "The Art of Implementation", Chapter 9 discusses how we can modify our analysis so that we can handle large, complex, messy problems and still deal effectively with administrative realities.

There is a great deal of overlap between the subject matter of these lectures and the fields of game theory, Operations Research, and Systems Analysis. In the last chapter of the book, "Further Perspectives, and a Guide to the Literature", I trace out some of the interconnections between these fields.

I refer to this book as "Lectures" because it is an edited composite of several series of lectures I have given over the past decade. My audiences for these series of lectures have been heterogeneous, and I have been more concerned with getting across a point of view or attitude than with developing detailed techniques for the analysis of decisions under uncertainty. Of course, it is hard to talk in generalities all the time and I have developed some special techniques in this book, but for the most part I have done this to help make the concepts more understandable and the overall approach more credible. I want you to believe the methodological approach I suggest is reasonable *and practical*.

Although the approach that I have taken in these lectures is not new, I hope the style of presentation is. Most books on this subject, including some of my own, present the analytical material in a formal mathematical style not easily understood by the nonmathematician. This is unfortunate, since most of the basic ideas of decision analysis can be understood with a mathematical background of high school algebra or less; and furthermore, in complicated applied problems the mathematical part of the analysis is not necessarily the most intellectually challenging or important part. I have therefore taken considerable pains to keep down the mathematical demands upon the reader, and most of the book is free from algebraic and symbolic manipulations. Still, some sophistication in logical analysis is undoubtedly required throughout; the presentation, after all, purports to be reasoned and logical. Although calculus, for example, is not required, I hope that the mathematically trained reader will not be bored. Unless he has read widely in decision analysis, he will find material here that is new to him. He might wish that I had presented some material in a more symbolic, compact form, but the criterion for effectiveness should not be pages-per-thought but time-taken-per-thought, and I hope that the better-prepared among you can read this material rather quickly. I also admit to a certain degree of logical sloppiness that might bother some who are mathematically sophisticated. At times I have been intentionally sloppy to keep down the mathematical level, and my rationalization is that if you are sophisticated enough to worry about pathological counterexamples that have not been ruled out with certain continuity assumptions, then you are sophisticated enough to take the next step and read the technical literature. I have not intentionally suppressed assumptions that really matter from an applied point of view.

If I have not failed completely in keeping down the mathematical level of these lectures, then there should be something of interest here for a wide audience. Indeed, the book should be suitable for independent reading by anyone who occasionally has to make important decisions of his own or anyone who has to help others in their decision-making processes. Businessmen, engineers, administrators, judges, doctors, and some scientists are in part professional decision makers and as such they may find the approach taken in this book relevant to the realities of their spheres of operation.

I did not write this book as a self-contained text for a full-semester course. It can be used as such, in my opinion, only if the instructor can furnish his own exercises or case material. However, I think it is appropriate to use it for short special courses (for example, in-service courses for management) or as supplementary reading matter in relevant courses.

Parts of the book can be omitted without interrupting the continuity of the whole. These parts have been clearly indicated by footnoting the titles of sections that can be skipped. Usually these sections develop side issues that I find interesting, and in some of these sections I have not felt compelled to hold down the mathematical symbolism to a bare minimum. Chapter 8, *Risk Sharing and Group Decisions*, is a case in point. This chapter is more symbolic and abstract than the rest of the book, but anyone who has struggled through any mathematics at the level of calculus should not be troubled. I wrestled with the thought of rewriting the chapter, or even deleting it, but since the material is both interesting (I think) and not essential for the succeeding chapters, I have left it just as is.

Acknowledgments. Although I have not received any financial support expressly for the preparation of this book, this project has been considerably helped indirectly by the generous support I have received for research on decision analysis from the Division of Research at the Harvard Business School and from a grant from the National Science Foundation. The earliest version of these lecture notes was prepared in 1961 as part of a course I gave on probability, statistics, and decision theory for the Institute of Basic Mathematics for Application to Business, sponsored by the Ford Foundation. Those notes were then revised and amplified a bit when I gave a series of lectures in the summer of 1963 at Gösing, Austria for a special symposium on Mathematics for Social Scientists sponsored by UNESCO.* In 1965, while I was a Visiting Professor at the Graduate School of Business Administration, Stanford University, I delivered a series of 15 two-hour lectures on decision analysis for which I completely reworked the '63 notes and added about half the material that now comprises Chapters 8, 9 and 10 of the present version. I hope by publishing this '68 version that I will finally bring to an end this escalating cycle of informal revisions.

In the last ten years I have collaborated closely with Robert Schlaifer and John Pratt, and I am grateful for the stimulation of their insights and ideas, many of which are reflected in this book.

On the basis of behavioral assumptions, Chapters 4 and 5 develop a justification for introducing subjective probabilities and utilities. I have adapted this particular development from a paper written by John Pratt, Robert Schlaifer, and myself entitled "The Foundations of Decision Under Uncertainty: An Elementary Exposition", which appeared in the *Journal of the American Statistical Association*, June 1964, Vol. 59.

The results in Chapter 8 date back to a series of seminar talks I gave in 1961. While perhaps I posed a few fundamental questions for research, most of the relevant answers came from contributions by John Pratt, Robert Wilson, and Richard Zeckhauser.

In preparing an earlier version of these lecture notes, Charles Zartman, who was then my research assistant, helped me with all sorts of tedious arithmetical and logical details. Through the years I have found errors in some computations, but invariably these seem to be my mistakes and not his.

Chapter 9 has profited considerably from my numerous discussions of the subject with John Hammond and Sigurd Andersen.

* These lectures were compiled by Sternberg *et al.*, and published in *Mathematics and Social Sciences I.* Proceedings of the Seminars of Menthon-Saint-Bernard, France (1–27 July 1960) and of Gösing, Austria (3–27 July 1962).

My special thanks go to John Bewick and Walter McBeth, who have made numerous suggestions that have improved both the clarity of the exposition and the style of writing.

My thanks also go to Mrs. Mary Gambolati, who typed the last draft of this book while juggling numerous other secretarial chores in an efficient and amiable manner.

Fred Mosteller, long before he became an editor of the Addison-Wesley Series on Statistics, encouraged me to publish the earliest version of these notes. I don't think I originally intended ever to work up the notes for publication; it was at Mosteller's gentle prodding that I finally decided to make the time to do the necessary polishing. In the process, the length of the notes grew by a factor of four and some of the original informality may have disappeared. Still, I hope that the final product will be readable, and that you won't get bogged down in the details that I have added.

Boston, Massachusetts   H. R.
June 1968

CONTENTS

INTRODUCTION

1. ORIENTATION

Here is the way these lectures will proceed. I shall first present a few thumbnail sketches of situations in which decisions must be made in the absence of complete information. I shall then point out that there is a structure of abstract elements that is common to all these illustrative decision problems under uncertainty. Chapter 1 states a concrete instance of this abstract structure by posing a basic problem in which *you*, the reader, will play the role of the decision maker. Initially, the basic problem is a noncontroversial one, theoretically speaking; practically all decision analysts would concur with the advice I shall give you to help you analyze this problem. Subsequent chapters introduce complicating features into this decision problem one at a time, complications that are designed to show you that you need more and more methodological concepts as the problem becomes more and more sophisticated. Some of this methodology is controversial, however, and you will find that any particular resolution of such controversy has both pragmatic and philosophical implications.

Expert statisticians, probabilists, and decision analysts differ from each other about the philosophical foundations of the subject of decision analysis, and also about the advice they think they should offer to a practitioner in a specific situation. It is only fair to state at the outset that I belong to a minority party, the so-called Bayesians* (an outright misnomer, but that is beside the point), and in the course of these lectures I shall set forth my party platform as I see it. There are some rough spots in our theory and we are not wholly invulnerable to attack, but it is infuriating to be attacked for the wrong reasons. I hope these lectures will serve to highlight certain philosophical issues over which intelligent professionals may respectfully disagree with one another and thereby place these issues in a more realistic perspective. This will also help to make it clear why a Bayesian might offer the advice he does in a specific situation.

Roughly speaking, the Bayesians, or *subjectivists*, wish to introduce intuitive judgments and feelings directly into the formal analysis of a decision problem. The non-Bayesians, or *objectivists*, feel that these subjective aspects are best left out of the formal analysis and should be used only, if at all, to bridge the gap between the real world and the objective results one obtains using a formal model. This is admittedly a gross oversimplification, but it should suffice to make you aware of the fundamental importance of the philosophical issues as they arise in the sequel.

2. THUMBNAIL SKETCHES OF DECISION PROBLEMS

An Oil Drilling Problem. An oil wildcatter must decide whether or not to drill at a given site before his option expires. He is uncertain about many things: the cost of drilling, the extent of the oil or gas deposits at the site, the cost of raising the oil, and so forth. He has available the objective records of similar and not-quite-so-similar drillings in this same basin, and he has discussed the peculiar features of this particular deal with his geologist, his geophysicist, and his land agent. He can gain further relevant information (but still not perfect information) about the underlying geophysical structure at this site by conducting seismic soundings. This information, however, is quite costly, and his problem is to decide whether or not to collect this information before he makes his final decision: to drill or not to drill.

Introduction of a New Drug. The president of a pharmaceutical firm must decide whether or not to market a newly developed drug for a skin allergy.

---

* Reverend Thomas Bayes, in "An Essay toward Solving a Problem in the Doctrine of Chance", *Philosophical Transactions of the Royal Society*, 1763, suggested that probability judgments based on mere hunches should be combined with probabilities based on relative frequencies by the use of Bayes' Theorem, a rather simple result using conditional probabilities.

He is uncertain about many things: the proportion of patients who will be cured, the proportion of patients who will have deleterious side effects, the demand for the drug at a given price assuming a given cure rate and a given side-effect rate, and so forth. He has available the scientific reports of his technical staff, the judgments of his marketing group, and the results of a pilot experiment conducted in a penal institution. He can gain further information about the cure rate and side-effects rate by conducting extensive experimental clinical trials with controls. Such trials, however, are costly and time consuming. Should he experiment further? If so, how much? Of course, he is not a completely free agent; he must act within the constraints set down by the Food and Drug Administration.

Introduction of a New Product. A large chemical company has successfully completed its research on the development of a new, long-lasting house paint. Its officers must decide whether they should manufacture this product themselves, and if so, what size plant to build, or whether they should sell or lease their patents and technical know-how to a firm that deals exclusively with the manufacture and distribution of house paints. Their principal sources of uncertainty are the proportion of the market they will get at a given price and advertising expenditure if they manufacture the product themselves, and the time before a competitor introduces a similar product. They can obtain some experimental information bearing indirectly on their future market penetration by interviewing a sample of paint distributors, but this information must be very carefully assessed because the distributors might not actually do what they say they will do. How should the company proceed?

Treatment of an Illness. A doctor does not know whether his patient's sore throat is caused by strep or by a virus. If he knew it were strep, he would prescribe penicillin pills or injection, whereas if he knew it were a virus, he would prescribe rest, gargle, and aspirin. Failure to treat a strep throat by penicillin (or other drugs) may result in a serious disease, such as nephritis or rheumatic heart disease. However, penicillin must not be administered indiscriminately since it may result in a penicillin reaction causing two to seven days of extreme discomfort, or, in very rare cases, death; and furthermore, penicillin-resistant bacteria might develop.

The physician may take a throat culture, which will indicate the presence or absence of strep. This test, however, is imperfect since (1) the bacteria may die before they are transplanted to the culture medium and (2) the presence of strep does not necessarily mean that the strep is causing the sore throat.

The physician must choose one of several possible strategies:

1) take no culture, treat the infection as viral;

2) take no culture, prescribe penicillin injection;

3) take no culture, prescribe penicillin pills for ten days;

4) take a culture, prescribe pills or injection only if positive;

5) take a culture *and* prescribe pills, and then continue pills if positive and stop pills if negative.

What should the physician do?

Government Investment in R&D.   A government official must decide whether to invest in a ten-year R&D program to develop fast-breeder reactors. Presently known supplies of low-cost uranium are sufficient for only eight years if the demand for nuclear power increases as expected. If no new sources of low-cost ore are discovered, the electricity costs in conventional nuclear power plants will rise rapidly. Now the point of the breeder reactor is that it acts as a source of fissionable fuel, generating more than it consumes; and therefore it reduces our dependence on natural ore. The use of breeder reactors would allow us to maintain present low electricity costs even if cheap ores were to become scarce.   Private industrial sources have suggested several different innovations for the construction of such reactors, all of which depend on different heat-transfer materials. The official is uncertain, however, whether a fast reactor can be built which is both safe and economical.

The decision maker must decide whether to launch a crash program of breeder development with the option of halting it later if new low-cost ore is discovered, or whether to launch a modest R&D program having a more distant completion date, in the expectation that there will be subsequent ore discoveries. He must also decide whether to concentrate all research on one innovation or to divide funds among several parallel projects until more information is available about the ultimate success of each.

The Common Abstraction

In these lectures, we shall discuss how a decision maker can make a deliberate, reasoned, and logical analysis of his problem, an analysis that can suggest to him his best course of experimentation and action in an uncertain environment. In each of the thumbnail sketches, I have assumed that the decision maker must make a choice, or a sequence of choices, among various possible courses of action; that the consequence of any course of action depends on an unpredictable event or "state of the world"; that the decision maker already has some information at hand that bears on the uncertainties of his problem and therefore can make some judgments about these uncertainties; and that he can obtain further information, at a cost, that bears on these uncertainties. We shall assume that the decision maker wishes to choose a strategy for experimentation and action that is logically consistent with 1) his basic preferences for consequences, and 2) his basic judgments about the unknown states or events.

CHAPTER 1

YOUR BASIC PROBLEM

1. INTRODUCTION

For many years, I have discussed and argued the foundations of probability, statistics, and decision theory, and have found that most people argue as though they are passive observers on the sidelines, as it were. They talk as though someone else, someone none too bright, some disembodied character, were the decision maker. Since there is no point in your getting prematurely embroiled in the psychological foibles of others, let us first concentrate on what choice *you*, the reader, would want to make in a given situation. Therefore let us discuss a concrete decision problem under uncertainty with *you* cast in the role of the decision maker, a decision problem in which *you* are asked to make the choice.

2. THE STATEMENT OF YOUR PROBLEM

Please imagine a collection of 1000 urns, each of which has one of the labels "theta sub one" (θ_1) or "theta sub two" (θ_2) pasted on its front.* Each urn contains red balls and black balls, the particular composition of the

---

* It would be more natural to label the urns as U_1 and U_2 (mnemonic for Urn) or as S_1 and S_2 (mnemonic for State), but we must reserve the symbols U and S for other purposes later on.

contents depending on whether the urn is of type θ_1 or type θ_2. In particular,

i) a θ_1-urn contains $\begin{cases} \text{four red balls,} \\ \text{six black balls,} \end{cases}$

and

ii) a θ_2-urn contains $\begin{cases} \text{nine red balls,} \\ \text{one black ball.} \end{cases}$

Now the gentleman to whom the 1000 urns belong (we shall call him the experimenter) selects one of them at random; by this we mean that each urn has the same chance of being selected. He places this urn on a table in front of you, but he removes the distinguishing label, θ_1 or θ_2, before you can note which type of urn it is. We shall assume that the urn is opaque and that you cannot see its contents. If the urn is of type θ_1, then we shall say in elliptical fashion that "the *true state* is θ_1". Analogously, when we say "the *true state* is θ_2", we shall mean that the urn is of type θ_2.

You are now asked to guess the type of urn that is on the table before you. If you guess correctly, you will win some money, but if you are wrong, you will lose money. You have three possible courses of action to choose from. They are

a_1: *Guess the urn is of type θ_1,*
a_2: *Guess the urn is of type θ_2,*
a_3: *Refuse to play.*

Now we come to the payoffs. If you choose a_3, then you get nothing and you pay nothing. However, if you choose either a_1 or a_2, then your monetary payment depends on whether θ_1 or θ_2 is the true state. In particular, if you choose

a_1, then $\begin{cases} \text{you win \$40.00 if } \theta_1 \text{ is the true state,} \\ \text{you lose \$20.00 if } \theta_2 \text{ is the true state,} \end{cases}$

and if you choose

a_2, then $\begin{cases} \text{you win \$100.00 if } \theta_2 \text{ is the true state,} \\ \text{you lose \$5.00 if } \theta_1 \text{ is the true state.} \end{cases}$

You might reasonably ask at this point, "Whom am I winning from or losing to?" The realism gets a little ticklish here, and we must guard against some possible misunderstanding. Let's say that you are winning from or losing to the experimenter, who is just manipulating the funds given to him by Foundation F to study decision behavior. Eventually all the funds will go to one subject or another or go back to the Foundation. The experimenter is neither trying to outguess you, nor playing a competitive game against you.

He is trying desperately to be neutral. Your only concern is your own monetary affairs, and you are not to worry about Foundation F or about such notions as "If I win, then someone else will not have an opportunity to win." Be single-mindedly selfish. Remember that it's your money that's at stake and not someone else's, and that not all the advice you will receive in these lectures is considered "good" advice by all the professionals in this game.

You may obtain additional information that will assist you in your basic choice between a_1 and a_2 and a_3 by selecting one of several *experimental alternatives*.

e_1: For a payment of $8.00, you can draw a single ball at random from the unidentified urn on the table.

e_2: For a payment of $12.00, you can draw two balls from the unidentified urn.

e_s: For a payment of $9.00, you can draw a single ball from the unidentified urn and *then*, after looking at the withdrawn ball, you can decide whether or not you want to draw out another for an additional $4.50. You can even have the privilege, free of charge, of deciding whether or not you should replace the first withdrawn ball from the urn before you make your second drawing.

You need to have one final but crucial piece of information. You already know that the experimenter has selected the urn on the table from a group of 1000 urns, some of which are of type θ_1 and some of which are of type θ_2. You also know that he has selected it at random. Now note this fact: *800 of the urns are of type θ_1 and 200 are of type θ_2.*

In Chapter 2 we (you and I) shall analyze the above problem in some detail. For your convenience we shall summarize the data of your problem in tabular display in that chapter.

3. VARIATIONS ON THE THEME OF YOUR PROBLEM

We shall introduce complicating features into your decision problem one at a time, starting in Chapter 3. The first part of that chapter will tell you that some monetary payoffs are not certain but are "fuzzy". We shall assume, however, that this fuzziness can be captured in terms of a probability distribution. You will then have to decide how much you would be willing to pay to eliminate some of this fuzziness.

In the second part of Chapter 3, we shall discuss the problem of *measurement bias*—in your decision problem, temporary color blindness. If a red is occasionally reported to you as a black or vice versa, then what are the implications for optimal sample design? How does it distort the results of sampling? How great does this bias have to become before you should give up sampling altogether?

Chapter 4 assumes that you, the decision maker, have an aversion to risk; for example, you would prefer not to take a 50-50 bet that loses or wins you $100.00. Although all probabilities remain crystal clear and objective, we shall assume that you do not wish to play the actuarial, long-run values. This chapter also shows you how you can use the modern theory of utility to help you select your course of action. You may decide not to follow the advice which is given, but remember: You *must* choose, for indecision or refusal to play will be interpreted as a definite choice that has a payoff and a consequence for you. It goes without saying that since *you* are the decision maker, you always have the right of peremptory challenge and you can refuse to follow any advice for no better reason than because it leaves you uncomfortable. In this chapter, we shall also discuss how nonmonetary payoffs, so-called intangibles, can be analyzed.

In Chapter 5, we shall begin to cloud the probabilities. First, the 800-to-200 breakdown of θ_1's and θ_2's will no longer be a sure fact; the breakdown might be 700 to 300, or 900 to 100, and each of these breakdowns is equally likely. Does the analysis of your problem change? Next we shall go to the case in which you are not told the original number of θ_1's and θ_2's; instead, the experimenter allows you a quick look at the thousand urns and their labels, too quick a look for you to do any systematic counting. Should you process your vague information or should you forget about these subjective appraisals and work with the hard objective numbers? We shall discuss whether you should treat subjective probabilities as if they were objective, and I shall try to persuade you that you should. Then, given your vague impressions about the number of θ_1's and θ_2's, we shall investigate how much you should be willing to pay for the exact count.

Chapter 6 discusses another way of analyzing the decision problem posed in Chapter 5. Instead of introducing judgmental probabilities (these are controversial!) at the outset of the analysis, we shall try to see how far you can go with a more objective analysis, and at the very end of this chapter I shall present you with an argument designed to convince you to process your feelings in terms of a judgmental probability distribution. Thus I shall make two efforts to persuade you to use judgmental probabilities in your analysis of a decision problem under uncertainty: one in Chapter 5 and one in Chapter 6.

I might remark that it is important that we maintain perspective throughout these deliberations. Obviously neither one of us is really concerned with the particular decision problem posed to you in these lectures. Our interest rather is in the class of real-world problems from which this allegorical abstraction has been created. Should subjective probabilities be used in a formal manner in analyzing real-world problems? This is the issue, and it is a major issue for both practitioners and theorists.

In Chapter 7, we shall assume that you have obtained some vague information about the proportion of θ_1-urns and then ask whether you should pay $5.00 for the exact count. The experimenter will then offer you the opportunity to take a random sample of these urns at $0.05 an urn. Such a sample will obviously enable you to refine your judgment concerning the proportion of θ_1-urns. Should you sample? If so, how much?

The genus of problem discussed in Chapter 7 is of great practical importance. Instead of the proportion p of urns of type θ_1, a decision maker might be interested in the proportion p of individuals in a target population who have a given attribute, or of heart patients who have a given symptom, or of students who learn more under one mode of instruction than under another, or of potential customers who will purchase a new product if it is introduced at a certain price, and so forth. By means of a dialogue I shall show how an individual can scale his judgments about an uncertain proportion and how his judgments should be modified in the light of sample information.

Chapter 8 treats the problem of risk sharing and selected topics in group decision-making. Suppose that because of your past industriousness and general business acumen, you have acquired the exclusive rights to a business venture which, when analyzed, turns out to have the same structure as your basic decision problem. Because this venture is larger in scale, however, all monetary amounts are multiplied by 1000; instead of paying $8.00 to take a single drawing, you now must pay $8000.00, and so forth. To engage in this venture you need more money than you have—still it looks like a good deal. Perhaps you should borrow the necessary capital, or perhaps you should share the risks with a partner, or perhaps you should incorporate and sell shares of stock. What happens if your newly acquired business associates have different attitudes towards risk, or disagree with your judgments about uncertain events? If you form a group, should its external behavior follow the same guidelines that I have suggested for so-called individual rationality?

In Chapter 9, I make the observation that real problems rarely fall into the simple mold considered thus far, and I try to correct some of the misconceptions that may have arisen because of the simplicity of the artificial problem posed for you. In this chapter we shall look at the art of implementation: how the theory must be bent, twisted, and extended, sometimes in a precarious fashion, to cope with the realities of complex problems. I summarize what I believe are some of the salient benefits, limitations, and dangers that arise from performing systematic analyses of decision problems.

The last chapter sketches some broader perspectives. The chapter starts with some historical background for different interpretations of probability, gives an overview of the field of statistics, and indicates the relationships that decision analysis has with game theory, with systems analysis, and with that field-of-many-names sometimes known as Operations Research. This chapter also presents a brief annotated guide to the literature.

Finally I should like to say a word in defense of our hypothetical and somewhat academic urn problem. Instead of this excessively artificial problem I might have chosen problems that are more realistic; for example, inventory control, medical diagnostics, market research, or personnel classification. The hard fact is that problems are realistic only if they are complicated, in fact *too* complicated for us to handle without a good deal of formal probability theory. The probability calculations we shall require for the urn problem are rather straightforward and are easily understood; the urn problem therefore allows us to focus our full concentration on the central controversial aspects of the methodology rather than on the complexities of probability computations. Furthermore, as an extra (and quite significant) dividend, we shall find that when many of these real problems are formulated mathematically, they turn out to be structurally similar to our idealized urn problem or variations thereof.

CHAPTER 2

ANALYSIS OF
YOUR BASIC PROBLEM

1. THE DATA OF YOUR PROBLEM*

Let us return to your basic decision problem, which doesn't have any complicating frills. The data and monetary payoffs for this problem are summarized in Table 2.1. (The last row of Table 2.1 should be ignored for the time being.) You will recall that State θ_1 represents the event that the randomly selected urn is of type θ_1, and that State θ_2 is similarly defined. Suppose, that is, the urns were transparent, and that you could actually see contents of the unidentified urn as it stands on the table: If the true state of the urn is θ_1, then you would see contents as indicated in Fig. 2.1(a); and if its true state is θ_2, then you would see contents as indicated in Fig. 2.1(b).

TABLE 2.1
Monetary payoffs for all state-act pairs

State	Act			Probability of state
	a_1	a_2	a_3	
θ_1	40	−5	0	.80
θ_2	−20	100	0	.20
EMV	28	16	0	1.00 (total)

---

* This information is displayed on the last page of the book for your convenience.

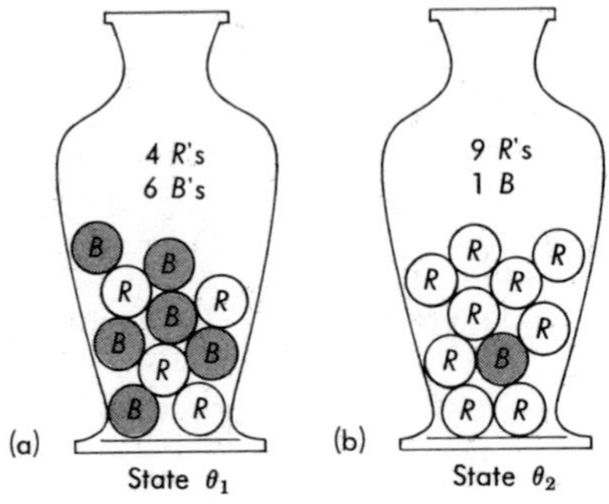

Figure 2.1

You will also recall that the unidentified urn on the table has been selected at random from a collection of 1000 urns: 800 of type θ_1, and the remaining 200 of type θ_2. The identity of the urn will of course influence your payoffs. You may take one of these experimental options:

e_0: no observations, at cost \$0.00,

e_1: a single observation, at cost \$8.00,

e_2: a pair of observations, at cost \$12.00,

e_s: a single observation at \$9.00 with the privilege of another observation at \$4.50. You also have the option of replacing the first ball. (The subscript s on e_s stands for "sequential".)

Finally, you will recall our notation for decisions on courses of action:

a_1: Guess the urn is of type θ_1,

a_2: Guess the urn is of type θ_2,

a_3: Refuse to play.

2. EXPECTED MONETARY VALUE (EMV)

You might answer the basic, uncomplicated problem posed to you without any hesitation whatsoever, by refusing to play (a_3). Some people will decide on a_3 right off because they think that if they do otherwise, there is some chance that they will lose at least \$5.00, and their potential winnings are not nearly high enough for them to justify the gamble. There is nothing irrational about this. Fairly frequently, for example, a person is not willing to pay \$10.00 for a fifty-fifty chance at \$0.00 or \$100.00. There are, however, other people who will pay \$49.00 or up to \$50.00 for this same gamble. There are still others who will pay \$52.00 because they are willing to pay a premium for the "thrill of the game", or, perhaps, because they feel that they can't do what they want to do with the \$52.00 of pocket money they now have, *but*, if they had \$100.00—

ah, then things would be ideal! Certainly it is unreasonable to expect that all people will gamble alike, *even* when the data are as objectively and unambiguously given as in your basic problem.

In this chapter, we shall analyze your basic problem from the point of view of the so-called EMV'ers. They constitute the class of people who are willing to act (so long as the stakes are not too large) on the basis of *expected monetary value* (EMV). The EMV of a gamble that results in a payoff of $0.00 or $100.00 with equal probabilities of $\frac{1}{2}$ is

$$\tfrac{1}{2}(\$0.00) + \tfrac{1}{2}(\$100.00) = \$50.00.$$

In general, one obtains the EMV of a gamble with several possible outcomes by multiplying each possible cash outcome by its probability and summing these products over all the possible outcomes. For example, deciding on a_1 in your problem without any experimentation would lead to a return of $40.00 if θ_1 is true (this has a probability .8), or a return of $-\$20.00$ if θ_2 is true (this has a probability of .2). Therefore this gamble is worth

$$.8(\$40.00) + .2(-\$20.00) = \$28.00,$$

and this is the figure in which the EMV'er is interested. For the purposes of this chapter, we shall assume that *you* are an EMV'er; but even if you aren't (and many are not), it will still be helpful for you to go through this preliminary stage before handling the complexities a non-EMV'er presents.

There is a technical expression, "certainty monetary equivalent" (CME), we often apply to an uncertain or risky prospect. For example, we might have said that for an EMV'er, the CME of the option that gives .8 probability of $40.00 and .2 probability of $-\$20.00$ is $28.00. This means that an EMV'er who enjoys the rights to this option would not sell or exchange these rights for less than $28.00, but would sell it for more than $28.00. A non-EMV'er might very well assign a CME to this same gamble at some such price as $15.00 or $10.00, or even $0.00.

3.　ANALYSIS OF THE NO-EXPERIMENT ALTERNATIVE

By referring to the first two rows of Table 2.1, you can see that if you do not experiment, then as an EMV'er you should evaluate a_1, a_2, and a_3 as follows:

a_1:　.8 ($40.00) + .2(−$20.00) = $28.00,
a_2:　.8(−$5.00) + .2($100.00) = $16.00,
a_3:　.8($0.00) + .2($0.00) = $0.00.

Therefore, provided that you do not experiment, your best choice is a_1, which is worth $28.00 to you.   These EMV's are displayed in the bottom row of Table 2.1 on page 7.

4.   THE DECISION-FLOW DIAGRAM

Your basic problem has now been stated and we are ready to start the first stage of the full analysis, which we shall work out in terms of a *decision-flow diagram* or "tree".   In this first stage, I shall present the anatomy or the qualitative structure of the problem as a chronological arrangement of those choices that are controlled by you, as decision maker, and those choices that are determined by Chance.

You have a choice at the very start: to play or not to play. (See Fig. 2.2.) If you refuse to play, that's it—we need go no further. If you agree to play, you then must decide whether to gather more information. Should you take no observations (e_0), take a single observation (e_1), take a pair of observations (e_2), or start on a sequential procedure (e_s)? These choices are shown in Fig. 2.3. If we wish, we can combine these two successive moves into one move with five branches: *Refuse to play, e_0, e_1, e_2, e_s.* (See Fig. 2.4.)

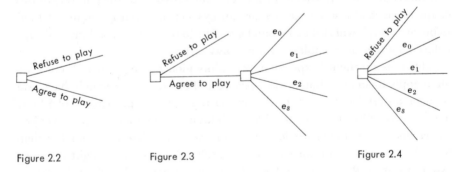

Figure 2.2   Figure 2.3   Figure 2.4

Now let's see what's in store for you if you choose to travel down the e_1-path. After paying your $8.00 toll (fee for sampling), you would encounter a fork in the road with branches marked R ("red") and B ("black"), as shown in Fig. 2.5. You are not master of your destiny at this point—Chance is in the driver's seat. Suppose, then, by chance, you draw a *red* ball from the un-identified urn on the table and thereby head down road R. You next encounter the fork that we shall denote by (e_1, R). At this point you control the steering wheel once again and can, at your own discretion, go down the a_1-road or the a_2-road. Suppose you go down a_2 and come to (e_1, R, a_2). Once again you

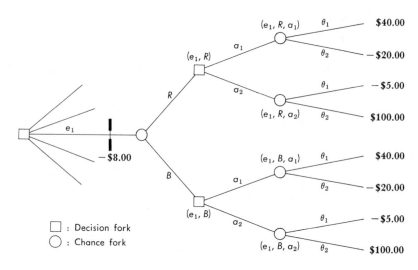

Figure 2.5

must relinquish control to Chance, who determines whether it shall be θ_1 or θ_2. If you journey over the route (e_1, R, a_2, θ_1), then, besides your toll of $8.00, you would also get the terminal payoff of $-$5.00; that is, you would lose $13.00. Observe that forks (junctures, nodes, or branching points) are of two types: *decision* forks and *chance* forks. A decision fork is designated by a small square and a chance fork by a small circle.

The decision-flow diagram of your basic problem is shown in Fig. 2.6. You can think of this display as the road map of your problem. We have already discussed the e_1-branch of Fig. 2.6. The e_2-branch is basically similar. To make sure you understand this presentation, let me lead you down the e_s-path. After paying your toll of $9.00, you will come to the fork (e_s). (See Fig. 2.6b.) Suppose Chance now leads you down path R to (e_s, R). At this point you can either stop or continue sampling. If you elect to stop sampling, then your view of the future at that point is identical in all respects with the one you would perceive at (e_1, R). If at (e_s, R) you go down the *Continue* path and pay an additional $4.50 toll, then at $(e_s, R, Cont.)$ you must decide whether or not to return the withdrawn red ball to the urn before the next drawing (*Replacement* or *Non-replacement*); and so on. These comments should suffice to make the flow diagram clear.

Ultimately we shall compute a value for each branch at each decision fork and this will enable you to choose your best set of alternatives. But we have things to do first.

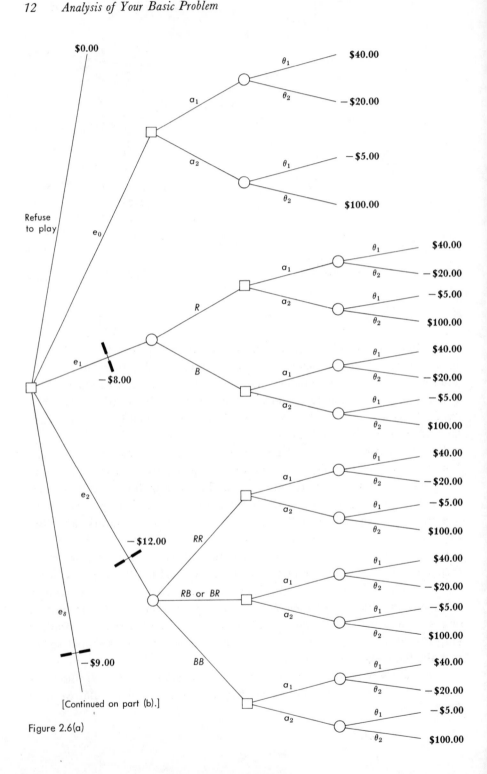

[Continued on part (b).]

Figure 2.6(a)

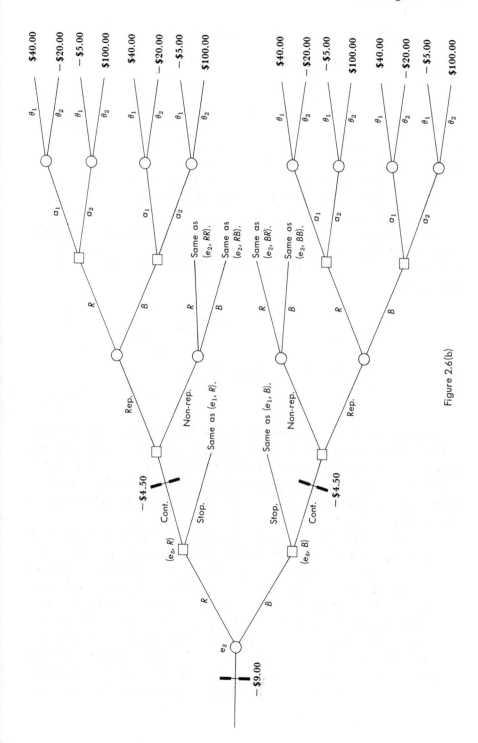

Figure 2.6(b)

5.   PROBABILITY ASSESSMENTS AT CHANCE FORKS

Let's take stock of where we are. We have begun our analysis of your problem by tracing out a decision-flow diagram that depicts in chronological order the alternative actions that are available to you as decision maker and the information that you acquire as you move through its various paths. We have likened this decision flow diagram to a road map and said that at some branch points you exercise control of your next choice, but at other branch points you relinquish control to Chance. The tolls you must pay are posted on your road map, and there are clearly designated prizes or penalties at the terminal ends (or tips of the branches). Your first problem, clearly, is to decide on your initial path. But there is something else we should add to the map: At each fork where Chance is in control, it is crucial to know what the probability is that Chance will choose any particular one of the alternative branches available. In this section, we shall discover how to make these probability assignments.

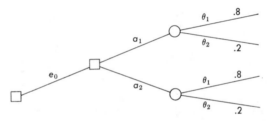

Figure 2.7

We first consider the e_0-branch (see Fig. 2.7), and the chance fork (e_0, a_1). What is the probability that Chance will select θ_1? Since the experimenter has selected the unidentified urn on the table at random from 1000 urns, 800 of which are θ_1's and 200 of which are θ_2's, the assignment for θ_1 is clearly .8. Similarly the assignment for θ_2 is .2. We make these same assignments at the chance fork (e_0, a_2).

Now let us look at branch e_1 (see Fig. 2.8). It is not so easy to make the appropriate probability assignments for this branch, and we must develop a very modest amount of probability theory. However, our probabilistic analysis of branch e_1 will form the basis of most of our further discussion on probability assessments. The analyses of branches e_2 and e_s will not present any further conceptual difficulties; they will not even depend on our analysis of branch e_1.

Suppose we imagine that you have selected the option e_1, that you have drawn a red ball from the unidentified urn (that is, Chance has sent you down path R), and that you have decided on act a_1. In other words, suppose you are perched at the chance fork (e_1, R, a_1). What is the probability of θ_1? We

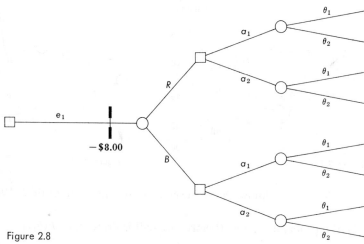

Figure 2.8

no longer can say that it is .8. At (e_1, R, a_1), we know that a red ball has been drawn from the unidentified urn. Since a θ_1 urn contains four red balls and six black balls, whereas a θ_2 urn contains nine red balls and one black ball, the information that a red ball has been drawn presumably should decrease the credibility that the unidentified urn is of type θ_1. In the next few paragraphs we shall discuss how you ought to revise your former assessment of the probability of θ_1 after you have obtained experimental evidence.

From Fig. 2.8 we see that we need to know these quantities:

a) the conditional probability of θ_1, given that e_1 results in a red ball being drawn, or $P(\theta_1|R)$, where the vertical bar "$|$" is read "given";

b) the conditional probability of θ_2, given that e_1 results in a red ball being drawn, or $P(\theta_2|R)$;

c) the conditional probability of θ_1, given that e_1 results in a black ball being drawn, or $P(\theta_1|B)$;

d) the conditional probability of θ_2, given that e_1 results in a black ball being drawn, or $P(\theta_2|B)$;

e) the probability that e_1 will result in a red ball being drawn, or $P(R)$;

f) the probability that e_1 will result in a black ball being drawn, or $P(B)$.

These six probability assignments can be arranged in the probability tree of Fig. 2.9. I have maintained the correspondence in labeling the branches from (a) to (f). (For the time being, please ignore the numbers labeled *Path probabilities*; these will be explained shortly.)

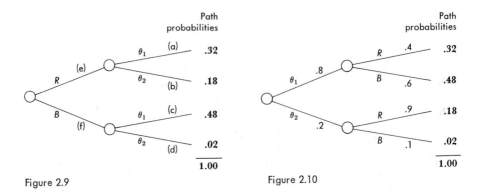

Figure 2.9   Figure 2.10

What do we know that can help us find these quantities? Well, we know

1) the probability of θ_1 (before any ball is drawn), or $P(\theta_1)$;

2) the probability of θ_2, or $P(\theta_2)$;

3) the conditional probability that e_1 will result in a red (R) if θ_1 is true, or $P(R|\theta_1)$;

4) the conditional probability that e_1 will result in a black (B) if θ_1 is true, or $P(B|\theta_1)$;

5) the conditional probability that e_1 will result in a red (R) if θ_2 is true, or $P(R|\theta_2)$;

6) the conditional probability that e_1 will result in a black (B) if θ_2 is true, or $P(B|\theta_2)$.

In particular, these values are

$$P(\theta_1) = .8, \qquad P(\theta_2) = .2,$$
$$P(R|\theta_1) = .4, \qquad P(B|\theta_1) = .6, \qquad P(R|\theta_2) = .9, \qquad P(B|\theta_2) = .1.$$

These six probability assignments can be arranged in the probability tree shown in Fig. 2.10. The probability of going down θ_1 *and* R (that is, the probability that the unidentified urn is of type θ_1 and that a random drawing from this urn results in a red) is $.8 \times .4 = .32$. The path probability of θ_1 *and* B is $.8 \times .6 = .48$, and so forth. These path probabilities are shown in Fig. 2.10.

Now let's return to Fig. 2.9. First we observe that although it is not clear how we are to assign probabilities to the six branches of this figure, it should now be clear how we are to assign probabilities to *paths*. For example, the path R *and* θ_1 in Fig. 2.9 is the same as the path θ_1 *and* R in Fig. 2.10, and

hence we must assign .32 to the path R *and* θ_1. The other assignments of path
probabilities in Fig. 2.9 follow analogously.

From Fig. 2.9 it should now be clear what probability assignment (e) we
must give to the R-branch: It must be $.32 + .18 = .50$, or .5. Similarly the
assignment (f) we give to the B-branch is $.48 + .02 = .50$, or .5. Having
assigned (e) and (f), we now can get assignments (a), (b), (c), and (d). Since
we know, for example, the path probability of R *and* θ_1 is .32, which is the
product of (e) $\times$ (a), and since we know that (e) is .50, it then follows that
(a) is $.32/.50$, or .64. Similarly (b) is $.18/.50 = .36$, (c) is $.48/.50 = .96$,
and (d) is $.02/.50 = .04$. These numbers appear in their proper positions in
Fig. 2.11.

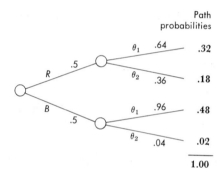

Path
probabilities

1.00   Figure 2.11

In the vernacular, we say that we have "flipped" the probability tree of
Fig. 2.10 to get the probability tree of Fig. 2.11. The former presents the data
in the form in which it was given to you; the latter presents processed data in
the form appropriate for further analysis. The appendix to this chapter gives
flipped trees for experiments e_2 and e_s.

Bayes' Theorem

There is an algebraic formula that lies behind some of the manipulations
we have just gone through in flipping the probability tree of Fig. 2.10 to the
tree in Fig. 2.11, and this formula ought to be stated explicitly. It bears the
illustrious name "Bayes' Theorem" or "Bayes' Formula", and it is considered
so basic by some that decision analysts like myself are called "Bayesians".
We shall generalize the formula for Bayes' Theorem later on, but it will be
helpful if we take a preliminary look at it at this point.

Bayes' Formula allows us to assess $P(\theta_1|R)$ from the quantities $P(\theta_1)$,
$P(\theta_2)$, $P(R|\theta_1)$, and $P(R|\theta_2)$. (We could of course replace R by B in this
formula.) For this development, we shall make use of two simple formulas

from probability theory: If A and B are any two events, then

i) $P(A|B) = P(A \text{ and } B)/P(B)$,

ii) $P(A) = P(A \text{ and } B) + P[A \text{ and } (\text{not } B)]$.

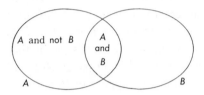

We may state these formulas in more specialized form, using the terms θ_1, θ_2, and R:

$$P(\theta_1|R) = P(\theta_1 \text{ and } R)/P(R), \tag{1}$$

$$P(R) = P(\theta_1 \text{ and } R) + P(\theta_2 \text{ and } R), \tag{2}$$

$$P(\theta_1 \text{ and } R) = P(R|\theta_1)P(\theta_1), \tag{3}$$

$$P(\theta_2 \text{ and } R) = P(R|\theta_2)P(\theta_2). \tag{4}$$

Working backwards, using the data of your basic problem, from Eq. (4) we get

$$P(\theta_2 \text{ and } R) = .9 \times .2 = .18;$$

from Eq. (3) we get

$$P(\theta_1 \text{ and } R) = .4 \times .8 = .32;$$

from Eq. (2) we get

$$P(R) = .18 + .32 = .50;$$

and finally from Eq. (1) we get

$$P(\theta_1|R) = .32/.50 = .64.$$

It is possible to put (1), (2), (3), and (4) together in a single formula:

$$P(\theta_1|R) = \frac{P(R|\theta_1)P(\theta_1)}{P(R|\theta_1) \cdot P(\theta_1) + P(R|\theta_2) \cdot P(\theta_2)}, \tag{5}$$

which is known as *Bayes' Theorem*. The quantities on the right-hand side of (5) can be assigned values in terms of the data of your basic problem.

Rather than flipping trees or using the algebraic approach just outlined, we could conveniently present all the necessary calculations in a table. By this time I hope that the figures in Table 2.2, together with its legend, can speak for themselves. Whether you flip trees, or do algebra, or write down joint tables doesn't matter. Sometimes one procedure is more convenient than the other. The point is that somehow or other we must obtain the necessary probability assignments and place them at all chance forks of the decision-flow diagram that describes your basic problem. These assignments appear on the decision-flow diagrams of Fig. 2.13(a, b).

TABLE 2.2
Joint and marginal probabilities of states and sample outcomes

Sample outcome	States		Marginal probability of sample outcome
	θ_1	θ_2	
Red	.8 × .4 = .32[c]	.2 × .9 = .18[e]	.50[g]
Black	.8 × .6 = .48[d]	.2 × .1 = .02[f]	.50[h]
Marginal probability of state	.80[a]	.20[b]	1.00 (total)

The items of the table are computed in the following order.

(a) $P(\theta_1) = .8,$

(b) $P(\theta_2) = .2,$

(c) $P(R \text{ and } \theta_1) = P(\theta_1) \times P(R|\theta_1) = .8 \times .4,$

(d) $P(B \text{ and } \theta_1) = P(\theta_1) \times P(B|\theta_1) = .8 \times .6,$

(e) $P(R \text{ and } \theta_2) = P(\theta_2) \times P(R|\theta_2) = .2 \times .9,$

(f) $P(B \text{ and } \theta_2) = P(\theta_2) \times P(B|\theta_2) = .2 \times .1,$

(g) $P(R) = P(R \text{ and } \theta_1) + P(R \text{ and } \theta_2) = .32 + .18,$

(h) $P(B) = P(B \text{ and } \theta_1) + P(B \text{ and } \theta_2) = .48 + .02.$

Now we can compute

(i) $P(\theta_1|R) = P(\theta_1 \text{ and } R)/P(R) = .32/.50 = .64,$

(j) $P(\theta_1|B) = P(\theta_1 \text{ and } B)/P(B) = .48/.50 = .96.$

Digression. I should like to pause to relate a personal anecdote that is relevant at this stage. Professor Ward Edwards, a psychologist at the University of Michigan, has investigated the intuitive reactions of many subjects to experimental, probabilistic evidence. In one of his experiments he poses the following problem.

> I have two canvas book bags filled with poker chips. The first bag contains 70 green chips and 30 white chips, and I shall refer to this as the *predominantly green* bag. The second bag contains 70 white chips and 30 green chips, and I shall refer to this as the *predominantly white* bag. The chips are all identical except for color. I now mix up the two bags so that you don't know which is which, and put one of them aside. I shall be concerned with your judgments about whether the remaining bag is predominantly green or not. Now suppose that you choose 12 chips at random with replacement from this remaining bag and it turns out that you draw eight green chips and four white chips, in some particular order. What do you think the odds are that the bag you have sampled from is predominantly green?

At a cocktail party a few years ago I asked a group of lawyers, who were discussing the interpretation of probabilistic evidence, what they would answer as subjects in Edwards' experiment. First of all, they wanted to know whether there was any malice aforethought in the actions of the experimenter. I assured them of the neutrality of the experimenter, and told them that it would be appropriate to assign a .5 chance to "predominantly green" before any sampling took place.

"In this case," one lawyer exclaimed after thinking awhile, "I would bet the unknown bag is predominantly *white*."

"No, you don't understand," one of his colleagues retorted, "you have drawn eight greens and four whites from this bag. Not the other way around."

"Yes, I understand, but in my experience at the bar, *life is just plain perverse, and I would still bet on predominantly white!* But I really am not a betting man."

The other lawyers all agreed that this was not a very rational thing to do—that the evidence was in favor of the bag's being predominantly green.

"But by how much?" I persisted. After a while a consensus emerged: The evidence is meager; the odds might go up from 50-50 to 55-45; but ". . . as lawyers we are trained to be skeptical, so we would slant our best judgments downward and act as if the odds were still roughly 50-50."

The answer to the question "By how much?" can be computed in a straightforward fashion (we do it below), and there is no controversy about the answer. The probability that the bag is predominantly green, given a sample of eight green and four white chips, is .967. Yes, .967. This bag is predominantly green "beyond a reasonable doubt". This story points out the fact that most subjects vastly underestimate the power of a small sample. The lawyers described above had an extreme reaction, but even my statistics students clustered their guesses around .70.

The analysis goes this way: Let us denote the predominantly green and white bags by GB and WB, respectively. We then have $P(GB) = .5$ and $P(WB) = .5$. Let A stand for the event "eight greens and four whites, in the particular order $g\,g\,w\,g\,w\,g\,g\,w\,g\,w\,g\,g$". (The particular order is actually unimportant; we give this example only for the sake of concreteness.) We then have

$$P(A|GB) = .7 \times .7 \times .3 \times \cdots \times .7 = (.7)^8(.3)^4,$$
$$P(A|WB) = .3 \times .3 \times .7 \times \cdots \times .3 = (.7)^4(.3)^8.$$

Now from Bayes' Theorem, with GB in place of θ_1, WB in place of θ_2, and A in place of R), we have

$$P(GB|A) = \frac{P(A|GB)P(GB)}{P(A|GB)P(GB) + P(A|WB)P(WB)}$$
$$= \frac{(.7)^8(.3)^4(.5)}{(.7)^8(.3)^4(.5) + (.3)^8(.7)^4(.5)} = .967.$$

6. AVERAGING OUT AND FOLDING BACK

Before we continue, let's once again take stock of where we are. Your basic problem has been organized in terms of a decision-flow diagram, or stylized road map, that depicts in chronological order the moves that you may choose as decision maker and the moves that are governed by Chance. This road map exhibits various tolls (which correspond to costs of experimentation) and also the payoff for following any road to its end. It indicates as well the probability assessments of the various possible branches at each chance fork, these assessments being *conditional* on the knowledge that would be available to you at that fork. Your problem can now be posed as follows: Given the road map in Fig. 2.13(a, b), including the tolls, probabilities at chance forks, and payoffs at the termini, how do you want to exercise your partial control? In particular, you must first decide whether you should go down e_0, e_1, e_2, or e_s, or whether you ought to refuse to play.

The analysis of your problem involves a sequence of calculations, and some of these intermediate steps are presented on the diagram in Fig. 2.13(a, b).

To ensure that we clearly understand the nature of the numbers that appear in the diagrams, we shall adopt certain typographical conventions. In the following list, the entry on the right is an example of how each particular kind of number will appear:

toll,	**− $5.00,**
intermediate monetary calculation,	*$40.15,*
payoff,	**$100.00,**
branch probability,	.5 or 144/145,
path probability,	.5 or **144/145.**

For the moment you should ignore the intermediate monetary calculations and the path probabilities; also ignore the double slash (//) marks on the diagram for the time being. Let's first analyze the e_0-branch, which is reproduced in Fig. 2.12.

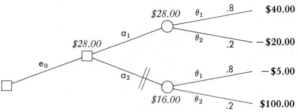

Figure 2.12

Averaging Out. Let's suppose, in conceptual time, that you are at (e_0, a_1) and that Chance is about to drive you down the θ_1- or θ_2-path. How much would you settle for at this point? How much is this risky option worth to you? You will collect $40.00 if you are lucky enough to be taken down the θ_1-branch, but perhaps Chance won't be so condescending and will take you down the θ_2-branch instead, for a penalty of $20.00. As an EMV'er (remember that for the time being you have agreed to cast yourself in such a role) who is perched at (e_0, a_1), the future looks as though it is worth

$$.8(\$40.00) + .2(-\$20.00) = \$28.00.$$

Symbolically we write

$$\text{EMV}(e_0, a_1) = \$28.00$$

and say, "The EMV of (e_0, a_1) is $28.00." Thus, in Fig. 2.12, I have written $28.00 beside (e_0, a_1). Similarly you can verify that

$$\text{EMV}(e_0, a_2) = .8(-\$5.00) + .2(\$100.00) = \$16.00.$$

Folding Back. Let's now back up and perch you at (e_0); here you must decide whether to choose a_1 or a_2. What do you see down the a_1-road? A risky option with an evaluation sign of $28.00. What do you see down the a_2-road? A risky option with an evaluation sign of $16.00. As an EMV'er, your choice is clear: You will go down the a_1-road and block off the a_2-road. (This is indicated on the diagram by the double vertical slashes.) The EMV of being at (e_0) is then $28.00 (the greater of $28.00 and $16.00), and we record $28.00 at (e_0).

Let's review what we have done. We first transported ourselves in conceptual time out to the very tips of the tree, where the evaluations are given directly in terms of the data of the problem. We then worked our way backwards by successive use of two devices:

1) an averaging-out process at each chance juncture, and

2) a choice process that selects the path yielding the maximum future evaluation at each decision juncture.

We call this the *averaging out and folding back* procedure.*

You should now be able to interpret and verify all the evaluations given in Fig. 2.13(a, b), found on pages 24 and 25, which are tinted for easy reference. For example, the fork (e_2, RR) is given an evaluation $58.00. By the averaging-out process, you should first verify that

$$\text{EMV}(e_2, RR, a_1) = .4(\$40.00) + .6(-\$20.00) = \$4.00,$$
$$\text{EMV}(e_2, RR, a_2) = .4(-\$5.00) + .6(\$100.00) = \$58.00.$$

Hence, by the folding-back process, path a_1 is then blocked off and you set

$$\text{EMV}(e_2, RR) = \$58.00.$$

Now what is the value of being at fork (e_2), after paying the $12.00 toll? At this node we can be sent down three paths: the RR-path, which has probability $24/90$; the RB- or BR-path, which has probability $42/90$; or the BB-path, which has probability $24/90$. Hence the value of being at (e_2) is

$$\tfrac{24}{90}(\$58.00) + \tfrac{42}{90}(\$34.86) + \tfrac{24}{90}(\$40.00) = \$42.40,$$

and we note down $42.40 at (e_2). Recall what this number means: Since you are an EMV'er, if someone offered you an amount greater than $42.40 for your option at this point, you would accept it; if someone offered you less than $42.40, you would refuse it.

---

*The averaging-out-and-folding-back process is often referred to as *the process of backwards induction in the theory of dynamic programming.*

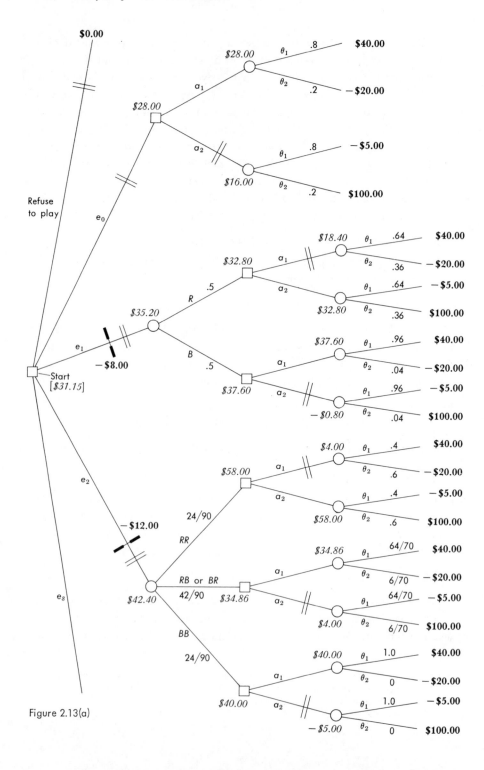

Figure 2.13(a)

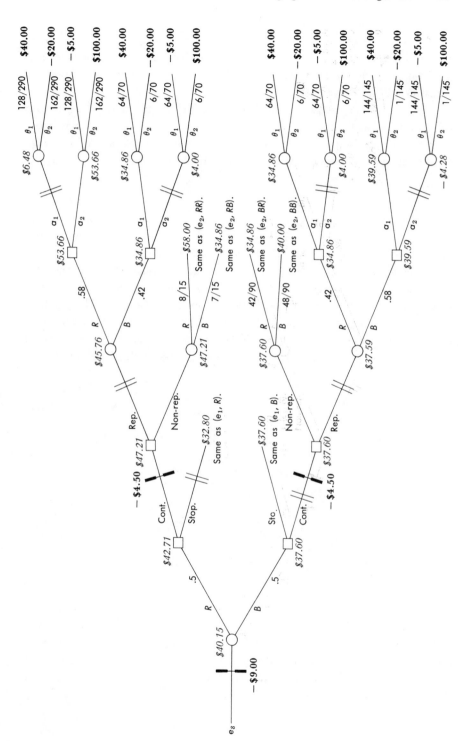

Have you verified enough of the evaluations given in Fig. 2.13(a, b) so that we can proceed with our analysis? Remember that all our deliberations have taken place in conceptual time and you are still at the starting point in real time. What do you see?

Figure 2.14 should show you that if you include the initial tolls in your calculations, you should decide that path e_8 is better than e_2, which is better than e_0, which is better than e_1 and all of which are better than *Refuse to play*. From your point of view, playing the game should be worth

$$\$40.15 - \$9.00 = \$31.15.$$

Now let's return to Fig. 2.13(b). Starting down e_8, you pay your $9.00 toll. Suppose that Chance takes you down R at (e_8). At this point the EMV of your future outlook has jumped to $42.71. Your optimal choice is then to continue sampling, to pay a toll of $4.50, and to choose *not* to replace the withdrawn red ball; this brings you to $(e_8, R, Cont., Non\text{-}rep.)$. Suppose that Chance here sends you down B. Your evaluation then drops down from $47.21 to $34.86. At this point your prospects are the same as they would be if you were at (e_2, RB). Hence you should go down the a_1-path and let Chance decide to give you $40.00 (with probability 64/70) or $-$20.00 (with probability 6/70).

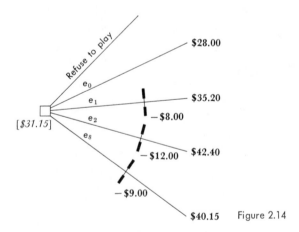

Figure 2.14

Figure 2.13(a, b) can also be used to determine the expected value of the information in any given sample plan. From the simpler Fig. 2.14 we see that the expected value of being at (e_0) is $28.00, while the expected value of being at (e_1) is $35.20. The difference between these figures ($7.20) is the expected increase in the value of the game effected by taking a sample of one ball and then choosing the best act on the basis of this sample information. In slightly different vernacular, we say that the *expected value of sample information* for experiment e_1 is \$7.20; symbolically, we may write

$$\text{EVSI}(e_1) = \$7.20.$$

Similarly we have $\text{EVSI}(e_2) = \$14.40$. The EVSI in a sequential experiment is more complicated and we shall not discuss it.

Digression. In the sequential procedure e_s, is it ever optimal to replace the withdrawn ball before the second drawing? Figure 2.13(b) shows us that it is not profitable to do so in this case. Is this *always* the case? Consider the following situation: Suppose urn θ_1 has two reds and one black, whereas θ_2 has 101 reds and 100 blacks. Let the first drawing from the unidentified urn be a red. Should it be replaced? The contents without replacement for θ_1 are one red and one black and for θ_2 are 100 reds and 100 blacks so that *if the withdrawn red ball were not replaced, no information about the original contents would be gained from a second drawing* because the probability of drawing a red (or black) is .5 for both θ_1 and θ_2. In this case it is clearly advisable to sample *with* replacement. I don't want to go into a long exposition of when it is desirable to replace or not to replace; my purpose here is rather to emphasize the fact that we have already discussed, in principle at least, the methodology for answering such questions.

7. EXPECTED VALUE OF PERFECT INFORMATION, AND OPPORTUNITY LOSS*

Before determining whether or not it is worth gathering experimental evidence, which, after all, is usually not completely decisive, it is first desirable to ask, "What is *perfect* information worth?" Suppose that in a given example perfect information is worth \$100.00 and the sampling experiment under consideration costs \$150.00. In this case we could forget about sampling without any further ado, since it would be foolish to pay \$150.00 for imperfect information when perfect information is only worth \$100.00. In analyzing your problem, we did not stop to ask this preliminary question. For completeness' sake we shall now do so, even though, strictly speaking, it is out of logical order. We shall find it convenient to approach the point in three different ways.

---

* We shall not use the contents of this section in the sequel and the reader can skip to the next. The reader who finds himself struggling with the material thus far is *especially urged to skip this section.*

1) Let's imagine that your basic problem has just been posed, that you have examined the table of payoffs (Table 2.1), and have concluded if you were to act without any experimentation, you would choose act a_1, which has an EMV of $28.00. Now the following questions are asked of you: "Suppose you no longer have the privilege of experimenting, but for a payment of $15.00 you could determine the identity of the unidentified urn. Would you pay $15.00 for this perfect information? Just how much would you be willing to pay for this perfect information?"

Note that if you decide to pay $15.00 for perfect information, you thereby eliminate *all the uncertainty*. If you learn the urn is of type θ_1, then you will choose a_1 and get $40.00; if you learn the urn is of type θ_2, then you will choose a_2 and get $100.00. It certainly is worth the $15.00 if you learn that the urn is of type θ_2, for then you will switch from a_1 to a_2 and get $100.00 instead of $-$ $20.00, thereby saving $120.00. However, if you learn it is of type θ_1, you will take a_1 just as planned, and you will have saved nothing. The crux of the situation is this: Is it worth it to you to make a certain payment of $15.00 for the possibility of a reward of $120, which obtains if the true state is θ_2 (this will happen with a probability of .2), or a reward of $0.00, which obtains if the true state is θ_1 (this will happen with a probability of .8)? But, as an EMV'er, your answer is now clear because you assess the value of this uncertain reward as $.2(\$120.00) + .8(\$0.00) = \$24.00$, *the expected value of perfect information*, which is greater than the cost of $15.00. Hence you ought to purchase this perfect information.

2) There is another way to view the problem of perfect information. If θ_1 is true, then a_1 is optimal and hence you suffer no *loss of opportunity* (or of payoff) in choosing a_1. There is loss of opportunity, however, in choosing a_2 or a_3. If you refer to Table 2.3, you can see that when state θ_1 obtains, there are 45 [that is, $40 - (-5) = 45$] units of lost opportunity if you choose a_2, and 40 units of lost opportunity if you choose a_3. These numbers are found in the row opposite θ_1. The numbers that appear in the row labeled θ_2 give the losses of opportunity incurred with choices of a_1, a_2, and a_3, respectively, when θ_2 is the true state. See if you can justify the values on the basis of the information given in Table 2.1.

Now we know how to interpret the *rows* of Table 2.3 in terms of loss of opportunity; it is also instructive to interpret the *columns* of this table. The entries under column a_1 have already been discussed, but we shall mention their significance once more: If you were going to choose a_1 without perfect information, then the value of obtaining the perfect information that θ_1 is true (with

TABLE 2.3

Loss of opportunity for all state-act pairs

State	Act			Probability of state
	a_1	a_2	a_3	
θ_1	0	45	40	.80
θ_2	120	0	100	.20
Expected opportunity loss	24	36	52	1.00 (total)

the privilege of switching acts) is zero, and the value of obtaining the perfect information that θ_2 is true (with the privilege of switching acts) is 120. See if you can interpret the numbers 45 and zero in column a_2 and the numbers 40 and 100 in column a_3 in terms of value of information. [Incidentally, you might note that instead of labeling Table 2.3 "Loss of opportunity" (you would incur), we could have also labeled it "Value of information" (you would receive).]

The *expected opportunity loss* (EOL) of a given act is found by multiplying the column entries for that act by the probabilities of the states and adding. For example, the EOL of a_1 is $.8(0) + .2(120) = 24$.

It is instructive to compare Tables 2.1 and 2.3. Note the following figures.

Act	a_1	a_2	a_3
EMV	28	16	0
EOL	24	36	52
Total	52	52	52

In general, the EMV plus the EOL is constant for all acts;* their sum, 52 in this case, will be interpreted below. Observe that act a_1 has a maximum EMV and minimum EOL. The minimum EOL (that is, the EOL which goes with the optimal act under present information) is called the *expected value of perfect information* (EVPI).

---

* For the mathematically curious reader: Try proving this!

3) We can look at the question, "How much is perfect information worth?" in a third way. First off, we have said that without perfect information, you will take a_1 and get an EMV of .8($40.00) + .2(−$20.00) = $28.00. We now ask, "What is your expected return if you can choose your act *after* learning the true state, that is, *after* obtaining perfect information?" Clearly the simple *availability* of perfect information allows you to look forward to a reward of $40.00 with probability .8 and a reward of $100.00 with probability .2, for an EMV of .8($40.00) + .2($100.00) = $52.00. (The EMV plus the EOL for any act is equal to this quantity.) The incremental EMV of perfect information is therefore worth $52.00 − $28.00 = $24.00, which is the EVPI.

Now let's reconsider your original problem. If the EVPI turned out to be much lower than it really is, for example, if the EVPI were $6.00, say, then you would certainly not pay $8.00 (option e_1) or more for imperfect sample information. Hence the calculation of the EVPI can tell you whether you should consider collecting sample information at all. In your basic problem, sampling costs a lot less than the EVPI ($24.00), and thus it is not clear from the EVPI-analysis whether or not it is desirable to collect sample information. Of course, if the cost of sampling were more than $24.00 for e_1, then the EVPI-analysis would indeed have saved us some time, since we should not have bothered to go through the full decision-tree procedure.

Now that we have developed the notion of the EVPI, it will be of interest to us to investigate how the EVPI changes after some imperfect information has been obtained. Let's suppose you have paid $8.00 and have drawn a red ball. Now would you still be willing to pay up to $24.00 for perfect information? To answer this, let's figure out what has changed in the structure of the problem *after* you have drawn a red ball. Since you have chosen option e_1 and have sunk the $8.00, future payments by you and to you are still given by Table 2.1. What has changed (I hope) is that you are no longer satisfied with the assignments of .8 and .2 for the probabilities of θ_1 and θ_2, respectively. Presumably getting a red should somehow force you to revise these probabilities—otherwise, why sample? The original (or prior) probability assessment of .8 for θ_1 will now give way to a new (or posterior) probability assessment for θ_1 which is lower than .8; analogously, the prior probability of θ_2 will go from .2 to a posterior probability higher than .2. ("Prior" and "posterior", as you can see, refer to points in time before and after experimentation, respectively.) This revision will make a_1 less attractive and a_2 more attractive, but is the shift great enough to induce you to switch your choice from a_1 to a_2?

In Section 5, we discussed how to revise the probabilities of the states θ_1 and θ_2 to allow for the fact that an R has been drawn. We can now decide whether you should switch to a_2 and how much you should be willing to pay

TABLE 2.4

	Value		Revised probabilities of state *after* a red ball is drawn	Opportunity loss		
	Act			Act		
State	a_1	a_2		a_1	a_2	State
θ_1	$40.00	−$5.00	.64	$0.00	$45.00	θ_1
θ_2	−$20.00	$100.00	.36	$120.00	$0.00	θ_2
EMV	*$18.40*	*$32.80*	Total = 1.00	*$43.20*	*$28.80*	EOL

for perfect information. We can carry out this analysis using the data given in Table 2.4.

Note that the EMV for a_2 is $32.80 = .64(−\$5.00) + .36(\$100.00)$. This is larger than the EMV for a_1, so that as an EMV'er you *should* now adopt a_2. Of course, we already know this from the decision-flow diagram. To find how much you should spend for perfect information at this point, we can argue as follows.

1) If you are told that the true state is θ_1 you will switch from a_2 to a_1, gaining for yourself $\$40.00 − (−\$5.00)$, or $45.00; and so far as you are concerned, the probability that you will be told that the true state is θ_1 is the *revised probability that you now give to θ_1*, namely .64.

2) If you are told the true state is θ_2, you will not switch and you gain nothing; and this has for you a probability of .36 of happening.

3) The EMV of this incremental gain from perfect information is therefore $.64(\$45.00) + .36(\$0.00) = \$28.80$. *Hence perfect information is worth more to you now that you have experimented and observed a red ball than it was before you experimented and observed the red ball.* Check the numbers and logic again if you do not believe it! What has happened is that the information has raised your prospective EMV *and* your EVPI as well.

Table 2.5 displays the basic information and revised probabilities for the case in which the withdrawn ball is black. From Section 5, we know that the revised probability of θ_1 after you draw a black ball is $.48/.50 = .96$; hence the revised probabilities in the middle column of the table. As an EMV'er you are now best off with a_1, and the incremental EMV of perfect information is now only $.96(\$0.00) + .04(\$120.00) = \$4.80$. I suggest that you check all the figures in Table 2.5 to verify that you fully understand these basic mechanical details.

TABLE 2.5

State	Value Act a_1	Value Act a_2	Revised probability of state *after* a black ball is drawn	Opportunity loss Act a_1	Opportunity loss Act a_2	State
θ_1	$40.00	$-$5.00	.96	$0.00	$45.00	θ_1
θ_2	$-$20.00	$100.00	.04	$120.00	$0.00	θ_2
EMV	$37.60	$- $0.80	Total $= 1.00$	$4.80	$43.20	EOL

The results we have developed about revised probabilities accord with common sense. Before seeing a sample of one ball from the unidentified urn, you assigned probability .8 to θ_1 and probability .2 to θ_2. Now an urn of type θ_1 holds more black balls than red balls, and an urn of type θ_2 holds more red balls than black balls. If you draw a red ball in your sample, it is more likely to come from an urn of type θ_2. In this case you would want to give less weight to the possibility that θ_1 is on the table. But reducing the .8 on θ_1 to .64 and increasing the .2 on θ_2 to .36 means that you must now be *less* certain which urn is before you. Therefore the value to you of knowing which urn is *really* on the table should increase, in view of the increase in your uncertainty.

We could use the same argument to show why a decrease in the incremental EMV of perfect information makes common sense if you were to draw a black ball. Drawing a black ball would only reinforce the judgment you made prior to the sample, that θ_1 is more likely than θ_2.

Prior Expectation of Posterior EVPI*

We have argued that if you are not given the privilege of sampling, then, as an EMV'er, you should be willing to pay $24.00 for perfect information. However, if you have already experimented and drawn a red, you should be willing to pay $28.80. If the withdrawn ball had been black, however, the value of perfect information would have plummeted down to a mere $4.80. I now pose the following question to you. How much would you pay for perfect information if you were given the privilege *at no cost* of first taking just a single observation from the urn? You haven't yet exercised this privilege, you understand; but you are aware that you have it. Well, we saw that perfect

---

* For those of you who have read thus far in this section despite my warning, I repeat: If you are having *any* trouble following the logic, don't bother reading the rest of this section. The benefits are not worth the cost.

information would be worth \$28.80 or \$4.80, depending on whether a red or a black were to materialize. But you now have to decide what perfect information is worth to you before you make your free experiment. What are the chances of red and black? In Section 5, we argued that the chance of getting a red on the first draw from the unidentified urn is .5, and similarly for black. Therefore perfect information is worth \$28.80 with probability .5 and \$4.80 with probability .5, for an EMV of

$$.5(\$28.80) + .5(\$4.80) = \$16.80.$$

This quantity is *the prior expectation of EVPI posterior to experiment e_1*.

Let's summarize. Perfect information is worth \$24.00 to you if you cannot take any drawing, and the value of this same perfect information goes down to \$16.80 if you can take at most a single free drawing. (Remember that this second figure applies only before the actual drawing has taken place.) The increment, \$24.00 − \$16.80 = \$7.20, can thus be thought of as the *expected value of the sample information* in this single drawing. This number, \$7.20, is no stranger to us. We got it much more directly from Fig. 2.14 (see Section 6). It is the difference \$35.20 − \$28.00 = \$7.20.

8. SUMMARY AND GENERALIZATION

I hope that if I were to change the monetary prizes, penalties, cost of sampling, and the contents of the urns at this point, you would be able to carry out all the necessary calculations and complete the analysis. In particular, you should be able to exhibit the decision-flow diagram, displaying the sequence of moves by the decision maker and by Chance in chronological order, assigning the economic payoffs and sampling costs to the tree, assigning probabilities to all the possible outcomes of a chance move conditional on being present at that chance move, and finally analyzing the tree by the process of averaging out and folding back.*

With a little imagination on your part you can now go a long way. We are not so enamored of our little urns that we would have spent all this effort on them if we could not generalize the ideas we have developed. The methodology we have applied to our artificial example is applicable to a wide class of problems that must be decided in the real world, which is after all a world of

---

* If you studied Section 7, you might prefer to start the analysis by first exhibiting a table giving the loss of opportunity incurred for each act given each state, computing the EOL of each of the acts, and then interpreting the minimum EOL as the EVPI. Only if the EVPI were considerably larger than the cost of experimentation would you then go on to determine the structure of the decision-flow diagram and analyze it.

uncertainty. However, many challenging complexities must be resolved before a real-world problem can be cast into the kind of framework discussed in this chapter.

1) One must strip away the irrelevant factors of a given situation and suppress other relevant but not crucial factors, so that the basic anatomy of the decision problem can be displayed in manageable form. It is not an easy task to identify the viable courses of action and the basic sources of uncertainty and to show how these interact in sequential order.

2) The economic payoffs and sampling costs are not usually given to the analyst on a silver platter; he has to work to get these appropriate figures. There may be considerations other than monetary ones that the decision maker will wish to consider in his analysis. Furthermore, even so far as the monetary payoffs are concerned, the decision maker may be averse to risk and choose not to work with EMV. I shall discuss these points in the next chapter.

3) The probability assignments are rarely presented in a clear-cut manner: the decision maker has to exercise considerable judgment to obtain appropriate figures. I shall discuss this in Chapter 5.

4) When there is a great multiplicity of alternatives at different forks, it may not be feasible to actually draw the tree diagram and hammer our way through to a solution by strictly primitive numerical means; but the conceptual framework can still be employed to great advantage and tractable solutions generated by suitable analytical techniques. I shall say more about this in Chapter 7.

5) Finally, I shall have much more to say about the *Art of Implementation* in Chapter 9.

9. PROJECT

As an exercise for the interested reader, I shall now make concrete a simplified version of the oil-drilling problem briefly described in the introduction. The oil wildcatter must decide either to drill (act a_1) or not to drill (act a_2). He is uncertain whether the hole is dry (state θ_1), wet (state θ_2), or soaking (state θ_3). His payoffs are given in Table 2.6. We assume here that the cost of drilling is $70,000. The net return of the consequence associated with the (*Wet*, a_1)-pair is $50,000, which is interpreted as a return of $120,000 less the $70,000 cost of drilling. Similarly the $200,000 amount is a net figure; it represents a return of $270,000 less the cost of $70,000 for drilling. (In a later project we shall make the cost of drilling uncertain.)

TABLE 2.6
Monetary payoffs

	Act	
State	a_1	a_2
Dry (θ_1)	$-\$70,000$	0
Wet (θ_2)	$\$50,000$	0
Soaking (θ_3)	$\$200,000$	0

TABLE 2.7
Joint and marginal probabilities

	Seismic outcome			Marginal probability of state
State	No S	Open S	Closed S	
Dry (θ_1)	.300	.150	.050	.500
Wet (θ_2)	.090	.120	.090	.300
Soaking (θ_3)	.020	.080	.100	.200
Marginal probability of seismic outcome	.410	.350	.240	1.000

At a cost of $10,000, our wildcatter could take seismic soundings (experiment e_1) which will help determine the underlying geological structure at the site. The soundings will disclose whether the terrain below has (a) *no* structure (outcome NS)—that's bad, or (b) *open* structure (outcome OS)—that's so-so, or (c) *closed* structure (outcome CS)—that's really hopeful. The experts have kindly provided us with Table 2.7, which shows joint probabilities. From it we can see, for example, that the probability of θ_1 (dry) and OS (open structure) is .150; the probability of θ_1 is

$$.300 + .150 + .050 = .500;$$

the probability of OS is

$$.150 + .120 + .080 = .350.$$

Assume the wildcatter is an EMV'er.

1) What is his optimal action without experimentation?

2) What is the EVPI? (The answer to this question depends on Section 7; skip it if you wish.)

3) What is the optimal strategy for experimentation and action? *Suggestion.* Exhibit a decision-flow diagram for the problem.

4) What is the expected value of seismic information?

APPENDIX

Probability Assessments for Branch e_2. The necessary probabilities for the e_2-branch can be obtained from Fig. 2.15(b), which in turn is obtained by flipping the tree in Fig. 2.15(a).

Probability Assessments for Branch e_s. There are two cases to consider.

Case 1. The second drawing is made without replacement. This is analyzed in Fig. 2.16.

Case 2. The second drawing is made with replacement. This is analyzed in Fig. 2.17. In each case, as before, we can flip the tree by computing the path probabilities in the (a)-part, by carrying these over to the (b)-part, by adding

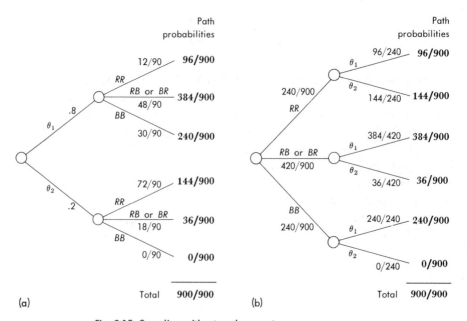

Fig. 2.15 Sampling without replacement.

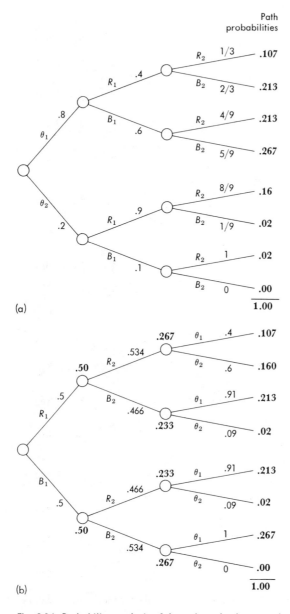

Path
probabilities

(a)

(b)

Fig. 2.16 Probability analysis of the e_s-branch when you draw without replace-ment. The path probabilities at the tips of the tree in part (b) come from Fig. 2.16(a). The probability of a partial path such as (R_1, B_2) is .213 + .020 = .233. The conditional probability of B_2 given R_7 is .233/.500, or .466.

to get the marginal probabilities of partial paths, and finally by computing the conditional probabilities of various branches by dividing appropriate partial

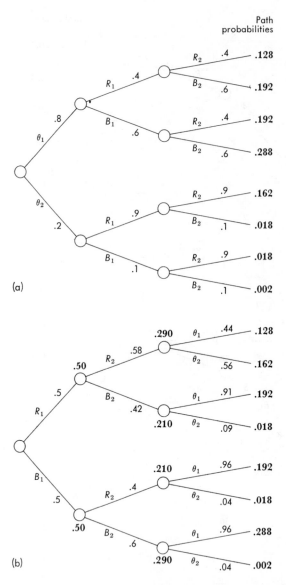

Fig. 2.17 Probability analysis of the e_s-branch when you draw with replacement.

path probabilities.   Conditional branch probabilities appear in sans-serif type (e.g., .4) and path probabilities in **boldface type** (e.g., **.128**). Subscripts on R and B denote the order of the drawing; for example, B_2 stands for a black on the second drawing.

CHAPTER 3

UNCERTAIN PAYOFFS
AND BIASED MEASUREMENTS*

1. INTRODUCTION

Although the basic problem analyzed in the previous chapter may have seemed complicated to you, we chose it because its structure is very simple in many important respects. There was never any doubt about such things as the payoff values or the cost of sampling. There were never any errors or distortions reported in the outcomes of experimentation, as there would have been in many real-world experimental situations. In this chapter, we shall discuss in a very tentative manner how we might relax some of these artificial simplifications. We cannot get too realistic, however, and perhaps all that we shall accomplish in this chapter is the substitution of one artificiality for another artificiality.

We shall consider three complicating factors: i) unknown payoffs, ii) unknown sampling costs, and iii) inaccurate reporting of outcomes of experiments (as, perhaps, through a noisy communications channel). In each case we shall make the rather artificial assumptions that we can always list all the events that might occur and that we can assign crystal-clear, objective probabilities to these eventualities. We shall find that with each of these complications the

---

* This chapter may be omitted without loss of continuity.

decision-flow diagram gets a bit more involved, but that we do not need any new conceptual techniques to analyze the modified problems.

In the ensuing chapters we shall gradually reduce the artificiality of our assumptions and develop some working notions to cope with these more realistic situations.

2.   UNCERTAIN PAYOFFS AND SAMPLING COSTS

To begin with, let's make this very simple modification in the original problem: Instead of getting a sure payoff of $40.00 if you take a_1 and θ_1 turns out to be the true state, suppose you get $30.00 or $50.00, depending on the toss of a fair coin. Here is the way we handle this very minor complication. Consider those tips of the trees in Fig. 2.13 at which the payoff is $40.00; for example, (e_2, RR, a_1, θ_1). At each such terminal position we must replace the certainty payment of $40.00 by the chance event of the type shown in Fig. 3.1. In the process of averaging out and folding back, an EMV'er would evaluate this chance event at $40.00, and therefore his ensuing backwards analysis and results would be identical with the analysis given in the previous chapter. A non-EMV'er (we shall consider his case in the next chapter) would probably prefer $40.00 outright, and so the minor modification under consideration would have an effect on his analysis.

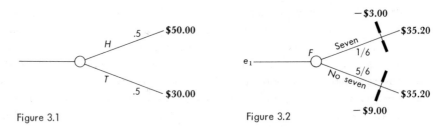

Figure 3.1   Figure 3.2

Let's analyze another minor modification, minor in the sense of being easy to analyze. Instead of an $8.00 toll for a single drawing, suppose the toll is either $3.00 or $9.00, depending on whether or not you roll a seven with a pair of fair dice. As any gambler knows, the probability of getting a seven is $\frac{1}{6}$. If you now proceed along the e_1-path, you meet a chance event of the type shown in Fig. 3.2, where the $35.20 is read from the e_1-fork in Fig. 2.1(a). But now it is a simple matter to get your EMV at point F. It is

$$\$35.20 - [\tfrac{1}{6}(\$3.00) + \tfrac{5}{6}(\$9.00)] = \$27.20.$$

You can see that there is no conceptual difficulty in handling uncertain payoffs or uncertain sampling costs, provided that the type of uncertainty involved can be crystallized as a chance event with precise terminal evaluations and precise probability assessments. In practice, it will be the assessment of probabilities that presents the greater difficulty. Consider, for example, the case where the payoff is changed from $40.00 certain to $40.00 certain *plus* five times the difference between tomorrow's and today's Dow Jones' averages. Here the probabilities are at best a bit fuzzy. We can make them fuzzier still if we make our payment partly dependent on whether our next lunar probe succeeds or not. We shall discuss this type of problem in Chapters 5, 6, and 7.

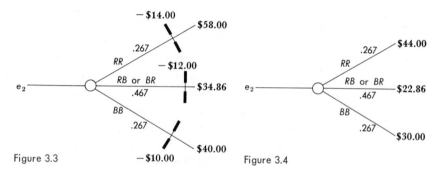

Figure 3.3   Figure 3.4

In some concrete problems, the cost of sampling depends on the outcome of the sample itself; a problem may involve so-called destructive sampling, for example, or following up not-at-homes in sample surveys. Let's return to your basic problem and suppose that for e_2 the cost of sampling is not a flat $12.00, but $10.00 plus a $2.00 penalty for each red ball withdrawn. One possible procedure for dealing with this complication is to replace the e_2-branch in Fig. 2.13(a) by the branch shown in Fig. 3.3; we could then work backwards to get an evaluation of e_2. Another suggestion, which we shall actually follow in the next chapter, is that we depart a bit from the chronological order of the flow diagram and eliminate all tolls, incorporating them with the payoffs at the tips of the tree. For example, on branch e_2, we could eliminate all tolls and subtract $14.00 from the payoffs at the tips of the (e_2, RR)-branch, subtract $12.00 from the payoffs at the tips of the $(e_2, RB$ or $BR)$-branch, and also subtract $10.00 from the payoffs at the tips of the (e_2, BB)-branch. After this modification, the averaging-out-and-folding-back process would lead to the partial decision-flow diagram shown in Fig. 3.4, which we can fold back as usual by using EMV's.

3.   THE VALUE OF INFORMATION ABOUT PAYOFFS

Let's return to the very simple complication stated at the beginning of Section 2, where we substituted a 50-50 chance at payoffs of $50.00 and $30.00 for the certainty of a payoff of $40.00. From the point of view of an EMV'er, we have not altered the strategic problem of optimal choice. But consider this question: Would you pay $2.00 to learn whether the actual payoff is $50.00 or $30.00 *before* you are required to commit yourself to a choice of experiment? Some people argue that their optimal strategy would not depend on whether they get $40.00 certain or get a 50-50 chance of $50.00 or $30.00; they do not see why they should pay $2.00 for useless information. What do you think of this argument? To get the logic clear, let us increase the difference between the prizes and make it much larger than $50.00 − $30.00 = $20.00. Suppose that instead of $40.00 certain, you are to receive $100.00 with probability .4 and $0.00 with probability .6. Now if you were to pay the $2.00 and were told that the prize would be $0.00, then you could and should exploit this added knowledge in making subsequent choices for experimentation and action. Intuitively speaking, doesn't it seem reasonable that you should be willing to pay $2.00 to find out whether the true payoff is $100.00 or $0.00? Would you pay $10.00 for this information? Getting back to the original problem, would you pay $2.00 to resolve the $50.00-$30.00 possibility? What maximum amount would you pay?

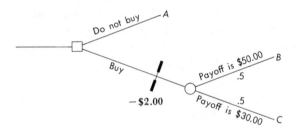

Fig. 3.5 Decision-flow diagram for analyzing whether or not it is worth $2.00 to find out the true payoff.

Conceptually, the problem we have just framed is easy to handle. At the outset you have two alternatives: to buy or not to buy information. If you buy, then you will learn whether the payoff is $50.00 or $30.00. The associated decision-flow diagram is shown in Fig. 3.5. At point *A*, looking into the future, you see ahead the flow diagram of Fig. 2.13. This future has a value to you (as an EMV'er) of $31.15. At points *B* and *C*, looking into the future, you see the identical thing except that on the appropriate tips of the *B*-tree you have replaced $40.00 by $50.00, and likewise on the appropriate tips of the *C*-tree you have replaced $40.00 by $30.00. By the averaging-out-and-folding-back process you are able to evaluate being at *B* and at *C*. It is time you did some of these calculations: As an EMV'er, would you be willing to pay $2.00 for this information?

4. BIASED MEASUREMENTS

Have you ever played Twenty Questions with a child who is never sure of his answers? Many years ago my son, who was then in kindergarten, was a bit annoyed with the slowness of his parents to catch on to this game, and he finally offered us a *real* hint: "I'm thinking of a vegetable that begins with the letter 'p'." After a long while we gave up trying, and with a big broad smile he unfolded to us his wonderful, secret word: "puhsghetti". Talk about noisy, distorted channels!

Researchers in sample surveys have long recognized that what people say they are going to do and what they do do are not always the same, to say the least. Naturally this inconsistency distorts the survey results. How can one cope with this measurement bias?

Let's take the suggestion from these two points and add this complication to your problem: Instead of choosing your own ball or balls from the un-identified urn, you let your friend Charlie offer you a helping hand and a not-so-helping eye. He will choose for you—quite legitimately at random—but don't be too sure of his reports. He is known to make mistakes. You see, Charlie is erratically color-blind. Here is some statistical data about Charlie's malady that will help you keep probability assignments crystal-clear: If he has the choice between red and black, he will identify red correctly only 80% of the time and black correctly only 70% of the time. You will find this information displayed in Table 3.1.

TABLE 3.1
Conditional probability of Charlie's guess

Actual color	Charlie's guess		Total
	Red	Black	
Red	.80	.20	1.00
Black	.30	.70	1.00

With this information at your disposal, to begin with, would you sample at all? If so, which experiment [e_1, e_2, or e_s] would you perform? Would you prefer to do your own sampling at full sampling cost or use Charlie at half-cost? (This is somewhat analogous to the problem of deciding between mail questionnaires and personal interviews in a sample survey, or of deciding between an inexpensive, highly variable testing instrument and an expensive precision instrument in a laboratory experiment.)   At this point, we are interested in the methodology you should use to answer such questions and not in the answers themselves. Therefore let us take a close look at Fig. 3.6, which shows a partial representation of the e_1-branch of the tree, given Charlie as your helper.

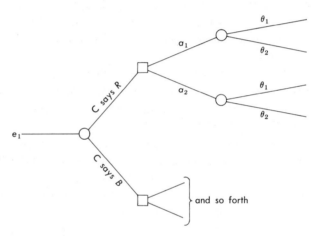

Fig. 3.6   Partial decision-flow diagram for analyzing the problem of biased reporting of sample information.

We must now calculate probability assignments for

[C says R] at (e_1),   (1)

θ_1 at (e_1, C says R, a_1),   (2)

θ_1 at (e_1, C says B, a_1).   (3)

But these are simple probability computations from the data you already have available, so to allow for such measurement bias in your analysis you should merely adjust the probability assignments on the chance moves. Then you

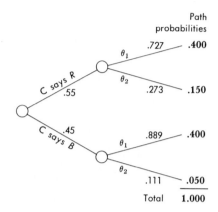

Fig. 3.7 Probability tree for the e_1-branch.

must work backwards by the averaging-out-and-folding-back process, just as before, but now using the modified probability assignments at the chance moves. To calculate the probabilities we need for the e_1-branch we shall use Figs. 3.7 and 3.8.

The probabilities on the branches of the probability tree of Fig. 3.7 are the ones that we need to analyze the decision-flow diagram. These probabilities, however, are not given directly; we must compute them. We must first arrange the sequence of events in such a way that we can make direct assessments from the data of the problem, which we have done in Fig. 3.8. Next we must compute the path probabilities, again as shown in Fig. 3.8, from the assessments on the branches of the tree. For example, we find that the probability that the unidentified urn is θ_1 *and* a black ball is drawn *and* Charlie says "Red" is

$$P(\theta_1) \times P(B \text{ if } \theta_1) \times P(C \text{ says } R \text{ if } B) = .8 \times .6 \times .3 = .144.$$

Then from the path probabilities in Fig. 3.8 we obtain the path probabilities in Fig. 3.7. For example, the path (C says R, θ_2) in Fig. 3.7 is the union of the paths

$$\{\theta_2, R, C \text{ says } R\} \qquad \text{and} \qquad \{\theta_2, B, C \text{ says } R\}$$

of Fig. 3.8, and this pair of paths has total probability of $.144 + .006 = .150$. You can calculate the other path probabilities in Fig. 3.7 in a similar manner.

Now that we have the path probabilities in Fig. 3.7, we proceed to compute the probabilities for the various branches. The probability for (C says R) is

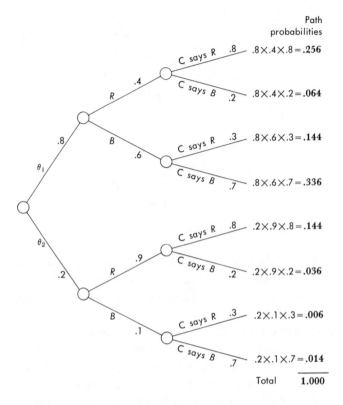

Fig. 3.8 Probability tree in sequence for direct assessment.

.400 + .150 = .55, and similarly the probability for (C says B) is .400 + .050 = .45. Next we observe that the probability of the θ_1-branch following (C says R) must be such that its product with the probability for (C says R), namely .55, must be the path probability .400. Here we use the formula

$$P(C \text{ says } R, \theta_1) = P(C \text{ says } R) \times P(\theta_1 | C \text{ says } R).$$

Hence

$$P(\theta_1 | C \text{ says } R) = .400/.550 = .727.$$

You can calculate the other probabilities in an analogous manner. You also could compute the probabilities on the e_2- and e_8-branches in a similar manner, by flipping probability trees. I think we had better avoid these details, however, although they do offer excellent exercises for anyone who is interested in carrying them out.

If you do not have the objective information about Charlie's past success ratios for identifying reds and blacks, then you can't assess or compute the appropriate probability assignments at chance forks so easily. But such a situation lies in the direction of "fuzzier" probabilities, and we shall hold off on this more complicated topic until we can discuss it in its proper context, in Chapters 5 and 6.

Observe that although we have shown that e_s is optimal for an EMV'er without measurement bias (in this case, without Charlie's services), the same is not necessarily true if measurement bias is present. Indeed, e_0 may now turn out to be optimal. Let's assume for the moment that your experimental cost is cut in half by using Charlie (e_1 with Charlie costs $4.00 instead of $8.00, and so forth). Figure 3.9 shows the fully analyzed decision-flow diagram for this situation. (You ought to be able to understand the averaging-out-and-folding-back analysis in this diagram; I have left the details for your verification.) Now we can go back to answer the question raised earlier: Would you sample if you had to use Charlie?

If you compare the tree shown in Fig. 2.13 (no bias in the samples) with the tree shown in Fig. 3.9 (Charlie is used at half price), you can see that a sequential sampling plan at full cost is to be preferred to using Charlie under any of the plans at half price. If we have to use Charlie, we won't sample at all. We should only use Charlie if his services cost less than $4.68 for two balls under alternative e_2, or if they cost less than $3.44 for the first ball and $2.25 for the second ball under alternative e_s. You can easily work out the implications of the various other sequential costs if you refer to Fig. 3.9.

The important fact here is that we do not place much confidence in Charlie's reports because we know that his reports are not always accurate. We can confirm this by observing that the conditional probability of θ_1 for each of the possible occurrences emanating from the e_1- or e_2-branches has not been appreciably modified from our original belief that there is a .8 chance of a θ_1 urn. Note that with e_1 none of the probability shifts are great enough for us to switch action. This is not true for e_2.

5. PROJECT

To create an exercise for the interested reader, we shall now make the following modifications in the oil-drilling problem we considered in Section 9 of Chapter 2. (*Note:* this project is continued on page 50.)

i) The cost of drilling is uncertain. It could be $40,000 with probability .2, $50,000 with probability .7, and $70,000 with probability .1.

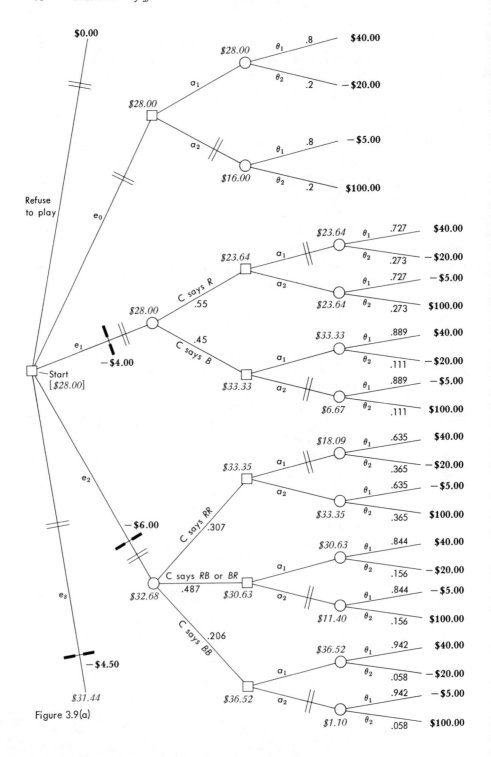

Figure 3.9(a)

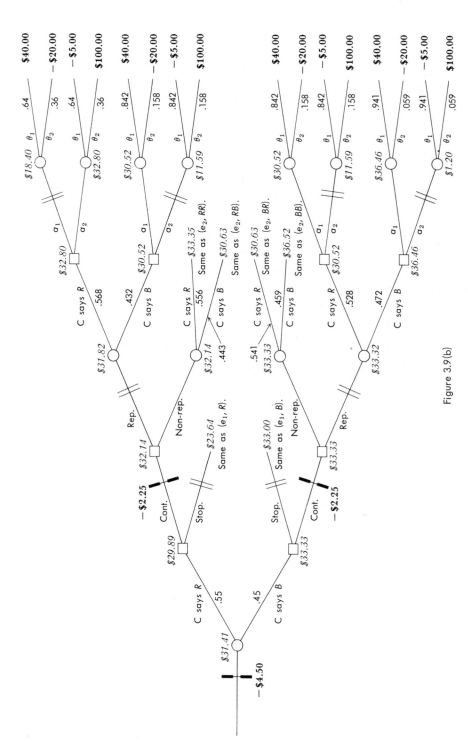

Figure 3.9(b)

TABLE 3.2

Conditional probability of getting apparent structure indication given true structure (using modified experiment)

True underlying structure	Structure indication from experiment			
	No structure	Open structure	Closed structure	Total
No structure	.90	.10	.00	1.00
Open structure	.20	.70	.10	1.00
Closed structure	.10	.30	.60	1.00

ii) Instead of using the standard seismic soundings, which are quite expensive but which will accurately disclose the true subsurface structure, the wildcatter can use a modified and cheaper experimental device which will also give an indication of the subsurface structure, but with occasional errors. This modified experiment costs only $3000 (instead of $10,000). Its results will be calibrated according to Table 3.2.

Should the wildcatter use the accurate seismic experiment at $10,000 or the modified, erratic experiment at $3000?

CHAPTER 4

UTILITY THEORY, OR WHAT TO DO ABOUT NON-EMV'ERS

1. INTRODUCTION

I asked this question of each of two experimental psychologists of my acquaintance: "Suppose you own the rights to a lottery ticket which gives you a 50-50 chance at $0.00 or $1000.00. What is the least amount you would be willing to take for this risky option? Don't answer on the spur of the moment— think it over; discuss it with your wife." After due reflection, my friends came up with very disparate answers. One was willing to sell the ticket for $450.00, but not for any lesser amount; the other was willing to sell his for any amount over $50.00.

"Are you sure," I asked one, "that you would not be willing to sell this option for any value less than $450.00? Your colleague would be willing to exchange it for $50.00."

"The trouble is," he retorted, "that it is very difficult to 'make believe'. So far as I am concerned, I would be willing to exchange this gamble for $450.00 and I personally think that my overly cautious colleague would have second thoughts if the money were on the table. I wonder if he and his wife thought hard about what they could get with that $1000.00?"

The other fellow defended himself in a very similar fashion. He insisted on the $50.00 limit and suggested that his reckless colleague and colleague's wife didn't take the whole thing seriously enough. "Imagine! Giving up a sure thing of $450 for an iffy prospect." And so on.

We may have our own private opinions about my subjects' responses; we might even attempt to make a predictive or psychological study of their underlying behavior. But if we are to advise each of them how they should behave in a decision problem similar to the one posed to you, then we had better simply accept the fact that they differ in their attitudes toward risk and that these differences should influence their choices.

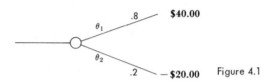

Figure 4.1

Suppose, now, that *you* fall in the largest category of people, that of the non-EMV'ers, people who would be delighted, like the two mentioned above, to accept $475.00, say, in exchange for a 50-50 chance at $0.00 or $1000.00. What can you salvage from the analysis of Chapter 2? Well, you can certainly go so far as drawing the decision-flow diagram, with the payoffs at the terminal points and the probabilities on the branches of chance forks. The trouble now is that you, a non-EMV'er, are not willing to use the averaging-out phase of the procedure of averaging out and folding back that we have described in earlier chapters. For example, suppose you place yourself at the chance fork with history (e_0, a_1). You would see ahead of you the *lottery*, as we may describe it, that is shown in Fig. 4.1. An EMV'er would be willing to assign

$$.8(\$40.00) + .2(-\$20.00) = \$28.00$$

as a certainty monetary equivalent (CME) for this gamble, as we already know. But now we are assuming that you are not an EMV'er and that if, for example, you were offered the possibility of exchanging your rights to this option for as little as $10.00, you might accept. You have one easy and natural way out of this dilemma, namely, you can use your *own* judgment to decide what specific amount *you* want to place at (e_0, a_1) in lieu of the gamble. Let's suppose you fix on $15.00. This means that if you were offered an amount in excess of $15.00 you would accept it in lieu of the option facing you at the (e_0, a_1)-fork; and if you were offered an amount less than $15.00 you would refuse it. In other words, $15.00 is your CME for this lottery. Now you might say that you are never actually so clear, that the $15.00 is really a very fuzzy quantity.

Well, imagine that you are working with an agent who is acting on your behalf; imagine that he will be offered some amount *x* in lieu of the lottery in Fig. 4.1. He wants instructions. No matter how fuzzy you are, you still might say to him: "Accept any value that is $15.00 or more; reject any value below $15.00." Certainly in analyzing *your* problem, you are better advised to work with *your* CME than to follow the dictates of EMV, which *you do not deem to be an appropriate guide to action for yourself*.

2. THE USE OF CME'S IN THE ANALYSIS OF A DECISION-FLOW DIAGRAM

Let me offer some advice on how you might proceed. First draw a decision-flow diagram of the basic problem and enter the payoffs at the tips of the tree, and enter as well all the appropriate probabilities at chance forks. Next work backward by using *your own* subjective judgment to replace each probabilistic fork of the type

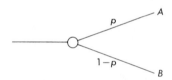

by your CME, which, incidentally, should depend on *A* and *B* (these numbers might in turn depend on judgments you have made further out on the tree), on *p*, on your financial assets (if any), on your attitudes toward risk, on your possible uses for (you hope) this extra money, on how you will explain this to your spouse if you lose, and so forth. Don't worry over the fact that your CME for an option may change with time. The question is: *What is it now*, at the time when you must decide what to do? In other words, you should proceed as suggested in Chapter 2 with this sole modification: Instead of using EMV's to compute values at each chance fork, you should use "seat of the pants" judgment to obtain CME's. You still work backward from the tips of the tree toward the start, just as before. Go ahead and try it! For your convenience, I have appended a decision-flow diagram with the necessary information at the end of this chapter.

Now you might reasonably argue that this formal analysis has not really helped you, if at the end you are forced to use your unaided judgment at so many junctures. But aren't you really better off now than before? Instead of having to use your unaided judgment on the whole tremendously complex problem, you now only have to use it on a host of simpler problems. You will further appreciate the gains as the whole decision problem increases in complexity. One of the troubles is, however, not that you have to use your judgment on a host of simple problems, but that these simple problems are *not simple enough*. Many people find it hard to think about giving a CME to the gamble

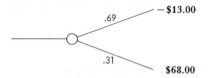

but not so hard for the gamble

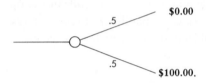

If possible, they would rather make up their minds to several of the latter gambles of the 50-50 type than to one of the former type. We shall consider this point in the next subsection.

Since the discussion must get a bit complicated anyway, we might as well handle a less specific problem with multi-fork gambles rather than one with only a two-fork gamble. After all, instead of two types of urns, θ_1 and θ_2, we could have started with three types or with 17 types. You might have been asked questions such as this: What CME would you give to the five-fork gamble shown in Fig. 4.2? If you *were* an EMV'er, the answer would be easy: The gamble would be worth

$$.13(-\$18.00) + .27(-\$7.00) + .23(\$3.00) + .17(\$16.00) + .20(\$72.00)$$
$$= \$13.06.$$

- $18.00

.13

.27   - $7.00

.23 $3.00

.17

.20 $16.00

$72.00   Figure 4.2

Indeed, an EMV'er could delegate authority to his representative by telling him exactly what calculations to make to find the CME of any gamble that is presented to him, no matter how many forks it has or what the monetary amounts are. For an EMV'er,

CME = EMV.

Could you, a non-EMV'er, do likewise? Not knowing what the gamble will be, could you give your representative inclusive instructions that would allow him to calculate a value that *you* would be willing to act upon as *your* CME of the gamble?

Slight Digression. We can represent the gamble shown in Fig. 4.2 in another way, in terms of a so-called *probability mass function* (see Fig. 4.3). The EMV, $13.06, is the *mean* or expected value of this distribution. Most subjects have a CME for this gamble that is below its EMV, or mean. One common suggestion, which is much too simplistic and often misleading, is to make allowance for the spread of the distribution by letting the CME for this gamble be the mean of the distribution (the EMV) *less* a proportion λ of the standard deviation (a common measure of spread of the distribution); or in more symbolic fashion,

CME = EMV − λ × standard deviation,

where the proportionality factor λ can be adjusted for individual differences of attitude toward risk. Besides its being terribly *ad hoc*, there is a lot that is wrong with this procedure. First of all, it is easy to give examples of two distributions that have the same mean and standard deviation but that have entirely

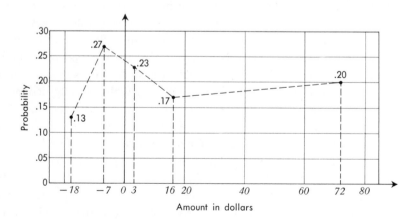

Figure 4.3

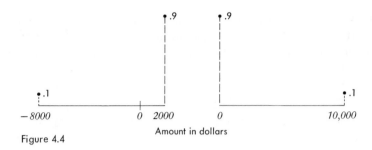

Figure 4.4

Amount in dollars

different financial implications.   (Figure 4.4 shows two such distributions.) Second, even if the distributions were symmetrically shaped on both sides of the mean, one would want the proportionality factor λ to depend on the placement of the whole distribution.   Not only is it important that one's CME be sensitive to the chances of getting an amount below $0.00, but below −$100.00, or −$500.00, etc., and, for that matter, it should also be sensitive to the chances of getting amounts above various positive values.   *The whole distribution counts.*

Where we are and where we plan to go.   For the moment you have agreed to change your stripes and become a non-EMV'er.   I think that you now realize that any non-EMV'er finds it difficult to assign a CME to such a complicated gamble as the one shown in Fig. 4.2.   We should like to find a procedure that you could use to think systematically about such problems.   Now if you, the non-EMV'er, were willing to disclose your attitude towards risk in broad terms, we could work out a method by which you could use this description of your attitude to analyze any specific gamble in routine fashion, however complex it may be.   We shall see that this can indeed be done, provided that you as non-EMV'er are willing to adopt certain consistency rules, rules which have some intuitive appeal.   You will see that if you reflect on your (brand-new) fundamental attitudes towards risk, you can use a surrogate commodity for money that works for you in very much the same way as money works for an EMV'er.   Instead of dollar bills, you will deal with specially designed lottery tickets, each of which will have a number between zero and one printed on its face.   To evaluate the desirability of a lottery, you simply substitute a ticket value (rather than a dollar value) for the prize at the tip of each branch of the tree, and then you multiply this ticket value by the probability of getting that branch; finally you sum these products over all the branches.   In other words, you average out over the ticket values to get an expected ticket value, and base your decision on a comparison of this resulting number with other numbers; you analyze a decision-flow diagram in terms of these surrogate ticket values by the same procedure of averaging out and folding back that we described in Chapter 2.

3. LOTTERIES WITH BASIC REFERENCE LOTTERY TICKETS AS PRIZES

In this section, our aim is to introduce and develop this new commodity that for all practical purposes behaves for the non-EMV'er as money does for an EMV'er. Shortly you will be asked to choose between two lotteries. Each of these lotteries has several prizes; the lotteries are *well defined* in the sense that you will be told the prizes and your chance at each of these prizes. What is peculiar about these lotteries is the nature of the prizes. A typical prize is a ticket, on one side of which is a number between zero and 1, inclusive; for example, the ticket with the number .38 on it will look like the one shown in Fig. 4.5(a). On the other side of the ticket is a description that tells to what this ticket entitles you; for example, the other side of the .38-ticket bears the message that appears in part (b) of the figure. For typographical reasons, we refer to the *basic reference lottery ticket* shown in Fig. 4.5 as a .38-BRLT, read "brilt" *and not* "b, r, l, t".

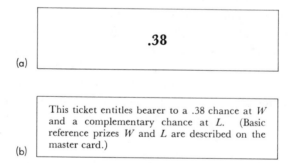

(a)

(b)

Fig. 4.5 The basic reference lottery ticket.

If you read the message in part (b), you will note that it refers to a master card. This master card might have the following descriptions.

W: Nontransferable rights for you and any companion of your choice to obtain (best) seats for any concert, play, opera, ballet, movie, sporting event, or lecture free of charge for a one-year period, starting now. You can go as often as you like.

L: Status quo.

All that you really have to keep in mind about W and L is that they are precisely defined consequences and that W is clearly preferable to L. (One student of mine actually preferred the status quo to the W described on this master card. He had scheduled a rigorous program of study for himself in the next year and he realized that he would succumb to the temptations of W at the expense of his academic work and end up unhappy in the long run. Let's rule out such aberrations.)

In order to execute the directions of the .38-BRLT, let's say that our friend the experimenter places 38 balls labeled W and 62 balls labeled L in an auxiliary urn and asks you to draw one of them at random. He has already made it clear to you that there is an equal chance that you will draw any one particular ball, and therefore you can see that the probability that you will draw a W is 38/100. (Note that this explains the symbolism on the lottery ticket, Fig. 4.5.) One additional point: You must realize that *any* ticket, regardless of the number on it, will ultimately result in one of the two basic reference prizes, W or L. *A 1.0-BRLT is identical to a W, and a 0.0-BRLT is identical to an L.*

We have assumed that you prefer W to L, and that given any two basic reference lotteries you would prefer the one with the higher number. For example, you would presumably prefer a .40-BRLT to a .38-BRLT because you would prefer drawing from an urn with 40 W's (and 60 L's) rather than from an urn with 38 W's (and 62 L's). The more winning balls, the better. Furthermore, *you feel this way even though you know the drawing will be done only once.*

Suppose you now have to make the choice described in Fig. 4.6. If you choose either a_1 or a_2, you will be confronted with a lottery whose prizes are basic reference lottery tickets. Consider the lottery associated with choice a_1.

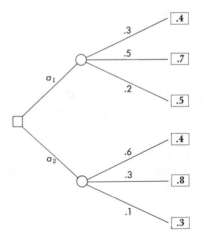

Figure 4.6

We can make the nature of this lottery clear if we proceed as follows. Let auxiliary urn A contain 30 balls marked ".4", 50 balls marked ".7", and 20 balls marked ".5". You then pick a ball at random from A, and if it turns out to be a ".7", then you get a .7-BRLT. This in turn means that the experimenter will place 70 balls marked W and 30 balls marked L in another auxiliary urn B, from which you will draw a second ball that determines whether you end up with W or with L. Note that the composition of the contents of urn B depends on the outcome of the drawing from urn A.

We could proceed, however, in another fashion, which I hope you will agree is strategically equivalent to the one I have just described. Suppose the experimenter places a total of 100 balls in an urn: The composition is 30 green, 50 yellow, and 20 orange. Of the 30 green balls, he labels .4 (i.e., 12 of them) with a W and 18 of them with an L; of the 50 yellow balls, he labels .7 (i.e., 35 of them) with a W and 15 with an L; and of the 20 orange balls, he labels .5 (i.e., 10 of them) with a W and 10 with an L. Figure 4.7 shows this composition. He now asks you to draw a ball at random from this urn, observe its color, and then immediately state whether it is a W or an L.

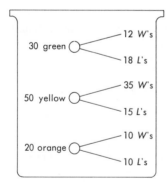

Figure 4.7

Of course, the important figure here is the number of W's in this urn. Since there are $12 + 35 + 10 = 57$ W's and 43 L's, drawing from this urn is equivalent to a .57-BRLT. We conclude therefore that the lottery associated with a_1 in Fig. 4.6 is equivalent to or *reducible to* a .57-BRLT. Observe that

$$.3 \times .4 + .5 \times .7 + .2 \times .5 = .57.$$

That is, .57 is a *weighted average of the ticket numbers* .4, .7, and .5, where the weights are the probability numbers on the branches: .3, .5, and .2, respectively. Hence we can say that .57 is the "expected BRLT value". In a similar fashion you can verify that the lottery associated with act a_2 in Fig. 4.6 is reducible to a .51-BRLT. Now your choice boils down to choosing a_1 and getting a .57-BRLT or choosing a_2 and getting a .51-BRLT. Clearly your choice should be a_1, and the whole venture is now worth a .57-BRLT.

It is important that you realize what we have just demonstrated. At first blush, one might have felt that in a one-shot situation it is not appropriate to use the weighted average of the BRLT numbers .4, .7, and .5, that some allowance should be made for how widely these numbers are dispersed, or the *spread* of these numbers. This is not so! Review once again the argument associated with Fig. 4.7. It says that it *is* appropriate to use the expected value (i.e., weighted average) of the BRLT numbers *without* any allowance for the spread of these numbers. This simple result would *not* be true if the prizes were in monetary values. Indeed, *this is why later we shall work in terms of BRLT values instead of money values.*

It is also important to keep in mind once again that the particular interpretations of the reference prizes W and L are not critical to the above arguments. All that is required is that you prefer W to L.

Let us summarize what we have argued* so far in terms of the following observation.

Fundamental Observation. You, as a decision maker, should be indifferent between the lottery which gives a

p_1-chance at a π_1-BRLT,
p_2-chance at a π_2-BRLT,
$\vdots$
p_m-chance at a π_m-BRLT,

(where $p_1 + p_2 + \cdots + p_m = 1$), and a $\overline{\pi}$-BRLT, where

$$\overline{\pi} = p_1\pi_1 + p_2\pi_2 + \cdots + p_m\pi_m.$$

All that matters is the weighted average (or expectation) of the π_i-values, where the weights are the p_i-values. The spread between these π_i-values is irrelevant. Furthermore, this is true even though it's understood that this

---

* The purist might worry at this point that our argument leading to the partitioning in Fig. 4.7 depended on the assignment of an *integral* number of balls in each category. If we had to deal with a .36247-BRLT, say, then we could not have used an urn with 100 balls, but we could have used an urn with 100,000 or 1,000,000 balls. We could handle irrational numbers as well, by considering an imaginary spinner (instead of an urn filled with balls) which for any given spin results in a real number on the continuum from 0.0 to 1.0.

lottery will be conducted just once and not repeatedly. No matter whether you are an EMV'er or a non-EMV'er, whether you like risk or are risk-averse, regardless of what monetary equivalent you associate with the basic reference prizes, it is appropriate for you to average out in terms of the units on the BRLT's.

Note that we could not assert a similar result if the lottery were given in terms of monetary prizes rather than BRLT values. For example, a decision maker would *not* necessarily be indifferent between a lottery which gives a

p_1-chance at $\$x_1$,

p_2-chance at $\$x_2$,

$\vdots$

p_m-chance at $\$x_m$,

and an amount, for certain, of

$$\bar{x} = p_1x_1 + p_2x_2 + \cdots + p_mx_m.$$

This would only be so for an EMV'er. The CME for a non-EMV'er would depend as well on the entire distribution of the monetary values.

4. SUBSTITUTABILITY

Consider the lottery ℓ shown in Fig. 4.8(a), that has these prizes:

C_1: a KLH table-model stereo record player,

C_2: $\$50.00$,

C_3: A used copy of the next-to-last edition of the *Encyclopedia Americana*. (This is included because it does not have an easily determinable market value.)

Now suppose that for C_1 the experimenter substitutes the prize C_1': a three-year subscription to *The New Yorker*. Let us keep C_2 and C_3 as before.

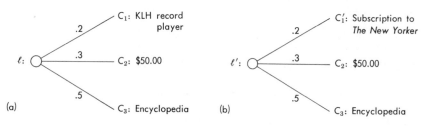

Figure 4.8

Would the modified lottery ℓ' shown in Fig. 4.8(b) be less desirable, more desirable, or indifferent to the original lottery ℓ? I personally would much prefer C_1 to C_1', and therefore I would prefer ℓ to ℓ'. It is not possible to *prove* that your choice should depend solely on your preferences between C_1 and C_1'; however, it seems reasonable that since C_2 and C_3 are common to both lotteries, they should not enter into your deliberations. Similarly the probabilities .2, .3, and .5 on the branches are irrelevant to the choice between ℓ and ℓ', so long as they are the same for both lotteries.

As we go on we shall constantly employ the following principle.

Substitution Principle. If a lottery is modified by substituting for one of its prizes another prize, everything else remaining fixed, and if you are indifferent between the original prize and its substitute, then you should be indifferent between the original lottery and the modified lottery.*

5.   THE SUBSTITUTION OF BRLT'S

I hope you now can foresee how we shall bring the material in the last two sections together. We can replace prizes such as C_1, C_2, or C_3, which may consist of items such as hi-fi equipment and encyclopedias, by equilibrated BRLT's, and we then can easily simplify the resulting lotteries with BRLT payoffs. Let us keep fixed the interpretations of W and L in Section 3, and C_1, C_2 and C_3 in Section 4. Consider the decision problem shown in Fig. 4.9, a problem similar to the one shown in Fig. 4.6, and let us first look at the lottery ℓ_1 associated with a_1. Let us assume that you would prefer W to C_3 and C_3 to L (the all-inclusive pass to the used encyclopedia to nothing). If a 1.0-BRLT, which is equivalent to W, were substituted for C_3, then the modification should make ℓ_1 more attractive to you. On the other hand, if a .0-BRLT, which is equivalent to L, were substituted for C_3, then this modification should make ℓ_1 less attractive to you. For high values of π, you will prefer the π-BRLT to C_3; and the opposite preference will hold for low values of π. You should have a hard time making up your mind whether you prefer C_3 or the π-BRLT for π somewhere in the interval between zero and 1. As π moves from 1.0 down to zero, your strong preference for the π-BRLT should evolve toward weak preference, and to weak disinclination, and to strong disinclination. We shall assume that somewhere along the line your feelings must pass through indifference. Suppose for the

---

* A stronger version of the Substitution Principle would state that if a lottery is modified by substituting for one of its prizes a *better* prize, then the modified lottery would be *better* than the original lottery. All we need for our purposes, however, is the version using indifferences.

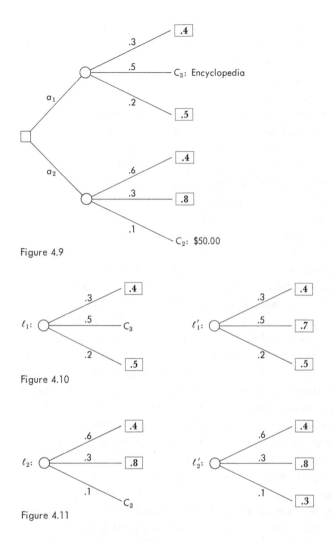

Figure 4.9

Figure 4.10

Figure 4.11

sake of argument that you are indifferent between getting C_3 outright and getting a .70-BRLT; then you ought to be indifferent between the two lotteries shown in Fig. 4.10. But now lottery ℓ'_1 is reducible to a .57-BRLT, since $.3 \times .4 + .5 \times .7 + .2 \times .5 = .57$, and therefore ℓ_1 is indifferent to a .57-BRLT.

How about a_2? For the sake of argument, suppose you are indifferent between C_2 and a .3-BRLT and therefore you are indifferent between the two lotteries shown in Fig. 4.11. Lottery ℓ'_2, however, is reducible to a .51-BRLT, since $.6 \times .4 + .3 \times .8 + .1 \times .3 = .51$, and therefore ℓ_2 is indifferent to a

.51-BRLT. Hence, to remain consistent with your previously expressed basic preferences, you ought now to conclude that you prefer a_1 to a_2, since you prefer a .57-BRLT to a .51-BRLT.

Before showing how all this relates to the analysis of the basic problem posed to you in the first chapter, let us consider a simpler problem that will consolidate what we have done in the last three sections. We shall formulate and analyze this simpler problem with the help of the decision-flow diagram shown in Fig. 4.12. As the decision maker you must, at the start, choose a_1 or a_2. If you choose a_2, then there is a .4 chance at consequence C_2 and a .6 chance at C_4; and if you choose a_1, then there is a .1 chance at C_4 and a .3 chance at C_3, and a .6 probability that you will arrive at the fork where you must choose between a_3 and a_4.

Choice a_3 at this fork leads to C_3 with certainty, and choice a_4 leads to C_1, C_4, or C_5 with probabilities .4, .2, and .4, respectively. Assume that each of the consequences $C_1, \ldots, C_5$ represents some complex bundle of rewards or penalties or both: money, tangible goods such as food and clothing; tasks to perform such as mowing the lawn, baby-sitting, and so forth.

Let's also assume that you have no trouble ranking consequences C_1 to C_5 when you have full description of them. So far as you are concerned, C_1 is preferable to C_2, which is preferable to C_3, which is preferable to C_4, which is preferable to C_5. There are undoubtedly cases where you cannot or will not, for some reason or another, rank the consequences according to your preferences. Let us talk about the cases where you can and are willing to do the ranking and where you are crystal clear in your preferences. It certainly should be self-evident, however, that ranking the consequences is not enough. Is your preference for C_1 to C_2 *stronger*, or *more compelling* (whatever that may mean), than your preference for C_3 to C_4, say? Lets analyze this problem in comparative preference.

First, we introduce a class of BRLT's where the reference prize W is taken as C_1 and the reference prize L is taken as C_5. This means that we already know that C_1 is indifferent to a 1.0-BRLT and C_5 is indifferent to a .0-BRLT. Suppose that after considerable probing of your preferences, you find that you feel indifferent between

C_2 and a .80-BRLT,

C_3 and a .50-BRLT,

C_4 and a .20-BRLT.

These equilibrating BRLT's appear at the tips of the branches in Fig. 4.12, in the positions where we would have placed consequences and payoffs before.

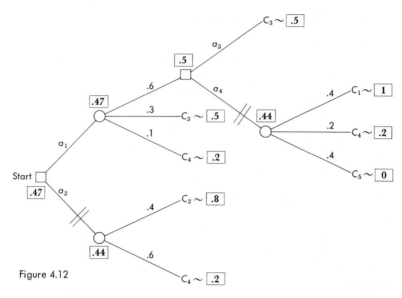

Figure 4.12

Now suppose that in conceptual time you are at the juncture where you must choose between a_3 and a_4. What future do you see? At the end of the a_3-road, you see a stimulus that you have subjectively evaluated as equivalent to a .5-BRLT. At the end of the a_4-road, you see a complex lottery with consequences C_1, C_4, and C_5 as prizes. You now know that by repeated substitution you can replace these prizes with equilibrating BRLT's; when you do so, this entire lottery reduces to a .44-BRLT, since

$$.4 \times 1.0 + .2 \times .2 + .4 \times 0 = .44.$$

Because you would prefer a .5-BRLT to a .44-BRLT, you ought to block off the a_4-road with double slashes. Then you can say that the "value" of being at the (a_3, a_4)-fork is a .5-BRLT. In other words, after substituting BRLT's for consequences, you merely have to average out and fold back just as you did in Chapter 2.

I hope the rest of the analysis is clear. By working backwards, you find that the a_1-branch is best and is worth a .47-BRLT. The critical factors in this analysis, of course, are the equilibrating π-values you associate with consequences C_2, C_3, and C_4. We shall say more about these measurements later.

In Chapter 2, we concluded that the averaging-out process in terms of money is only legitimate for EMV'ers. But the averaging-out process in terms of BRLT values is always legitimate for non-EMV'ers as well as EMV'ers—that's why we chose to work with these values.

6.   THE π-INDIFFERENCE FUNCTION FOR MONEY

Let us return to the analysis of your basic decision problem and now assume that you, the readers, are all non-EMV'ers. It is impossible for me to carry out the details of the analysis of the decision problem for each of you since your subjective evaluations will differ, but I shall discuss with you one such analysis for a particular non-EMV'er to help you to go ahead on your own. Let's refer to him as the Decision Maker, or D.M. for short.

We first select two monetary values, $-\$50.00$ and $\$100.00$ say, that are sufficiently wide apart that they encompass all the rewards and penalties in your (as well as D.M.'s) basic decision problem, and we introduce the class of basic reference lottery tickets with lower reference prize $L = -\$50.00$ and upper reference prize $W = \$100.00$. Thus a π-BRLT gives D.M. a π-chance at $\$100.00$ and a $(1 - \pi)$-chance at $-\$50.00$.

Next, we ask D.M. what amount $\$x$ he would want for certain in lieu of a π-BRLT. His answer sets up a correspondence, appropriate for him, that relates

$$x \qquad \text{and} \qquad \pi.$$

We can graph this correspondence in the form of a curve, where for each x on the abscissa, there is a corresponding π on the ordinate axis. (See Fig. 4.13.) This curve is called a π-*indifference curve for money* and represents D.M.'s evaluations. Thus, for example, the point (10, .575) lies on the curve, and this means that D.M. is indifferent between getting $\$10.00$ for certain and getting a .575-BRLT.

The π-indifference curve for an EMV'er is simply a straight line connecting the point $(x = -50, \pi = 0)$ with the point $(x = 100, \pi = 1)$. We can verify this by observing that for an EMV'er,

$$x = (\pi)(100) + (1 - \pi)(-50)$$
$$= -50 + 150\pi,$$

or

$$\pi = \tfrac{1}{150}(x + 50),$$

which is an equation of a straight line.

We shall explain a couple of points on this π-indifference curve. In reply to our questioning, D.M. has indicated that he is indifferent between $\$0.00$ (that is, the status quo), and a .5-BRLT. Hence his curve goes through the point

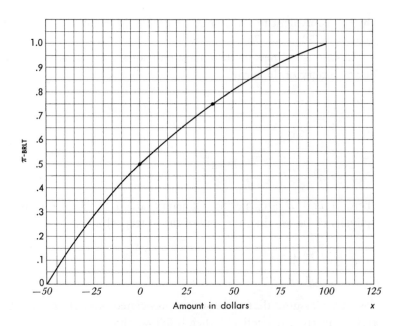

Fig. 4.13 Mr. D.M.'s π-indifference curve for money. For any (x, π)-value on the curve, Mr. D.M. is indifferent between getting x dollars for certain and getting a π-BRLT. The π-BRLT gives him a π-chance at $100.00 and a (1 − π)-chance at − $50.00.

(x = 0, π = .5). We asked D.M. to use this value of $0.00 and the upper prize of $100.00 to give his CME for the lottery

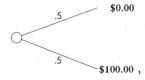

and he settled on the value of $38.00. If we substitute the .5-BRLT for $0.00 and the 1.0-BRLT for $100.00, we see that D.M. should be indifferent between $38.00 for certain and the lottery

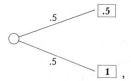

which is equivalent to a .75-BRLT. Hence D.M.'s curve also goes through the point $(x = 38, \pi = .75)$.

In serious business matters, most individuals are *risk-averse* in the sense that for any lottery of the form

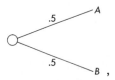

where A and B are specific monetary amounts, their certainty monetary equivalent C is less than the EMV of the lottery; that is,

$$C < \frac{A + B}{2} . \tag{1}$$

Now if we assume that the π-values associated with A, B, and C are $\pi(A)$, $\pi(B)$, and $\pi(C)$, respectively, then it follows that

$$\pi(C) = \frac{\pi(A) + \pi(B)}{2} . \tag{2}$$

What does all this imply about the shape of π-indifference curve for a risk-averse individual? Properties (1) and (2) imply that such a curve must be concave, that is, it must be shaped

everywhere this way: ⌐ , and nowhere this way: ⟋

To see this, refer to Fig. 4.14. From (1) we observe that the point C must be to the left of $(A + B)/2$. From (2) we observe that the point on the curve with coordinates $(C, \pi(C))$ must be to the left of the midpoint of the chord connecting $(A, \pi(A))$ with $(B, \pi(B))$. We therefore conclude that this curve must pass through the three points designated by crosses in Fig. 4.14. We can also observe that if the curve were not concave everywhere in its range, it would be possible to choose an A and B so that (1) and (2) would be contradicted.

Now let's follow D.M.'s own course of analysis as he works to construct his own π-indifference curve. Since D.M. has indicated that he is risk-averse, he knows that his curve must be concave and must pass through the four

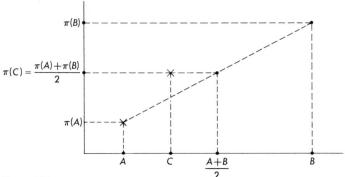

Figure 4.14

points $(-50, 0)$, $(0, .5)$, $(38, .75)$, $(100, 1)$. He also wants his curve to rise in a smooth fashion, without any sharp corners. These guidelines will help him to fill in the curve in Fig. 4.13. He can then test his curve by looking at different lotteries of the form

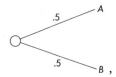

determining the certainty monetary equivalent C for each (see Fig. 4.14), and checking to see if each of these results meets with his approval. Occasionally a certainty monetary equivalent C may not agree with his personal judgments, which naturally take into account his economic well-being at the time as well as his predilections for gambling; when this occurs, he would bend or straighten out his π-indifference curve, as the case warrants. After such jockeying, he ends up with the curve as it is drawn in Fig. 4.13.

Let us return to the question posed at the end of Section 2: Could D.M. delegate his authority to a representative, telling him exactly what calculations to make in order to find D.M.'s CME for any lottery that is presented (where the monetary prizes range in the interval from $-\$50.00$ to $\$100.00$)?

The answer is, "Yes". Let us consider the lottery shown in Fig. 4.15. The representative would refer to D.M.'s π-indifference curve and would substitute for each monetary prize D.M.'s indifferent π-BRLT. He would then be instructed to compute

$$.13 \times .35 + .27 \times .45 + .23 \times .52 + .17 \times .62 + .20 \times .89 = .57,$$

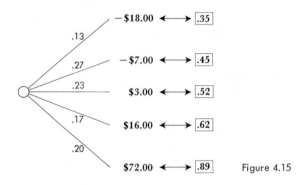

Figure 4.15

and he would conclude that D.M. would be indifferent between this lottery (Fig. 4.15) and a .57-BRLT. Furthermore, by referring once again to D.M.'s π-indifference curve, he would conclude that this ticket is worth $11.00. Incidentally the EMV of this lottery is $13.06. The difference between D.M.'s CMV and the EMV would of course be more dramatic if either the π-indifference curve were more bent than it is, or if the stakes were larger.

To summarize; We have just shown that if you can systematically associate a CME with every special lottery of the form

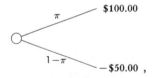

then you can *compute* the CME that you *ought* to associate with *any* lottery having any number of branches and any payoffs, so long as these payoffs lie in the interval between −$50.00 and $100.00. Although there are still an infinite number of π-BRLT's for you to consider, we have reduced your problem to a manageable form; we have done this by specifying that your π-indifference curve must satisfy some very stringent structural properties (for example, it must be monotonically rising in a continuous manner), and suggesting that perhaps you might want your curve to have a certain shape, i.e., concavity. Later we shall discuss other structural properties that you might want your curve to have, and this of course will be an opening for further simplification. Finally, then, to obtain a suitable π-curve you only have to locate a few points, police these to see that they line up nicely on a smooth curve of the structural kind you are seeking, and "fill in" the rest by a smooth eye-ball process.

7. ANALYSIS OF
YOUR BASIC DECISION PROBLEM FOR A NON-EMV'ER

Now let's analyze your basic problem for a decision maker having the
π-indifference curve for money shown in Fig. 4.13. First, we draw the decision-
flow diagram for the problem, which shows how decision choices and chance
choices unfold sequentially. Second, we enter the payoffs at the tips of the
branches, but in these payoffs we now include all the sampling costs. In other
words, we eliminate the sampling tolls and incorporate these payments at the
ends of the tree. The reason for this is rather subtle and we shall explain it
later, in Section 11. Next, we substitute a π-BRLT for each monetary payment x
at the tips of the tree; here π and x are of course related by the π-indifference
curve. Fourth, just as before, we assign the appropriate probabilities to the
branches at every chance fork. Finally, we analyze the tree by the usual
procedure of averaging out and folding back. This procedure gives the value
of being at any fork in π-BRLT terms. At any fork, however, the decision maker
can also determine his CME for any π-BRLT; this would tell him in monetary
terms what it is worth to be at any given fork on the tree.

Before we examine the details of this entire program, let us analyze just
the e_1-branch, which is shown in Fig. 4.16. If, for example, D.M. follows the

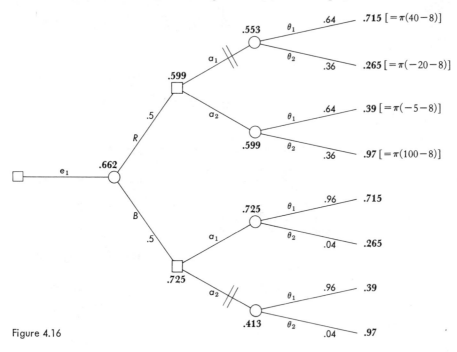

Figure 4.16

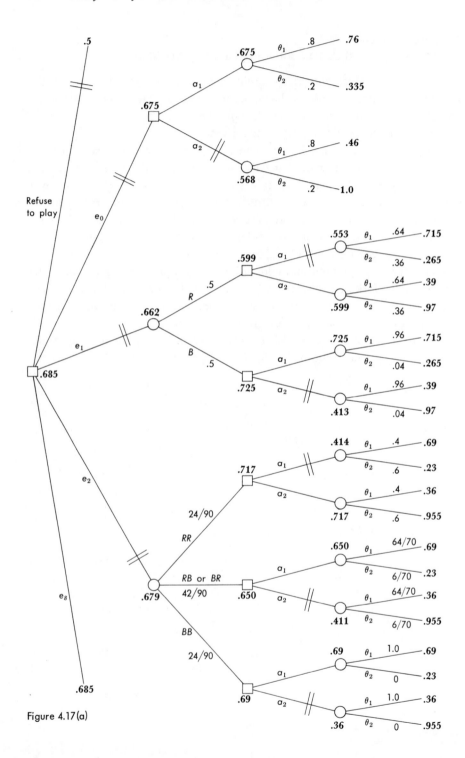

Figure 4.17(a)

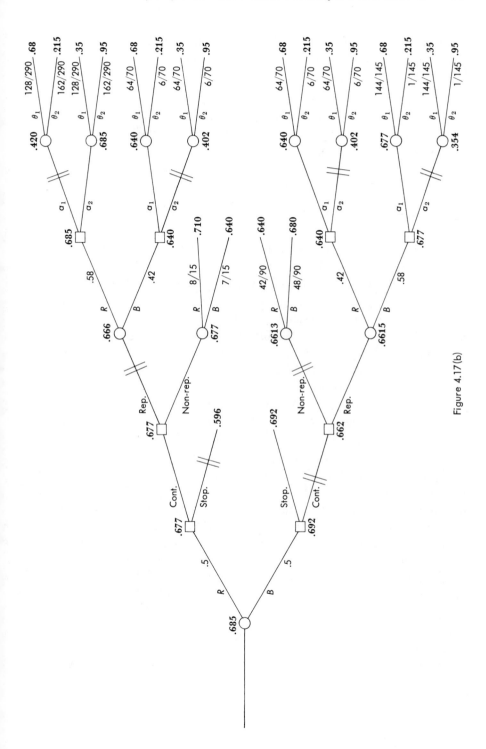

Figure 4.17(b)

(e_1, R, a_1, θ_1)-path, the payoff will be \$40.00 less the \$8.00 toll, or \$32.00. Using his π-indifference curve for money, we obtain

$$\pi(32) = .715.$$

At (e_1, R, a_1), D.M. encounters a lottery that yields a .715-BRLT with probability .64 and yields a .265-BRLT with probability .36. Thus being at (e_1, R, a_1) should be worth a .553-BRLT to him, since

$$.64 \times .715 + .36 \times .265 = .553.$$

From this result we see that his CME at (e_1, R, a_1) should be \$7.00, since $\pi(7) = .553$. Working backward, we finally obtain the result that the e_1-path should be worth a .662-BRLT, and since for him $\pi(22) = .662$, his CME of the e_1-path should be \$22.00.

In Fig. 4.17 we present the entire analysis. From this figure we see that the sequential experiment e_s is optimal for D.M., and his optimal strategy has the value of a .685-BRLT. Referring to Fig. 4.13, we see that an x-value of 26 corresponds to a π-value of .685, and hence we conclude that D.M.'s CME for this entire enterprise is \$26.00. If someone were to offer him more than \$26.00 for the rights to this monetary venture, he ought to accept; if anyone were to offer less, he ought to refuse.

Note that the strategy D.M. ought to select agrees with the strategy an EMV'er ought to select; however, D.M.'s evaluation of the venture is \$26.00, whereas an EMV'er's evaluation is \$31.15. Not a very striking difference. When I worked out these results I thought at first I might change some payoffs or sampling costs or bend D.M.'s π-indifference curve a bit more to get a more dramatic contrast, or at least a shift in optimal strategy. It isn't very hard to change some of the numbers so that e_0 is optimal for an EMV'er and e_s is optimal for D.M., given his curve as shown in Fig. 4.13; but I refrained from making such changes because there is a message to be learned here that these figures bring out clearly. In many decision problems, so long as the decision maker's π-indifference curve is not too drastically bent, the EMV-analysis of a problem does not differ markedly from the full π-indifference analysis, and the EMV-analysis can be used as a first-order approximation that *may* stand up in a more detailed analysis. This point notwithstanding, there are loads of problems where an EMV-analysis will be plainly misleading. We shall discuss some of these situations in Chapter 8 when we consider risk sharing; in these cases we shall find the full essence of the problem to be the curvature of the π-indifference curves of the decision makers.

8.   TRANSITIVITY

Please refer to Fig. 4.18 and decide which act you would prefer, a_1 or a_2. You certainly would rather not play, but suppose you *have to choose*. Now refer to Fig. 4.19; which act would you prefer here, a_2 or a_3?

Many subjects say they prefer a_1 to a_2 and a_2 to a_3. They argue that rather than lose \$45.00 for certain (Fig. 4.18), they would take the gamble. As regards Fig. 4.19, they report that since the gamble that pays \$45.00 or −\$50.00 with equal chances is unfair, they would rather not play if they had to choose, even after losing \$45.00; hence they would prefer a_2 to a_3.

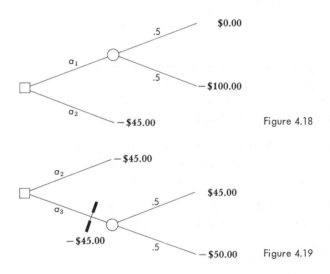

Figure 4.18

Figure 4.19

Now let's consider a_1 versus a_3 (see Fig. 4.20). Note that with a_3 you actually are being given a 50-50 chance at \$0.00 or −\$95.00, so clearly a_3 should be preferred to a_1. You may have recorded a preference for a_1 to a_2, for a_2 to a_3, and for a_3 to a_1. Such a set of cyclic preferences we shall call *intransitive*.

Some subjects who registered intransitivities on these three paired comparisons said they would not alter their original expressions of preference even after their intransitive choices were pointed out to them. They felt that if they were to make changes for the sake of consistency, they would not be revealing their primitive, true tastes, however illogical these might be, but would instead be playing a game that might result in their being tricked into saying things they really did not believe. Other subjects, after their intransitive choices were pointed out, became increasingly uncomfortable with them; on

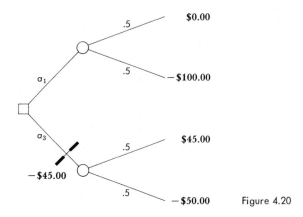

Figure 4.20

reexamining their basic feelings they felt that they gained a better appreciation of the complexities of the choice situation, and many subsequently changed their choice, preferring a_2 to a_1, thus eliminating the intransitivity.

At this point it will be helpful to formalize the

Transitivity Principle. Let A, B, C be any three alternatives. If the decision maker has any preferences among these alternatives, then these preferences should be consistent in the following sense:

a) If he is indifferent between A and B and between B and C, then he is indifferent between A and C; symbolically,

$$\left.\begin{array}{l} A \sim B \\ B \sim C \end{array}\right\} \Rightarrow A \sim C.$$

b) If he prefers A to B and prefers B to C, then he also prefers A to C; symbolically,

$$\left.\begin{array}{l} A > B \\ B > C \end{array}\right\} \Rightarrow A > C.$$

c) If he prefers A to B, and is indifferent between B and C, then he prefers A to C; symbolically,

$$\left.\begin{array}{l} A > B \\ B \sim C \end{array}\right\} \Rightarrow A > C.$$

We have used the Principle of Transitivity implicitly many times already. For example, in comparing the lottery ℓ_1 in Fig. 4.10 with the lottery ℓ_2 in

Fig. 4.11, we used a procedure of successive simplifications that invoked the Transitivity as well as the Substitution Principle. Recall that we argued that

$$\ell_1 \sim \ell'_1, \qquad \text{by substitution,} \qquad (1)$$

$$\ell'_1 \sim .57\text{-BRLT}, \qquad \text{by reduction,} \qquad (2)$$

$$\ell_2 \sim \ell'_2, \qquad \text{by substitution,} \qquad (3)$$

$$\ell'_2 \sim .51\text{-BRLT}, \qquad \text{by reduction,} \qquad (4)$$

$$.57\text{-BRLT} > .51\text{-BRLT}, \qquad \text{by monotonicity.} \qquad (5)$$

From this we concluded that $\ell_1 > \ell_2$, but to do this formally we must invoke the full power of the Transitivity Principle. Using (1), (2), and part (a) of the Transitivity Principle, we get

$$\ell_1 \sim .57\text{-BRLT}. \qquad (6)$$

From (6), (5), and part (c), we get

$$\ell_1 > .51\text{-BRLT}. \qquad (7)$$

From (7), (4), and part (c), we conclude

$$\ell_1 > \ell_2. \qquad (8)$$

It seems a bit pedantic to use all this formality to get such an intuitively appealing result. But it is important to recognize that we have used the Transitivity Principle rather liberally in the past, and that this principle is part of what we mean by "consistency".

It's easy to give examples that illustrate intransitivities of choices. Very often, however, one gives examples that really do not violate the Transitivity Principle if one is careful to specify fully enough the stimuli that are being compared. For example, Mr. Smith preferred A to B yesterday, prefers B to C today, and will prefer C to A tomorrow. Tastes shift, and such shifts should not necessarily be construed as intransitivities. The stimulus "A yesterday" is not necessarily the same as the stimulus "A tomorrow".

The following example will help to illustrate how intransitivities may arise in *descriptive* choice behavior and why in a *prescriptive* theory of choice this type of behavior should be discouraged. Suppose A, B, and C are three properties that a potential buyer, Mr. Jones, is considering. Jones is concerned about cost, space, and convenience. His evaluations are summarized in Table 4.1. Suppose Jones does not know whether his realtor will offer him any one, two,

TABLE 4.1
Rankings of three properties on three attributes

	Attribute		
Properties	Cost	Space	Convenience
A	Best	Worst	Middle
B	Middle	Best	Worst
C	Worst	Middle	Best

or all three of these properties. After thinking about what he would do if he were offered any pair, Jones decides that he would prefer: A to B, B to C, and C to A. Each of these seems reasonable to him since, he argues, in each paired comparison the preferred alternative has a higher ranking on two of the three important attributes; for example, A is better than B on cost and convenience.

It's fun to argue with someone like Jones who registers these choices and obstinately refuses to change his mind.

"Suppose, Mr. Jones, that you have just been given the deed to property A and now the realtor offers you C for a small premium. If your preferences mean anything, they certainly mean that you would be willing to pay this tiny premium to exchange A for C . . . Okay, now you have C. Next suppose the realtor offers you B for another tiny premium. Certainly you should be willing to pay this premium to get B rather than stay with C . . . Okay, now you have B. But why stay with B when for a small premium you can switch to A? After all, you say you prefer A to B . . . Okay, now you have A. But why stop here? Do you still insist you prefer C to A? You do? . . . Well, for a small premium . . . Are you sure, Mr. Jones, you don't want to change your mind?"

Mr. Jones is known in the vernacular as a "money-pump". Although we can rationalize why Jones acts the way he does, would *you* act this way? Or, more precisely, would you ever maintain a set of intransitive choices, if you were made aware of this and had the opportunity to change?

[A few years ago I tried to convince a friend of mine that he should vote for plan A rather than plan C for school construction in our town. He was truly undecided because there were so many factors that had to be considered. I asked him how he would feel if he had to choose between plan A and a hypothetical alternative plan B. He was clearly in favor of A over B. He also clearly favored B over C, all things considered.

"Well, doesn't this help you to make up your mind for A over C?" I asked.

"Not really. After all, plan B is *not* under review and is purely extraneous at this point."

"I don't agree. There's nothing illegitimate in adding hypothetical alternatives for our deliberation, provided they can help us think more systematically about the issues."

We bandied this around for a while and then he said, rather heatedly, "If *you* favored C over A, I suspect you would try to concoct a plan D in such a way that I would favor C over D and D over A, and by this tricky procedure you would try to lead me down the path of C over A."

"Yes, I would try. But could I deliver? That's the issue! I don't think I could."

He finally voted for A, but I must confess not because of my appeal to logic. It was more a case that the "bad guys" were for C.]

The following example illustrates that a long series of *indifferences* can lead to a real *difference* when they are strung together. So beware. Jones has a choice between a two-week paid vacation in Mexico (alternative M) or Hawaii (alternative H). He can't decide, and he concludes that he is really indifferent between them. Now if we add a $1.00 bonus to M, then he still might say he is indifferent between H and $M + \$1.00$. Symbolically,

$$H \sim M + \$1.00.$$

But now we can start a series of paired comparisons such that at each stage Jones will be indifferent between the alternatives. Jones might record

$$(M + \$1.00) \sim (H + \$2.00),$$
$$(H + \$2.00) \sim (M + \$3.00),$$
$$\vdots$$
$$(M + \$9999.00) \sim (H + \$10,000.00).$$

By transitivity of indifference this would imply that Jones should be indifferent between H and $H + \$10,000.00$, which is patently ludicrous. Should we say that the Transitivity Principle is not appropriate for Jones? I think a better way out of this dilemma is to have Jones agree that for some specific amount d he will be *strictly* indifferent between M and $H + \$d$ and that when any amount, however small, is added to either side he will change this strict indifference to an ever-so-slight preference, just enough of a preference to break the chain of indifferences.

If a decision maker asserts he is indifferent between A and B and between B and C, then our behavioral assumption states that he should be indifferent between A and C. In practice, this must be checked. If for some reason or other the decision maker prefers A to C, then he must go back and review his previous assertions. Somehow he must agree to police his basic preference structure for consistency if he wants to employ the decision techniques developed in these lectures. If in a given context he cannot find a comfortable compromise that assures consistency, then he will be better advised to use other less formal methods for decision making. Of course, he might very well adopt the methodology described in these lectures for one class of problems and not for another.

9.   A CRITICISM OF THE BEHAVIORAL ASSUMPTIONS

M. Allais, a French economist, posed the following pair of intriguing decision problems. Before reading further, decide without any calculations which choices you would make in Problems 1 and 2, Fig. 4.21.

M. Allais reports—and I as well as others have verified with hundreds of subjects that what he asserts is quite true—that most subjects prefer a_1 to a_2 in Problem 1 and prefer a_3 to a_4 in Problem 2. Most of these subjects reason as follows: "In Problem 1 I have a choice between \$1,000,000 for certain and a gamble where I might end up with \$0.00. Why gamble? In Problem 2 there is a good chance that I will end up with \$0.00 no matter what I do. The chances of getting \$5,000,000 are almost as good as getting \$1,000,000, so I might as well go for the \$5,000,000 and choose a_3 over a_4."

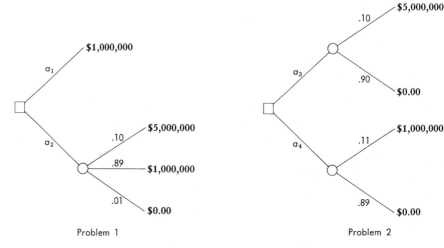

Problem 1   Problem 2

Figure 4.21

Now let's analyze this problem in the light of the advice offered so far in this chapter. Let's introduce a basic reference lottery with reference prizes $5,000,000 and $0.00, so that a π-BRLT stands for the lottery

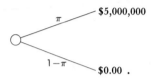

The methodology requires that the decision maker assign a π-indifference value for $1,000,000. This is not easy to do, so let's defer this ticklish assessment for a while, and meanwhile symbolically assert that $1,000,000 is indifferent to a π_1-BRLT. Substituting tickets for dollars and reducing lotteries with BRLT prizes, we then have

Act	Equivalent π-BRLT
a_1	π_1
a_2	$.10 + .89\pi_1$
a_3	$.10$
a_4	$.11\pi_1$

Now we conclude that

1) a_1 should be preferred to a_2 if and only if $\pi_1 > .10 + .89\pi_1$, or, equivalently, if and only if $\pi_1 > 10/11$,

2) a_3 should be preferred to a_4 if and only if $.10 > .11\pi_1$, or, equivalently, if and only if $\pi_1 < 10/11$.

From these two assertions, we see that a decision maker who follows the advice in this chapter could *never* prefer a_1 to a_2 in Problem 1 *and* a_3 to a_4 in Problem 2. (Neither could he prefer a_2 to a_1 and a_4 to a_3, for that matter.) So we see that descriptively speaking, most people do *not* behave in conformity with the principles of this chapter. But no one claims that most people *do* behave as they *ought* to behave. Indeed, the primary reason for the adoption of a prescriptive or normative theory (that is, an "ought to do" theory) for choice behavior is the observation that when decision making is left solely to unguided judgment, choices are often made in an internally inconsistent fashion, and this indicates that perhaps the decision maker could do better than he is doing. If people always behaved as this prescriptive theory says they ought to, then there would be no reason to make a fuss about a prescriptive theory. We could then just tell people, "Do what comes naturally."

The important issue is whether the Allais problems point out a serious weakness in the prescriptive theory. Let's take a closer look. I shall present two independent arguments designed to convince those who prefer a_1 to a_2 and a_3 to a_4 to change their minds.

First argument.* Imagine that our friend the experimenter has an urn that contains 89 orange balls and 11 white balls. Tomorrow morning at 9:00 a.m. you will draw one of these balls at random. If it is orange, you will receive prize Q. If it is white, he will offer you the choice between receiving $1,000,000 for certain (alternative A) and receiving the lottery

which we label alternative B, and you will have to make this choice at 9:05 a.m. The structure of this problem is shown in Fig. 4.22.

> *Question 1.* If you obtain a white ball, would your choice between alternatives A and B then depend on the detailed description of prize Q?
>
> *Question 2.* If at 8:55 a.m. the experimenter asks you to announce which alternative you will choose if you draw a white ball, will your decision depend on Q? Would it differ from the choice you would actually make at 9:05 when the chips were down?

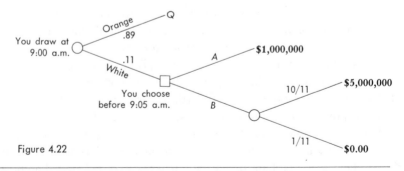

Figure 4.22

---

*Robert Schlaifer has offered this argument in slightly different form.

Most individuals (including myself) answer these questions negatively, and we shall investigate the implications of these responses. If you draw a white ball and if at 9:05 a.m. you prefer alternative A to B, regardless of Q, then you would be willing to announce at 8:55 a.m. that this would be your choice *if you draw a white ball*. But now let's see what this strategy implies. On the one hand, if Q is set equal to \$1,000,000, then this strategy is equivalent to a choice of a_1 over a_2. (Check this!) On the other hand, if Q is set equal to \$0.00, then this strategy is equivalent to a choice of a_4 over a_3. (Check this!)

If everything were the same except that at 9:05 a.m. you were to choose B over A, then by shifting the value of Q from \$1,000,000 to \$0.00 this would be equivalent to a choice of a_2 over a_1 in Problem 1 and a_3 over a_4 in Problem 2. In any event, if you agree with the negative answers to Questions 1 and 2, the logic seems to indicate overwhelmingly that you should not persist in choosing a_1 over a_2 *and* a_3 over a_4. Something must give. If you initially recorded preferences for a_1 over a_2 and a_3 over a_4, then perhaps you should admit that you made a judgmental slip, that you were dazzled by some of the numbers, and that you should change your preferences. Well, what do you think?

Second Argument. Suppose you strongly prefer a_1 to a_2 in Problem 1 and a_3 to a_4 in Problem 2. If you feel so strongly, presumably you would not change your mind if the experimenter were to add \$10.00 to each of the prizes in a_2 and a_4. Suppose now that he tosses a fair coin: heads you get Problem 1, tails you get Problem 2. If heads come up, will you still take a_1?... Yes. If tails come up, will you still take a_3?... Yes. If the experimenter asks you to announce your intention before the toss of the coin, would you assert that you would take a_1 if heads and a_3 if tails?... Yes. Would it therefore be fair to conclude that so far as you are concerned, the pair (a_1, a_3) is your most preferred, or *best*, strategy and the pair (a_2, a_4) is your least preferred, or *worst*, strategy?... Yes. Now let's investigate this.

The experimenter places 10 green balls, one white ball and 89 orange balls in an urn. You will draw a ball at random, with payoffs as given in Table 4.2.

TABLE 4.2 (M: million)

Outcome of drawing	Choice in Problem 1		Choice in Problem 2	
	a_1	a_2	a_3	a_4
Green (10)	\$1M	\$5M + \$10	\$5M	\$1M + \$10
White (1)	\$1M	\$0M + \$10	\$0M	\$1M + \$10
Orange (89)	\$1M	\$1M + \$10	\$0M	\$0M + \$10

Check the table to make sure that the choices and payoffs shown in the table agree with those shown in Fig. 4.21.

Now let's examine the payoffs (see Table 4.3) for your *best* and your *worst* strategies, supposing that the experimenter will toss a coin to determine which problem he will assign to you. Suppose the experimenter draws a ball without disclosing the result to you and holds it in his left hand; he then tosses a coin, also without disclosing the result to you, and holds it in his right hand. If you use your best strategy and if he has a green ball in his left hand, what stimulus confronts you? Simply a $1M or $5M return, depending on whether he has "heads" or "tails" in his right hand. If we now use the symbol $\langle A, B \rangle$ for the lottery that gives a .5 chance at A and a .5 chance at B, then the payoff corresponding to *Green* and *Best* is $\langle \$1M, \$5M \rangle$. The remaining payoffs in Table 4.3 should now be clear.

TABLE 4.3

Outcome of drawing	Your best strategy (a_1, a_3)	Your worst strategy (a_2, a_4)
Green (10)	$\langle \$1M, \$5M \rangle$	$\langle \$5M + \$10, \$1M + \$10 \rangle$
White (1)	$\langle \$1M, \$0M \rangle$	$\langle \$0M + \$10, \$1M + \$10 \rangle$
Orange (89)	$\langle \$1M, \$0M \rangle$	$\langle \$1M + \$10, \$0M + \$10 \rangle$

Would you prefer your best or your worst strategy if the experimenter discloses a green ball in his left hand (keeping the contents of his right hand still secret)? If he discloses a white? If he discloses an orange? In each of these cases, your *worst* strategy is *better* than your *best*!

Would you not agree at this point that something is drastically wrong? Check the logic once again and see if you agree that the weak link in the chain is the assertion that you strongly prefer a_1 to a_2 *and* a_3 to a_4. Would you still persist in choosing a_1 over a_2 *and* a_3 over a_4?

A student who heard my reasons for saying that the worst pair seems better than the best pair exclaimed, "Wait a second, I don't understand your argument. What if I had originally chosen a_2 over a_1 and a_4 over a_3, so that (a_2, a_4) would be my best pair and (a_1, a_3) my worst? Couldn't you switch the $10.00 bonus from the (a_2, a_4) pair to the (a_1, a_3) pair and then use the same argument to show (a_1, a_3) is really better than (a_2, a_4)? What does this prove?"

"Sure, I would argue that way," I responded. "If you take either (a_1, a_3) or (a_2, a_4) as your best pair, then the argument I used should undermine your confidence in your choices. But I could *not* use the same trick to undermine a choice of (a_1, a_4) or (a_2, a_3) as your best pair. These strategy pairs are *consistent*; the pairs (a_1, a_3) and (a_2, a_4) are *not* consistent, and that's the reason either pair can be upset."

A Counterargument

We have now discussed two arguments that show that the pair of simultaneous choices of a_1 over a_2 in Problem 1 and a_3 over a_4 in Problem 2 is incompatible with the behavioral assumptions we have adopted in these lectures. There is a counterargument that asserts there is *no incompatibility* if one is a bit more delicate in his interpretation of some of the consequences. Basically this argument says that one "zero" is not necessarily the same as another "zero". Here is the counterargument.*

From a descriptive point of view, one simply cannot say that zero dollars is zero dollars regardless of the psychological setting. The possible return of $0.00 stemming from the a_2-choice is a vastly different stimulus than the return of $0.00 stemming from an a_3- or a_4-choice. The subject who chooses a_2 and by chance gets a return of $0.00 may have all sorts of guilt feelings. "If only I had taken a_1," he moans, "I would have been *sure* of getting $1,000,000. This is what happens to greedy types like myself. My wife will never forgive me, and I'll have a guilty conscience for a long time to come. I just should not have let $1,000,000 slip through my fingers."

But now one could retort, "Well, if you would feel that way about getting a $0.00 return with a_2, should you not *also* feel equally guilty if you happen to get $0.00 with the choice of a_3? After all, the very ball you drew with a label of $0.00 might have had a $1,000,000 label on it if you had chosen a_4 instead of a_3."

"Ah, but I would never be certain. The balls are not colored green, white, and orange. If I chose a_3 and drew a ball marked $0.00, how could I tell this is *the* 'eleventh' ball which would magically turn to $1,000,000 if only I had chosen a_4? I would never know and therefore I would not feel guilty afterwards."

There are individuals for whom the stimulus of $0.00 on the a_2-branch is *just different* from the stimulus of $0.00 on the a_3- or a_4-branches. If the subject

---

* See Donald G. Morrison, "On the Consistency of Preference in Allais' Paradox", *Behavioral Science*, **12**, September 1967.

insists that this is the case, we can introduce new consequences C_0: "$0.00 and a terribly guilty conscience," and C_1: "$0.00 and a guiltless conscience". In these terms the subject's preferences will be

$$C_0 < C_1 < \$1,000,000 < \$5,000,000,$$

where we read the symbol $<$ as "is less preferred than". If we now use C_0 and $5,000,000 as reference prizes for basic reference lottery tickets, then we can let C_1 be indifferent to a π_1-BRLT and $1,000,000 be indifferent to a π_2-BRLT. Of course, in this case C_0 will be indifferent to a 0.0-BRLT and $5,000,000 to a 1.0-BRLT. If we now substitute equilibrating BRLT's for consequences, then it is possible to find π_1- and π_2-values such that he prefers a_1 to a_2 in Problem 1 and prefers a_3 to a_4 in Problem 2. Hence there is *no* inconsistency in these choices! This flexibility, however, has been bought at a price: No longer is zero the same as zero, the same as zero . . .

10. THE MAXIMIZATION OF EXPECTED UTILITY

Suppose that our friend the experimenter shows you a collection of lotteries and asks you which one you most prefer. Since you are no longer an EMV'er, it is *not* appropriate for you to associate with each lottery its expected *monetary* value and to choose the lottery that maximizes this value. Note that the emphasis here falls on the word "monetary". We now ask whether there is some way of transforming monetary values into values expressed in some new and different units such that it *is appropriate* for you to associate with each lottery its expected value in these new units and to choose the lottery that has the best showing on this new scale of expected values. For the sake of the discussion, let's agree to call the units of these new values *utilities*, or *utiles* (here we are borrowing terminology from the theory of utility). This sounds like a good idea, but how are we to find these new utility values? In other words, is there a suitable procedure for transforming dollar values into values expressed in utiles? We are already familiar with the π-indifference function shown in Fig. 4.13, which is just such a procedure; therefore let's suppose that this particular function is appropriate for you. You could use it to associate a "utility", in utiles, with each amount in dollars and compute the expected value of any lottery, and then choose the lottery that maximizes this index. For example, in the lottery ℓ of Fig. 4.15 you would make the associations

$$-\$18.00 \rightarrow .35 \text{ utiles}, \quad -\$7.00 \rightarrow .45 \text{ utiles}, \quad \$3.00 \rightarrow .52 \text{ utiles},$$
$$\$16.00 \rightarrow .62 \text{ utiles}, \quad \$72.00 \rightarrow .89 \text{ utiles}.$$

You would then associate with this lottery its expected utility value

$$.13(.35) + .27(.45) + .23(.52) + .17(.62) + .20(.89) = .57.$$

Finally, you would choose the lottery with the largest associated expected utility value.

If we look at the question in this manner, it is clear that there is nothing *unique* about the association of utility values with monetary amounts. We could add any constant to *all* these numbers and not affect the relative ranking of the lotteries. For example, -3.40 units could be arbitrarily added to each association, giving the following utility values for the consequences of ℓ:

$$-\$18.00 \rightarrow .35 - 3.40 = -3.05 \text{ utiles,}$$
$$-\$7.00 \rightarrow .45 - 3.40 = -2.95 \text{ utiles,}$$
$$\$3.00 \rightarrow .52 - 3.40 = -2.88 \text{ utiles,}$$
$$\$16.00 \rightarrow .62 - 3.40 = -2.78 \text{ utiles,}$$
$$\$72.00 \rightarrow .89 - 3.40 = -2.51 \text{ utiles.}$$

The expected utility value for ℓ would then be

$$.13(-3.05) + .27(-2.95) + .23(-2.88) + .17(-2.78) + .20(-2.51)$$
$$= -2.83.$$

But this new value of -2.83 is merely the previous value of .57 minus the constant 3.40. Subtracting or adding a constant to each of the π-values merely subtracts or adds this same constant to the index associated with each lottery. When we deal with these associated numbers we no longer have nice probabilistic interpretations, but no matter; all we are interested in is using these associated indices to rank the desirabilities of lotteries, and these rankings will not change. We can go further: If we uniformly multiply all the π-values by a positive constant and uniformly add any positive or negative constant, then once again the rankings of the associated indices for the lotteries will not be altered. Of course, we must use the same constants for each lottery.

There is another instructive way of looking at this process. Refer back to the π-indifference curve for money in Fig. 4.13. When we interpret this curve as a means of transforming monetary values into utility values, forgetting about the interpretation of the π as a break-even indifference probability, we see clearly that the only thing that is essential is the shape of the curve. The units of measurement on the vertical axis are immaterial. Just as we can change centigrade temperatures to Fahrenheit by multiplying by $\frac{9}{5}$ and adding 32, we can arbitrarily change one utility scale into another, so long as we consist-ently use one scale throughout the analysis of a given problem.

In analytical work this free choice of origin and of unit of measurement for a utility curve adds a little flexibility that allows us to use slightly simpler numbers or formulas. Suppose we start with a correspondence that associates a utility value $u(x)$ with each amount x. Let x_1, x_2, and x_3 be any three amounts, where $x_1 > x_2 > x_3$. The individual numbers $u(x_1)$, $u(x_2)$, and $u(x_3)$ mean nothing in themselves, but it does follow that $u(x_1) > u(x_2) > u(x_3)$. Further-more, there is some value π such that one is indifferent between getting x_2 for certain and getting the lottery

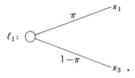

But this means that the index for the degenerate lottery that gives x_2 for certain, namely $u(x_2)$, must be the same as the index for lottery ℓ_1, which gives a π chance at x_1 and complementary chance at x_3. This means that

$$u(x_2) = \pi\, u(x_1) + (1 - \pi)\, u(x_3),$$

or

$$\pi = \frac{u(x_2) - u(x_3)}{u(x_1) - u(x_3)}.$$

Now if the scale of measurement of u is such that $u(x_3) = 0$ and $u(x_1) = 1$, then

$$\pi = \frac{u(x_2) - 0}{1 - 0} = u(x_2);$$

that is, x_2 is indifferent to the basic reference lottery ticket

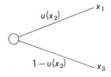

or to a $u(x_2)$-BRLT with $W = x_1$ and $L = x_3$.

Let's take a closer look at this last result. Suppose you draw your π-indifference curve for money with reference consequences $L = -\$50.00$ and $W = \$100.00$. Now suppose you want to change your reference consequences to $L = -\$25.00$ and $W = \$80.00$. You need not redraw your π-curve or ask yourself new questions. All you need to do is change the vertical scale so that the curve has a value of zero at $x_3 = -\$25.00$ and a value of one at $x_1 = \$80.00$. If x_2 is some value between x_3 and x_1, and if the value of the curve at x_2 (with this scale change) is $u(x_2)$, then you should be indifferent between getting x_2 for certain and getting a $u(x_2)$-BRLT with reference consequences $L = -\$25.00$ and $W = \$80.00$.

11. BUYING AND SELLING PRICE*

Consider the lottery ℓ that pays 0.00 or 1000.00 with equal probabilities:

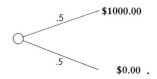

For the sake of argument, suppose your CME for this lottery is 400.00. This means that if you owned the rights to this lottery you would be willing to exchange them for any amount greater than or equal to 400.00 but not for any amount below 400.00. In other words you would "just be willing" to sell ℓ for 400.00, or, stated more succinctly, your CME is your *selling* price.

If you did not own the rights to lottery ℓ, would you be willing to *buy* ℓ for 400.00? Are you inconsistent if you would not? Not at all. Conceivably you might only have 200.00 in liquid assets and you might only be willing to spend 100.00 for the rights to this lottery. Your selling price s of a lottery is not necessarily the same as your buying price b of the same lottery. In terms of your utility function u for incremental monetary amounts, we can argue that

1) since you are indifferent between the lottery ℓ and the amount s for certain, you are indifferent between the two choice branches shown in Fig. 4.23. In utility terms, this means that

$$u(s) = \tfrac{1}{2}u(1000) + \tfrac{1}{2}u(0);$$

2) since you are indifferent between buying the lottery ℓ for the amount b and not buying it, you are indifferent between the two choice branches shown

---

* This section is not used in the sequel and can be skipped.

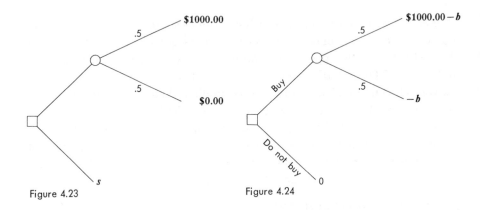

Figure 4.23   Figure 4.24

in Fig. 4.24. In utility terms, this means that b is such that

$$u(0) = \tfrac{1}{2}u(1000 - b) + \tfrac{1}{2}u(-b).$$

In particular, if we arbitrarily set $u(0) = 0$, then s and b satisfy the equations

$$u(s) = \tfrac{1}{2}u(1000) \qquad \text{and} \qquad u(1000 - b) = -u(-b).$$

Clearly s and b will not in general be the same.

The buying price b and the selling price s of any lottery will be the same for an EMV'er. However, we *cannot*, in general, conclude that if $b = s$ for any lottery, then the decision maker is an EMV'er; there is a class of so-called exponential utility functions where the buying price is always equal to the selling price and the decision maker in question might be employing one of these utility functions.

Mathematical Digression. We can show that if the decision maker's selling price is the same as his buying price for any lottery ℓ, then his utility function is very special: It is either linear, as

$$u(x) = x,$$

or exponential, as

$$u(x) = 1 - e^{-\lambda x},$$

where λ is a measure of *risk aversion*. In general, if the buying price for favorable lotteries is *less* than the selling price, then this places a qualitative restriction on the utility function, but one that does not type it quite so neatly as the qualitative restrictions in the case when the selling and buying prices are exactly the same. The next section has more to say about this.

Suppose you did not own the rights to play the basic problem posed to you in these lectures but rather you had to *buy* the rights to engage in this venture. How much would you be willing to pay for these rights? Alternatively, suppose you had the chance to bid in an open auction for the rights to this venture: What would be your maximum bid?

This is not an easy problem to solve exactly. For an EMV'er or, more broadly, for a decision maker with exponential utility, the solution is easy: His buying price equals his selling price. There are shortcuts one can employ to solve this problem for special types of utility functions but in general one can proceed as follows.

1) Let $u(0) = 0$.

2) Let b_0 be a guess at the solution.

3) Subtract b_0 from all the payoffs at the tips of decision tree, with the understanding that these payoffs include all the tolls for experimentation.

4) Convert monetary payoffs into utility payoffs.

5) Average out and fold back in terms of utility units to get the overall utility evaluation of the prospect (with b_0 subtracted out as in step 3). Call this utility number $\bar{u}$.

6) Compare $\bar{u}$ with 0; if $\bar{u} > 0$, then b_0 is too small; and if $\bar{u} < 0$, then b_0 is too large.

With a few iterations one can zero in on the correct buying price.

12. DECREASING RISK AVERSION*

Your CME (or equivalently, your selling price) for a sizable gamble usually depends on your present asset position, your monetary worth. In this section we shall be concerned with this dependence.

Let ℓ be a lottery that pays off \$500.00 or $-\$500.00$ with equal probabilities. Let's assume that you, like myself, are risk-averse and that if you had a choice, you would rather not participate in this lottery. Indeed, if you were saddled with the obligations of this lottery, let's say you would be willing to pay an insurance premium of \$100.00 to avoid the burden. In other words, you would be indifferent between the two choice branches shown in Fig. 4.25. If your asset position were very much higher than it is, if you were a much

---

* This section is not used in the sequel and can be skipped.

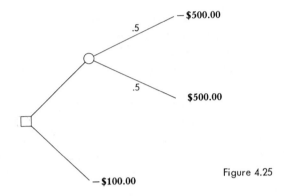

Figure 4.25

richer man, you would probably not be willing to pay a $100.00 insurance premium to relieve yourself of the responsibilities of *ℓ*—you would rather take your chances. The insurance premium you would be willing to pay for this lottery presumably *decreases* toward zero as your asset position increases. I must include the modifiers "presumably" or "probably", since not everyone would agree with the above statements. Qualitatively speaking, if I were to plot a curve of the insurance premium I would be willing to pay as a function of my assets *A*, the result would be a curve like the one shown in Fig. 4.26. We say that such behavior exhibits *decreasing risk aversion*. If you desire to be decreasingly risk-averse, then, as we shall show, your utility curve for money must be qualitatively structured in a rather restricted manner. Not every concave utility function is compatible with the requirement of decreasing risk aversion.

In drawing a *π*-indifference or utility curve for money, we have adopted the convention that the horizontal axis refers to monetary increments from your present asset position. Thus an *x*-value of $100.00 refers to an outcome that would add $100.00 to your present assets. Now if you want to see how an incremental change of $5000.00 in your assets might affect your attitude toward

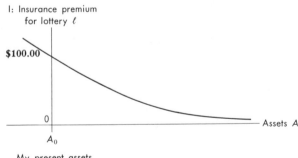

Figure 4.26

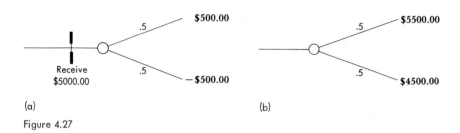

Figure 4.27

the given lottery ℓ, you can proceed by first observing that the two lotteries in Fig. 4.27 are strategically equivalent. (Again we are assuming that all transactions are done sequentially, without any delays. If there were delays, we should have all sorts of complications, such as new financial obligations and getting used to a new way of life.)

According to Fig. 4.27(a), you receive a $5000.00 bonus before confronting ℓ. In Fig. 4.27(b), this $5000.00 bonus is added into the payoffs of lottery ℓ. Using your utility curve you can compute your CME for the lottery of Fig. 4.27(b). Say it comes out to be $4950.00. We then can conclude that your CME for the lottery ℓ, after receiving a bonus of $5000.00 or, equivalently, assuming a sudden increase of $5000.00 in your asset position, is $-$50.00. In other words, your insurance premium for ℓ would be $50.00 if your assets were to increase by $5000.00.

In summary, we have shown how you might use your utility curve to ascertain what insurance premium you should be willing to pay if you receive a sudden change in assets. But we shall exploit this observation *by exactly reversing it*. Suppose for the moment that your insurance-premium curve is identical with mine, that is, with the one shown in Fig. 4.26. You are quite certain that you want *this* curve to give the premiums you would be willing to pay as your assets change, and hence you must see to it that your utility curve is so constructed that it gives this premium curve as the answer! If it does not, then you will have an inconsistency in your preferences and you will want to change either your utility curve or the qualitative nature of your insurance premium curve.

Thus we see in particular that if you want to be decreasingly risk-averse, you must constrain your utility curve to guarantee this requirement. This places a severe limitation on the structure of your curve and this can be exploited in the assessment of your utility curve. How do we do this? Unfortunately we can't say just now, because such a discussion would get us bogged down in mathematical detail that is not in the spirit of these lectures. All we need say here is that when we assess a utility function, it is imperative that we keep in mind such qualitative restrictions as risk aversion (which implies concavity of shape) and, more stringently, decreasing risk aversion. (We assume throughout, of course, that the decision maker agrees with the reasonableness of these qualitative desiderata.)

13. BEHAVIOR THAT IS NOT RISK-AVERSE*

There is nothing inconsistent about a subject who refuses to sell for $550.00 a lottery that pays off $1000.00 with probability .5 and $0.00 with probability .5. All we can say is that we should not describe such a subject as risk-averse. If we arbitrarily assign a utility of 1 to $1000.00 and a utility of zero to $0.00, which entails no loss of generality, then the utility of $550.00 would be less than .5. This implies that the utility curve of the subject must have a dip in it somewhere (that is, it cannot be concave everywhere) in the interval from $0.00 to $1000.00 The utility curve shown in Fig. 4.28 is such an example.

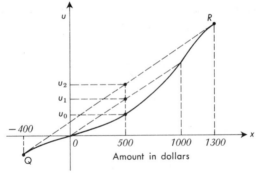

Figure 4.28

Friedman and Savage,[†] Mosteller and Nogee,[‡] Siegel,[§] and Grayson,[||] in that order, have demonstrated that utility functions with convex portions are quite common. Indeed, it is not uncommon to find utility curves that are quite kinky, like the one shown in Fig. 4.29. Some of the oil wildcatters whom

---

* This section is not used in the sequel and can be skipped.

† Friedman, M., and L. J. Savage, "The utility analysis of choices involving risk", *Journal of Political Economy*, April 1948, 279–304.

‡ Mosteller, F., and P. Nogee, "An empirical measurement of utility", *Journal of Political Economy*, October 1951, 371–404.

§ Siegel, S., "Level of aspiration and decision making", *Psychological Review*, **64**, 1957, 253–262.

|| Grayson, C. J., *Decisions Under Uncertainty*. Boston: Harvard Business School, 1960.

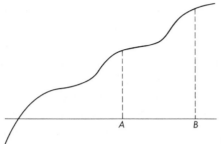

Figure 4.29

Grayson interviewed talked about a critical amount of money (such as *A* in Fig. 4.29) that they thought represented an achievement level that would mean a new way of life; to them it represented something worth gambling for. "Why, at *A* I can get my own yacht." I suppose *B* is also worth gambling for— if the wildcatter could achieve it, he could be the head of a two-yacht family, or perhaps even give away a yacht or two as Christmas presents. Siegel identifies inflection points of utility curves with "levels of aspiration".

Now let's add some cautious words about using such noncautious utility curves. Suppose you had the utility curve shown in Fig. 4.28 and you wanted to compute your CME for the lottery ℓ shown in Fig. 4.30. You would then (1) refer to your curve to find $u(-\$500.00)$, $u(\$500.00)$, and $u(\$1400.00)$, (2) compute the expected utility $\bar{u}$,

$$\bar{u} = .3 \; u(-\$500.00) + .4 \; u(\$500.00) + .3 \; u(\$1400.00),$$

and (3) refer to your curve to find the monetary amount *A* whose utility value is $\bar{u}$. This amount *A* is your CME for ℓ. But the amount *A* you have calculated for the CME of ℓ might be quite misleading if actuarially fair gambles were available to you in the open market place. For example, at Reno or Las Vegas you can get almost, but not quite, "fair" gambles at the casinos. The house likes to take a modest bite out of a wager. They would bet even money with you if they had a .51 probability of winning. While there may not be really "fair" (objective) gambles available, "almost fair" gambles are abundant.

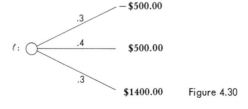

Figure 4.30

Actually there are "super-fair" gambles available on the stock market but these involve subjective considerations that we shall defer until the next chapter.

Let's suppose that there are fair gambles available, that your utility function is as shown in Fig. 4.28, and that you want to get your CME of lottery ℓ shown in Fig. 4.30. If perchance you get a payoff of $500.00 as you proceed with ℓ, you wouldn't stop there. You would, for example, prefer to bet the whole $500.00, win or lose. If you were to remain at $500.00, your utility index would be u_0; if instead you stake your $500.00 in a 50-50 gamble that brings you to a net position of $0.00 or $1000.00, then your utility for this prospect would be u_1, which is larger than u_0. (See Fig. 4.28.) You can even do better. Rather than end at $500.00, it would be preferable if you were to arrange subsequent fair gambles that would either give you a net asset position of $-$400.00 or $1300.00. To accomplish this you would engage in the fair bet where you could lose $900.00 (ending you up at $-$400.00) with probability $\frac{8}{17}$ or win $800.00 (ending you up at $1300.00) with probability $\frac{9}{17}$. This is an actuarially fair gamble since

$$\tfrac{8}{17}(-\$900.00) + \tfrac{9}{17}(\$800.00) = \$0.00.$$

The utility index for this prospect is the amount u_2 shown in Fig. 4.28; it represents your best exploitation of the availability of fair gambles and the peculiarities of your utility curve. Hence when the environment offers fair gambles for your exploitation, your operational utility index for $500.00 should be u_2 and not u_0.

In summary: If you have convex dips in your utility function, and if fair gambles are available in the marketplace, then when you analyze a decision problem you should fill in these dips in your utility function by straight line segments like the one shown connecting points Q and R in Fig. 4.28.

If this were an advanced treatise in decision analysis, we could go on to examine the case in which a given class of almost-fair gambles is available. Indeed, we could go further. The particular problem posed in this section suggests an interesting class of more complex problems. The utility function that a person works with today should be sensitive to the demands or investment opportunities that he perceives will be available to him in the future. When a subject assesses his utility function for current operations he should incorporate these future possibilities, if not formally, then at least informally. However, this is more easily said than done, and once again we must avoid an advanced topic that is not appropriate for these elementary lectures.

The availability of a market for gambles suggests the possibility of a more extensive market where risky ventures might be bought, sold, traded, and shared. This will be the subject matter of Chapter 8.

14. RISK CONTROL THROUGH PORTFOLIO SELECTION AND DIVERSIFICATION*

If an investor is offered an opportunity to buy a share of a given investment, he naturally will be concerned with his perceived probability distribution of the uncertain returns from that investment. But, equally important, he must consider the interaction of this investment with his other investments, those to which he is already committed and those he may wish to consider in the future. He should not evaluate a given investment in isolation, but rather as an integral part of a balanced portfolio of investments. A few illustrations will help set the perspective.

A businessman who is in a certain line might actively pursue new investment opportunities that tend to complement those investments he already holds. To diversify his holdings, for example, he might join his business with someone else's, especially if by so doing he and the other party to the merger can hedge themselves against some possible contingencies. Again, if an insurance company holds several large policies, all of which will be payable if a given misfortune strikes (for example, a devastating fire in a certain locality), this company should try to share its risk with other insurance companies in a similar position. In this section we shall briefly discuss a class of problems suggested by these illustrations.

A dramatic and highly oversimplified hypothetical example will bring some of the issues to the fore. Let's suppose an investor has under review a new investment contract which he perceives will pay off either a net sum of $1M (one million) or a net loss of $1.5M after taxes. It seems to him that both possibilities are equally likely. Note that the EMV of this investment is negative;

$$.5(1M) \cdot .5(-\$1.5M) = -\$0.25M.$$

Our investor happens to be risk averse, and therefore it seems clear that he should reject such an investment. But wait! Suppose he is already committed to an old investment that is just as likely to pay off $3M as $-$1M and he is particularly worried about that potential $1M loss. Furthermore, let's assume

---

* This section is not used in the sequel and can be skipped.

TABLE 4.4

State of the World	Probability	Investments		Total
		Old	New	
S_1	.5	$3M	−$1.5M	$1.5M
S_2	.5	−$1M	$1.0M	$0.0M

that if the old investment turns out unfavorably, the new investment will turn out favorably; in other words, the new investment is a perfect hedge against the old. Table 4.4 summarizes this state of affairs. Two equally likely states of the world are possible: state S_1, which is favorable to the old investment and unfavorable to the new, and state S_2, which is unfavorable to the old and favorable to the new. While the new investment is a poor bet in isolation, a risk-averse investor might deem it a marvelous opportunity since he can combine it with his old investment to make up an extremely attractive package.

Let's generalize. Instead of two states, let there be m states $S_1, S_2, \ldots, S_m$ with assigned probabilities $p_1, p_2, \ldots, p_m$; let I_0 denote the old investment, and let $I_1, I_2, \ldots, I_n$ be n new investments under review; if state S_k prevails, let the net monetary return from I_0 and I_j be x_{k0} and x_{kj}, respectively. Table 4.5 summarizes this situation. If the investor adds I_j to I_0, then his payoff is $x_{k0} + x_{kj}$ when state S_k prevails. Let u be the investor's utility function. We can then express his expected utility from adding I_j to I_0 as

$$u(x_{10} + x_{1j})p_1 + \cdots + u(x_{k0} + x_{kj})p_k + \cdots + u(x_{m0} + x_{mj})p_m.$$

Assuming he can only choose one new investment, the investor's problem is to select j to maximize his expected utility. Of course, this maximum might not

TABLE 4.5

State	Probability	Investments				
		I_0	I_1	$\cdots I_j$	$\cdots I_n$	
S_1	p_1	x_{10}	x_{11}	$\cdots x_{1j}$	$\cdots x_{1n}$	
$\vdots$	$\vdots$	$\vdots$	$\vdots$	$\vdots$	$\vdots$	
S_k	p_k	x_{k0}	x_{k1}	$\cdots x_{kj}$	$\cdots x_{kn}$	
$\vdots$	$\vdots$	$\vdots$	$\vdots$	$\vdots$	$\vdots$	
S_m	p_m	x_{m0}	x_{m1}	$\cdots x_{mj}$	$\cdots x_{mn}$	

be good enough, and then the investor would make no investment at all. It will be easier, however, if we think of his doing nothing as an available null investment that pays off $0.00 for each state; if he uses this convention, the investor need only consider maximization over j and can avoid any subsequent comparison with the status quo.

Now let's imagine that our investor has certain funds to invest. If he invests all of them in I_j and if S_k then occurs, his gross return will be $x_{k0} + x_{kj}$ (we still are assuming his continuing involvement in I_0). In general terms, if he invests a proportion π_1 of his investment funds in $I_1, \ldots,$ a proportion π_j in $I_j, \ldots,$ and a proportion π_n in I_n, where

$$\pi_1 + \cdots + \pi_j + \cdots + \pi_n = 1 \qquad \text{and} \qquad \pi_j \geq 0 \quad \text{for all } j,$$

then his return when S_k occurs is

$$x_{k0} + \pi_1 x_{k1} + \cdots + \pi_j x_{kj} + \cdots + \pi_n x_{kn}.$$

By converting this gross amount into a utility value, multiplying it by p_k (the probability of state S_k), and adding over k, we get the investor's expected utility for his portfolio of selections. He then is faced with a mathematical programming problem, how to select the π_j that will maximize his expected utility value. This problem is known in the literature as the *portfolio selection problem*, and if you are interested you should consult the pioneering work by Harry Markowitz, *Portfolio Selection*, John Wiley and Sons, 1959.

As a variation of this problem, we can allow our investor to divest himself of a proportion of his old investment I_0 (which may be a package of individual investments) and to use the proceeds for new investments. In particular, other investors might buy into I_0 if this would make their portfolios more attractive, and our investor could always sell to them. The more they want of I_0, the higher the price our investor can charge and the more he can demand in a merger contract.

Let's consider another variation. Instead of a single investor, consider a corporation consisting of two divisions A and B. The division manager of A has a choice between I_1 and I_2 and the division manager B has a choice between I_3 and I_4. If their selections are I_1 and I_4, say, then the corporation will be engaged in the triplet of investments $\{I_0, I_1, I_4\}$, where once again we use I_0 to designate the totality of previously committed investments. In general, the comparative merits of investments I_1 and I_2 in division A will depend on I_0 and on the choice of investment made by division manager B. In some very special cases it is possible to decentralize the choice of investments (or projects) without loss of efficiency; in other cases it may still be worthwhile for diverse administrative reasons to decentralize the decision-making process, even if this entails some loss of efficiency.

In this section, we have talked about only a very small part of the mammoth subject commonly called "capital budgeting". We have ignored problems of time, of the unfolding dynamics, of the existence of market mechanisms that are external to a firm, of the possible introduction of market-like mechanisms that are internal to a firm (for example, incentive schemes, transfer pricing, goal selection), of differing perceptions of future possibilities, of differing attitudes towards risk, of distortions of information flow, of the creation of contingent contracts, and so on. The deeper one goes into this area, the harder it becomes to isolate a problem for prescriptive analysis—everything seems to be intertwined with everything else. But still, decisions have to be made; and by studying various paradigms in detail one can begin to get a sense of perspective and begin to know what are first-order and what are second-order effects, what must be included and what can be left out of an analysis.

15. PROJECT

Let's modify the project posed at the end of Chapter 2 by making the following changes. The oil wildcatter has $100,000 in present assets. Keeping in mind his future opportunities, he asserts:

a) "At this period in my life I want to be risk-averse. I don't want to participate in fair gambles. I would not bet at Las Vegas even if the house cut were reduced to zero."

b) "On a 50-50 bet I would just be willing to risk losing my whole $100,000 bankroll if I could possibly net $300,000. If I were lucky, I would then have $400,000 to play with."

c) "What would I pay for a deal where there is a .5 chance at winning $300,000 and .5 chance of breaking even? Well, since I don't have to worry about dipping into my own bankroll, I would exchange this for $100,000 certain."

d) "How much would I be willing to spend of my own money to insure against a .5 chance of losing my entire working capital of $100,000? This is a tough one. It would be a catastrophe if I lost everything; but then there is also a .5 chance of losing nothing. Okay, I would give up $60,000 of my own money. With the other $40,000 I would have left I could get started again, somehow."

Analyze the oil wildcatter's decision problem. What is his optimal strategy for experimentation and action? How much is the whole venture worth to him?

Suggestion. Draw the wildcatter's utility-for-money curve on graph paper. The information given does not specify his curve exactly, and you should investigate how sensitive your answers are to the arbitrary features of the curve you draw.

16. DATA FOR THE PROJECT SUGGESTED IN SECTION 2

In Section 2, we discussed how *you* might analyze your basic problem by working backwards down the tree, using CME's rather than EMV's. For your convenience I append on the following pages a decision-flow diagram of your basic problem with all payoffs and probability assessments included. This figure is the same as Fig. 2.13, but has been drawn without the intermediate monetary calculations and without double slash marks. Everything is ready for you to express your very own judgments. But before you begin, you may wish to make an intuitive guess at what the whole game is worth to you at the start. Now work backwards and see what you get.

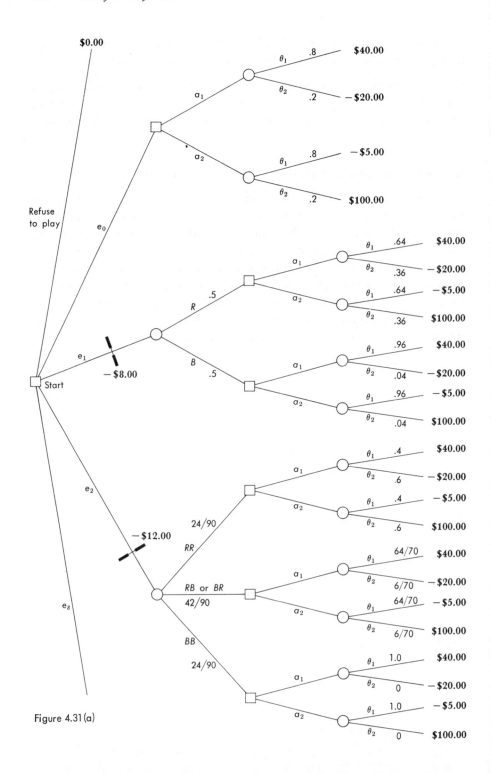

Figure 4.31(a)

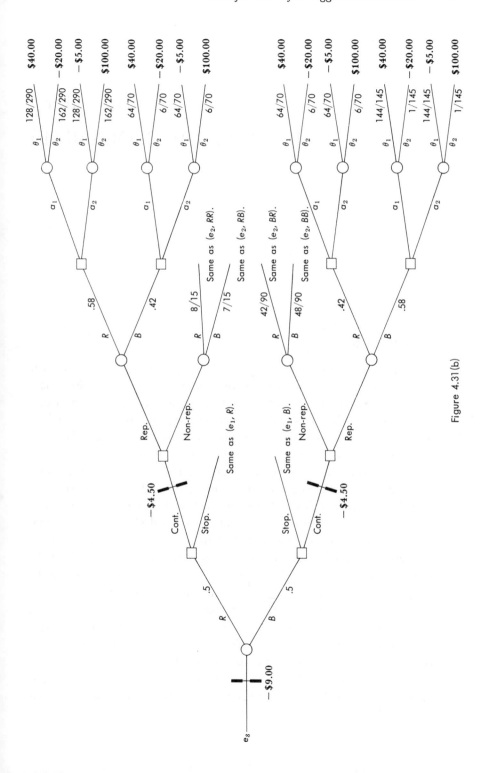

Figure 4.31 (b)

CHAPTER 5

THE USE OF
JUDGMENTAL PROBABILITY

1. INTRODUCTION

In Chapter 0, I drew several thumbnail sketches of decision problems to get us started on the subject matter of these lectures. These problems have one essential ingredient in common: In some form or another, they all involve *uncertainty*. The difficulties of analyzing most of these problems would evaporate if only the decision maker could gain enough insight to change these uncertainties into certainties. But, alas, this he cannot always do.

There are uncertainties and there are uncertainties. At one polar extreme is the uncertainty about the outcome of a toss of a die, a die tooled as perfectly as we can imagine and with which we have had loads of previous experience; or similarly, the uncertainty of the color of a ball we draw from an urn that contains a specified number of red and black balls. At the other polar extreme is the uncertainty of the state of our economy two decades hence, and the uncertainty about whether the U.S. will land a man on the moon before the Russians, and the uncertainty whether the marginal cost of producing a new piece of equipment will be less than $5.00, and so forth. Opinions differ as to whether we can or ought to incorporate subjective feelings or hunches about uncertainties of the latter type into the formal analysis of a decision problem. In this chapter, we shall argue that if you are the decision maker and you are involved in your private practical-action problem, then indeed you should scale your subjective feelings about vague but relevant uncertainties in terms of judgmental probabilities and you should use these probabilities to analyze your problem and to decide which action you ought to adopt. You will have noted that until now we have diligently avoided complications that arise because of vagueness about probability assignments. In this chapter we shall emphasize this aspect of the subject.

Let us return to consider the problem I originally proposed to you. I now ask you to consider two variations, both of which turn on your information about the composition of the 1000 urns from which the experimenter randomly chooses the unidentified urn. Originally you understood that there were 800 θ_1 urns and 200 θ_2 urns. Now consider these specifications for Variations 1 and 2:

Variation 1. You do not know exactly how many θ_1 urns and θ_2 urns there are, but you do know that the breakdown is either 700 θ_1's and 300 θ_2's or 900 θ_1's and 100 θ_2's. You should consider each possibility equally likely.

Variation 2. You are never told how many θ_1 urns and θ_2 urns there are. However, the experimenter has strewn all the urns around the floor of the next room, and each one still displays a θ_1 or θ_2 label. Before he chooses an urn at random for you to identify, he will open the door of the next room just long enough for you to take a quick look at those urns. Since he won't give you enough time to do any counting, all you will be able to do is get a rough impression.

This chapter is primarily concerned with the analysis of problems that are like the one suggested by Variation 2. The question, once again, is whether you should calibrate your hunches or vague impressions, and if so, how these should enter into the formal analysis of your problem. Before we discuss this question itself, however, we ought to go through an analysis of Variation 1—this will help us avoid some preliminary misconceptions.

2. OBJECTIVE VAGUENESS

We first assert that leaving probability assignments aside, the structure of the decision-flow diagram given in Fig. 2.13 is still appropriate for Variation 1. We next assert that *your old probability assignments are also the appropriate ones for this new problem.** (We shall discuss this assertion below.) These two assertions together imply that the best action for you to take in this new problem should

---

* In general: If the proportion of θ_1's were known to be any of $a_1, a_2, \cdots, a_m$ with probability $b_1, b_2, \ldots, b_m$, respectively, and if $a_1 b_1 + \ldots + a_m b_m$ were also .8, then the analysis given for $P(\theta_1) = .8$ would apply without modification.

be the same as the one you chose in the original problem, when you knew for certain there were 800 urns of type θ_1.

Let us take a closer look at some of the probability assignments. Consider the assignments on the e_1-branch. First you need the probabilities of red (R) and black (B) and later you need the updated probabilities of θ_1 and θ_2 if Chance gives you a red and if Chance gives you a black. Figure 5.1 indicates the probabilities you want.

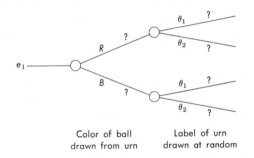

	Color of ball drawn from urn	Label of urn drawn at random

Figure 5.1

To get the probability assignments for Fig. 5.1, let's first consider the flipped probability tree shown in Fig. 5.2. The conditional probability assignments for R and B given θ_1 and given θ_2 are obviously correct as they appear. The question is: What assignments should we give to θ_1 and θ_2 at the first stage? We answer this by considering the details of Fig. 5.3. The probability that the urn chosen at random is type θ_1 is the sum of the two path probabilities .35 and .45, or .80. Similarly the probability of a θ_2 urn is the sum of path probabilities .15 and .05, or .20. Hence the probabilities of θ_1 and θ_2 in Fig. 5.2 should be .80 and .20, respectively. But if we now supply these probabilities

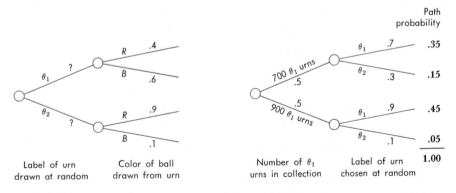

Figure 5.2   Figure 5.3

in Fig. 5.2, then we get the numbers identical to the ones that appear in Fig. 2.10, and hence the probability assignments that we *must* make in Fig. 5.1 are exactly the same as the ones we made in Fig. 2.11. The same mode of argument applies to the e_0-, e_2- and e_8-branches of the tree.

In summary: The probability that the unknown urn is a θ_1, denoted by $P(\theta_1)$, is clearly .8 in the original problem, and it *still* ought to be *.8 for Variation 1*; also, mathematically speaking, .8 is .8 is .8 is . . . , and it's of no avail to say that one .8 is fuzzier than another .8. Furthermore, you ought to treat the original problem and its first variation as strategic equivalents.

Of course, we might add a factor to the problem that would establish a strategic difference between these two cases. Suppose that you can elect to count the number of θ_1 urns in the original 1000 urns for a fee of $0.50 before the experimenter selects an urn at random and removes its label. In the original problem, you would be throwing away your $0.50 because you already know that there were 800 θ_1's. In the first variation, however, your count will come out as either 700 θ_1's or 900 θ_1's. Your decision-flow diagram for this variation on Variation 1 is shown in Fig. 5.4.

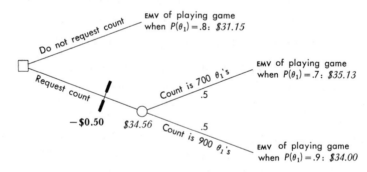

Figure 5.4

For an EMV'er, the value of the game with $P(\theta_1) = .8$ is $31.15, as we saw in Fig. 2.13. Later we shall show that the EMV of playing the game with $P(\theta_1) = .9$ is $34.00 and the EMV of playing the game with $P(\theta_1) = .7$ is $35.13. Therefore the expected value of playing the game after the toll has been paid, but before you have received the specific count, is

$$.5(\$35.15) + .5(\$34.00) = \$34.56.$$

Therefore an EMV'er would be wise to buy a complete count for $0.50 in this problem.* The expected value of this information is $34.56 − $31.15 = $3.41.

---

* The form of the optimal strategy will depend on whether $P(\theta_1) = .7$ or .9. See Table 6.1.

I repeat—and this is important enough to repeat—the original problem and its first variation are strategically different problems *if* you are given the opportunity to buy information about the original count; however, they are strategically equivalent problems *if* you do *not* have the opportunity to get any further information about the original count.

Perhaps I am laboring a point that is already clear, but let me drive it home by bringing up an analogous problem. Suppose you are confronted with two options. In option 1, you must toss coin 1 (which is fair and true), guess heads or tails, and win $1.00 if you match and lose $1.00 if you fail to match. In option 2, you have a 50-50 chance of getting coin 2, which has two heads, or of getting coin 3 which has two tails. Not knowing whether you are tossing coin 2 or 3, you must call, toss, and get the payoffs as in option 1. With option 1, the probability of the toss coming out heads is .5; with option 2, the same probability is either 0 or 1, and since the chance of each in turn is .5, the probability of heads is ultimately .5 once again. Nothing is to be gained by saying that one .5 is sharply defined and that the other is fuzzy. Of course, *if*, and this is a big "if", you could experiment with the coin you will toss before you are obliged to declare, then the two options are manifestly asymmetrical. Barring this privilege, the two options are equivalent.

3. THE CALIBRATION OF SUBJECTIVE VAGUENESS

We are now ready to discuss the controversial problems of subjective probability. Variation 1 was our foil and now we are ready for Variation 2. The door is open: Take a quick look at those 1000 urns strewn around the floor! That's all the time you get! . . . Now the experimenter has selected an urn at random, removed its label, and placed it on the table in front of you. Do you want to guess at this point, or would you like to buy e_1-, or e_2-, or e_s-information? Clearly your action should in some sense depend on your impression of the proportion of θ_1's in the original collection. But how can you calibrate your vague impressions?

Here is one possible procedure. When you have an unknown length to estimate, you can calibrate it by placing it in juxtaposition to some more familiar objectively known length. You might try to apply this technique here. Let us once again introduce the class of basic reference lottery tickets, where a π-BRLT gives you a chance of π at prize W (for *win*) and a complementary chance of $1 - \pi$ at prize L (for *lose*). Throughout this discussion we shall assume that $W = \$100.00$ and $L = -\$50.00$. We have already used this class of lottery tickets to scale your attitudes towards money in a risky environment; it is important for later manipulations that the two reference prizes $W = \$100.00$ and $L = -\$50.00$ be the same as the ones we used before.

Now we can proceed. First of all, suppose you say that you have the distinct impression that there are a majority of θ_1's. We can formalize this statement by considering the following two options.

Option 1. You receive reward W if the unknown urn turns out to be a θ_1, and L otherwise:

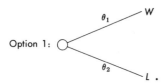

Option 2. You receive a .5-BRLT, that is, you receive W if you pick a blue ball from a so-called *calibrating urn* and L otherwise, where the calibrating urn contains 50 blue and 50 orange balls.

When you say you have the impression that a majority of urns are θ_1's, this presumably means that *if you were to make a side bet*, you would prefer Option 1 to Option 2.

Would you feel the same way if the calibrating urn had 99 blues and one orange? Now it should be obvious what the game is. We can manipulate the contents of the calibrating urn until you have a difficult time deciding between the two options, that is, until you are *indifferent* between the two options. Of course, it would be very difficult for you to decide whether you would be more comfortable with 75 blues or 76 blues or 77 blues, ..., or 85 blues in the calibrating urn; however, we need not be unduly concerned about such critically fine distinctions.† A break-even value of 80 blues in the calibrating urn is a central value in the range of your indecision, so let's follow out its implications. Let's assume that you are indifferent between Option 1 and a .80-BRLT.

Here let's take stock of where we are. On this side bet, you are willing to act *just as if* the probability of a θ_1 were (about) .8. For the sake of brevity we'll just say that your "judgmental probability" of θ_1 is .8 and write $P^*(\theta_1) =$ .8. The asterisk on the operator P will help to remind us that all you have agreed to do is apply a suggestive label to a dubious concept; you have in no way committed yourself to work with this judgmental probability as if it were a bona fide, objective, tangible, real-world, frequency-based probability. The remaining part of this chapter aims at convincing you that *so far as action is concerned*—and this is all that is of interest here—you should feel free to use

---

† We shall later show that for an EMV'er, the optimal strategy for the game is the same if $P(\theta_1)$ is .75 or .80. For $P(\theta_1) = $ .85, the optimal strategy changes. The loss from acting as if $P(\theta_1) = $ .80 when in fact $P(\theta_1) = $ .85 is $1.84.

these judgmental probabilities just as if they were the "real" thing, and you should not worry about mixing some objective and some subjective or judgmental probabilities together in the same formula.

In the previous section, we argued that if it is equally likely that $P(\theta_1) = .7$ or $.9$ (both objective), then so far as action is concerned, you should behave just as if $P(\theta_1) = .8$. The arguments in the next sections are designed to demonstrate that in the case in which the vagueness is of the subjective variety, this vagueness should not influence your behavior in making a choice.

Before we push on, we ought to have a formal definition of judgmental probability.

> **Definition of Judgmental Probability.** Let E be some uncertain event in the real world, and let ℓ_E be the lottery which gives prize W if E occurs and prize L if E does not occur. If ℓ_E is indifferent† to a p-BRLT (that is, to a lottery that gives an objective probability p at W and a complementary probability at L), then we say that the *judgmental probability* of E is p. We write this symbolically as $P^*(E) = p$.

Later we shall prove that if the decision maker wishes to behave in a manner that is consistent with certain principles, then the number $P^*(E)$ should not depend on the reference prizes W and L.

4.   A CONSISTENCY PROPERTY FOR JUDGMENTAL PROBABILITY

It is tempting to conclude without any further ado that if $P^*(\theta_1) = .8$, then $P^*(\theta_2)$ must be $.2$, since it "stands to reason" that

$$P^*(\theta_1) + P^*(\theta_2) = 1.$$

Unfortunately this argument is not very convincing,‡ and the point at issue is

---

† Recall that the statement "ℓ_E is indifferent to a p-BRLT" is an elliptical form for this more complete statement: "The decision maker is indifferent between having ℓ_E and a p-BRLT." Henceforth we shall use this ellipsis without apology.

‡ Excerpt taken from *N.Y. Times:* Robert Moses has appealed to the Weather Bureau here to take a more "positive" approach in its forecasts to avoid discouraging attendance at the World's Fair.

Instead of forecasting that there will be "a 20 percent chance of precipitation," Mr. Moses said in a letter to the bureau, the weathermen should say that there is an "80 percent chance of fair weather."

Mr. Moses, president of the World's Fair, sent his letter on May 7 to Anthony E. Tancreto, head of the Weather Bureau here. Mr. Moses wrote that he was supported in his campaign by the Chamber of Commerce of the Rockaways to persuade the weathermen to "accentuate the positive." © 1964 by the New York Times Company. Reprinted by permission.

so very critical that we require a more substantial analysis. First, however, we shall cite an example that is put forward by some in defense of the notion that the judgmental probability assessments of θ_1 and θ_2 should not necessarily add up to 1:

$$P^*(\theta_1) + P^*(\theta_2) \neq 1.$$

Suppose the experimenter asks a subject whether he thinks that the American League or the National League team will win the first World Series baseball game, which is scheduled to start in just a few minutes. "I know so little about baseball," the subject responds, "that I hesitate to give an answer. I do not know, for example, who the teams are, and I don't know how well they have done this past season."

"That's just fine," the experimenter exclaims. "I wanted to choose a situation just like this. Suppose I offer you a choice between the following two options:

Option 1. Select a team, American or National, and place your choice in a sealed envelope. If the team you select wins the game about to get under way, you get $100.00. Otherwise you get nothing.

Option 2. Draw a ball from an urn containing 50 orange and 50 blue balls. You will receive $100.00 if you draw an orange ball and $0.00 if you draw a blue ball. (All balls are equally likely to be drawn.) The drawing will take place at the conclusion of the game.

Which option would you prefer?"

After thinking a while the subject responds, "I would naturally prefer the drawing."

"Why?"

"Because with the urn I *know* the probability of winning. I think I would choose the American League team but the probability that this team will win can be anything. How do I know it isn't .2?"

"You don't. Would you still prefer to choose the second option if the number of orange balls were 10 and the number of blues were 90? Twenty oranges and 80 blues? Thirty oranges and 70 blues? Where is your break-even point?"

Some subjects argue that there is nothing inconsistent about choosing American over National and at the same time, in terms of a break-even analysis with an objective calibrating urn, choosing

$$P^* \text{ (American)} = .40,$$

say. In this case,

$$P^* \text{ (National)} < P^* \text{ (American)},$$

and therefore

$$P^* \text{ (National)} + P^* \text{ (American)} < 1.$$

After all, the argument goes, there is no scientific or behaviorist law that says that judgmental break-even probabilities obey the rules of ordinary probabilities.

In experiments I have personally conducted, I have found that a majority of subjects prefer the crisp objectivity of Option 2 to the vagueness of Option 1. Many subjects, for example, are willing to pay up to $40.00 for Option 2 (that is, for an objective 50-50 chance at $100.00 or nothing), but would not pay more than $10.00 for Option 1. Such reasoning is quite common, and one can offer rationalizations of it. However, a person who has the liberty in Option 1 to choose his team and who will pay substantially more for Option 2 than for Option 1 has simply made a slip in logic. Furthermore, just as such a person will change his answer if we point out to him that he has added a column of figures incorrectly, he ought also in this case to change his response if we point out to him his logical error. Let me state why I am being so dogmatic about this issue. Suppose that in Option 1 the subject would prefer to choose the American League team. Presumably this means that he would prefer to decide outright on the American League team rather than decide Option 1 by tossing a coin, say, where he will choose American if heads and will choose National if tails. But let's look at this randomized procedure: No matter whether the American team wins or loses, he has an objective 50-50 chance of picking the winner with the toss of the coin. (Check this!) The fact that he has tossed the coin first should not matter. But if this *is* a question of concern, then perhaps he could get a friend to toss the coin and secretly place the outcome in the sealed envelope that he will open after the game. But this thinking argues that the randomized procedure is equivalent to Option 2. If in Option 1 the subject would *prefer* a free choice of the American League team rather than resort to the vagaries of the tossed coin, then by transitivity he should *prefer* Option 1 to Option 2. Don't you think so? Should he not change his mind? *I* think he should. Now let's prove the following proposition formally.

If you wish to act consistently with the principles of substitutability and transitivity, then you ought to assign values to $P^*(\theta_1)$ and $P^*(\theta_2)$ such that

$$P^*(\theta_1) + P^*(\theta_2) = 1.$$

▷ *Proof.* For simplicity, let's denote $P^*(\theta_1)$ and $P^*(\theta_2)$, respectively, by p_1 and p_2. Consider the lottery whose outcome is W or L, depending jointly on the

TABLE 5.1

	Type of urn	
Toss of coin	θ_1	θ_2
H	W	L
T	L	W

outcome of a fair coin and on the occurrence of θ_1 or θ_2, as described in Table 5.1. Thus, for example, if the unidentified urn on the table before you is a θ_1 *and* the coin comes up heads (H), you get prize W. You would also get W with the (θ_2, tail)-combination. Otherwise you would get L. Now to prove that $p_1 + p_2 = 1$, we shall show that (**1**) when we analyse ℓ in one fashion, it is reducible to a BRLT that gives a $(p_1 + p_2)/2$ chance at W, and (**2**) when we analyse ℓ in another fashion, it is reducible to a .5-BRLT. But by transitivity this means that

$$\frac{p_1 + p_2}{2} = \frac{1}{2}, \quad \text{or} \quad p_1 + p_2 = 1.$$

1) Figure 5.5 will be used to demonstrate that ℓ is reducible to a BRLT with a

$(p_1 + p_2)/2$

chance at W. (The symbol $\sim$ is read "is indifferent to".) The indifference between (1) and (2) in Fig. 5.5 follows from the definition of ℓ in Table 5.1. The indifference between (2) and (3) follows if we substitute a p_1-BRLT for the lottery that gives W if θ_1 is the true state and L if θ_2 is the true state and if we substitute a p_2-BRLT for the lottery that gives W if θ_2 is the true state and L if θ_1 is the true state. The indifference between (3) and (4) follows from the standard type of reduction argument, which we have already given in Chapter 4.

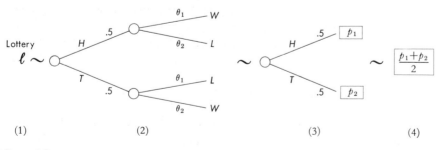

(1)   (2)   (3)   (4)

Figure 5.5

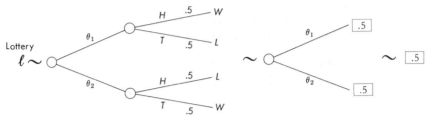

Figure 5.6

2) We shall use Fig. 5.6 to demonstrate that ℓ is reducible to a .5-BRLT. The first indifference follows from the definition of ℓ in Table 5.1. The second indifference is self-evident. Finally a lottery that yields a .5-BRLT regardless of whether θ_1 or θ_2 obtains is obviously equivalent to a .5-BRLT, and that explains the third indifference.

This completes the proof of the statement that if you want to satisfy the principles of substitutability and transitivity, then your $P^*(\theta_1)$- and $P^*(\theta_2)$- assignments must add to unity. ◁

5.   THE ADDITIVITY OF JUDGMENTAL P^*-MEASURE

In essence, in Section 4, we showed that if E is any uncertain event and $\overline{E}$ is the event "not E", then

$$P^*(E) + P^*(\overline{E}) = 1.$$

All we need to do is identify E with θ_1 and "not E" with θ_2 and use the previous proof. Before we can demonstrate that judgmental probability follows the same rules as ordinary probability, however, we must generalize this result to the following statement.

Let E_1 and E_2 be two uncertain events that are mutually exclusive in the sense that if one event occurs, then the other cannot. (We do not assume, however, that these events are exhaustive; some other event E_3 might occur.) To be consistent with the principles of substitutability and transitivity, the judgmental measure P^* must be such that

$$P^*(E_1) + P^*(E_2) = P^*(E_1 \text{ or } E_2).$$

▷   *Proof.*† Let E_3 be the event that $(E_1 \text{ or } E_2)$ does not occur. Hence one and only one of the events E_1, E_2, or E_3 will occur. Now consider two lotteries

---

† You may omit the proof since we have already described the basic idea in Section 4.

TABLE 5.2

	Lottery ℓ_1				Lottery ℓ_2		
		Outcome of toss				Outcome of toss	
Event				Event			
		Heads	Tails			Heads	Tails
E_1		W	L	E_1		W	L
E_2		L	W	E_2		W	L
E_3		L	L	E_3		L	L

ℓ_1 and ℓ_2, whose prizes depend on which one of the E events occurs *and* on the outcome of the toss of a fair coin (which has nothing to do with the E-events), according to the schedules in Table 5.2. Figure 5.7 depicts two tree representations of lotteries ℓ_1 and ℓ_2.

First tree representation for lottery ℓ_1

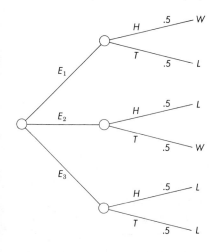

First tree representation for lottery ℓ_2

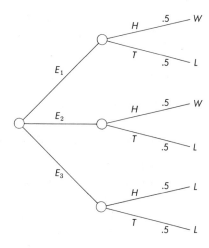

Second tree representation for lottery ℓ_1

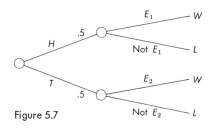

Second tree representation for lottery ℓ_2

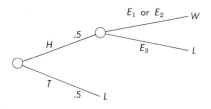

Figure 5.7

From the first tree representation we conclude that $\ell_1 \sim \ell_2$, since ℓ_2 results from ℓ_1 by keeping the prizes for E_1 and E_3 the same, and substituting an indifferent prize for E_2. From the second representation, we get

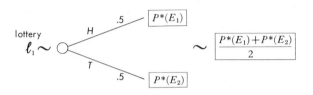

and

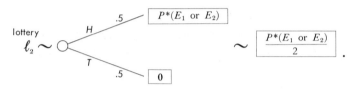

Now by transitivity we conclude that

$$\frac{P^*(E_1) + P^*(E_2)}{2} = \frac{P^*(E_1 \text{ or } E_2)}{2},$$

or

$$P^*(E_1) + P^*(E_2) = P^*(E_1 \text{ or } E_2),$$

which is what we set out to prove.   ◁

6.   THE ANALYSIS OF THE e_0-BRANCH

Now that we have established the principle that judgmental P^*-measure satisfies the usual rules of probability, let us return to the analysis of your basic decision problem and ask whether it is legitimate for you to use these judgmental probabilities in the process of averaging out and folding back. Can we proceed in the same way as we did in the last chapter, substituting judgmental probabilities for objective probabilities, or when it comes to the choice of action should we make allowances for the vagueness of our judgments?

Let's see what happens in the simplest case. If you go down the (e_0, a_1)-branch in your basic problem, you come to this lottery:

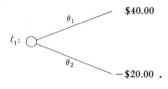

For the sake of argument, let us assume that you feel indifferent between getting \$40.00 certain and a .76-BRLT, and between $-\$20.00$ certain and a .35-BRLT. Recall that $W = \$100.00$, $L = -\$50.00$, and a π-BRLT gives you a π chance at W and a complementary chance at L. If it were legitimate to use $P^*(\theta_1) = .8$ as though it were an objective probability, then the lottery ℓ_1 would be indifferent to this one:

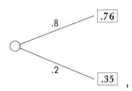

which is equivalent to a .678-BRLT, since

$$(.8)(.76) + (.2)(.35) = .678.$$

We shall now argue that you *should* be indifferent between ℓ_1 and a .678-BRLT. Keep in mind the meagerness of our set of building blocks: We have the behavioral assumptions of substitutability and transitivity, and we can substitute a $P(E)$-BRLT for the very specific lottery that pays off W if E and L if $\overline{E}$.

In the first place, if we substitute a .76-BRLT for \$40.00 and a .35-BRLT for $-\$20.00$, you should be indifferent between ℓ_1 and the lottery

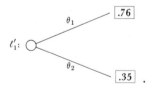

Next, let us put into an auxiliary urn 35 green balls, $76 - 35 = 41$ yellow balls, and $100 - 76 = 24$ orange balls. Let ℓ_1'' be a lottery with a schedule of prizes as given in Table 5.3. In ℓ_1'', the prize depends on whether θ_1 or θ_2

TABLE 5.3

Outcome of drawing from auxiliary urn	Type of urn	
	θ_1	θ_2
(35) green	W	W
(41) yellow	W	L
(24) orange	L	L

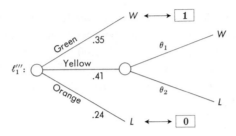

Figure 5.8

is the true state, and also on the color of the ball you draw from the auxiliary urn. It should be clear that ℓ_1'' is just another way of looking at ℓ_1', and that therefore ℓ_1' and ℓ_1'' are equivalent. But you can look at ℓ_1'' still another way: The lottery ℓ_1'' is the same as the lottery ℓ_1''' shown in Fig. 5.8. However, if you draw a yellow ball, the lottery that results is merely our old friend Option 1 of Section 3, which you will remember gives W if θ_1 and L if θ_2. You will also remember that you are indifferent between receiving this option and an .80-BRLT. If we substitute an .80-BRLT for this lottery and reduce ℓ_1''', you should be indifferent between getting ℓ_1''' and a .678-BRLT, since

$$(.35)(1.0) + (.41)(.80) + (.24)(0) = .678.$$

How nice—just what we wanted!

It is instructive to manipulate the left-hand side of this equality:

$$\begin{aligned}
(.35)(1) + (.41)(.80) + (.24)(0) &= (.35)\,(.80 + .20) + (.41)(.80) \\
&= (.80)(.35 + .41) + (.20)(.35) \\
&= (.80)(.76) + (.20)(.35) = .678.
\end{aligned}$$

We did this last bit of arithmetical juggling so that we could interpret the numbers in the next to last equality. There .80 is the P^*-equilibrating value for θ_1; .76 is the π-equilibrating value for \$40.00; .20 is the P^*-equilibrating value for θ_2; and .35 is the π-equilibrating value for $-\$20.00$. From this we

TABLE 5.4

Outcome of drawing from auxiliary urn	Type of urn	
	θ_1	θ_2
(46) green	W	W
(54) yellow	L	W

conclude that in analyzing your (e_0, a_1)-branch, it is appropriate for you to work with your judgmental probability $P^*(\theta_1) = .8$ just as if it were an objective probability.

We now can analyze the (e_0, a_2)-branch in a similar manner. Choices e_0, a_2 lead to the lottery

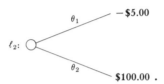

If we assume, for the sake of argument, that you are indifferent between $-\$5.00$ certain and a .46-BRLT, then that substitution tells us that you are indifferent between ℓ_2 and

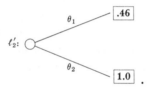

Now let us put into an auxiliary urn 46 green balls and $100 - 46 = 54$ yellow balls. Let ℓ_2'' be a lottery with the schedule of prizes given in Table 5.4. Since ℓ_2'' is just another way of looking at ℓ_2', you ought to be indifferent between them. But there is still another way to look at ℓ_2''. (See Fig. 5.9.) Since we have shown in the previous section that

$$P^*(\theta_2) = 1 - P^*(\theta_1) = 1 - .8 = .2,$$

it is legitimate for you to substitute a .2-BRLT for the lottery at the end of the "yellow" branch. If you do so, you will finally discover that ℓ_2''' is indifferent to a .568-BRLT, since

$$(.46)(1) + (.54)(.2) = .568.$$

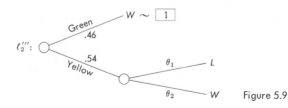

Figure 5.9

If you merely assumed that it is legitimate to treat $P^*(\theta_1) = .8$ in the same way that we treated $P(\theta_1) = .8$, then you would have found that ℓ'_2 is indifferent to the lottery

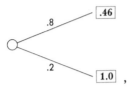

which is equivalent to a .568-BRLT, since

$$(.8)(.46) + (.2)(1.0) = .568\text{-BRLT}.$$

Thus we have demonstrated for the e_0-branch what we have been trying to show generally in this chapter: For decision-making purposes, it is appropriate for you to use your judgmental assessment $P^*(\theta_1) = .8$ in exactly the same way you used the objective assessment $P(\theta_1) = .8$ in previous chapters. The vagueness you feel about the .8 measurement does not enter into the analysis. Furthermore it is *not* appropriate to attempt to skew or slant your judgmental probabilities in any way to compensate for this vagueness.

7. THE REDUCTION OF A GENERAL LOTTERY

In the previous section we proved the following statement, essentially:

1) If ℓ is a lottery that yields C_1 if event E_1 occurs and C_2 if event E_2 occurs, where either E_1 or E_2 must occur but both cannot simultaneously occur;

2) if you are indifferent between C_1 and a π_1-BRLT and between C_2 and a π_2-BRLT; and

3) if your judgmental probabilities of E_1 and E_2 are, respectively, p_1 and p_2, where $p_1 + p_2 = 1$; then you should be indifferent between ℓ and a $\overline{\pi}$-BRLT, where

$$\overline{\pi} = p_1 \pi_1 + p_2 \pi_2.$$

To demonstrate this we used the principles of substitutability and transitivity. In this section we shall generalize and formalize this result.

Let $E_1, \ldots, E_i, \ldots, E_m$ be m mutually exclusive and exhaustive uncertain events (that is, one and only one of these events will occur). Let ℓ be the lottery that results in consequence C_1 if E_1 occurs, $\ldots$, C_i if E_i occurs, $\ldots$, and C_m if E_m occurs:

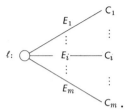

Let W and L be two reference prizes for a class of BRLT's such that W is more preferred than each of the C's and L is less preferred than any one of the C's. For each i, let C_i be indifferent to a π_i-BRLT, and let the lottery that gives W if E_i occurs and L if it does not occur be indifferent to a p_i-BRLT. In other words, let π_i be the utility of consequence C_i and let p_i be the judgmental probability of event E_i. Then consistency with the principles of substitutability and transitivity requires that ℓ be indifferent to a $\bar{\pi}$-BRLT, where

$$\bar{\pi} = p_1\pi_1 + \cdots + p_i\pi_i + \cdots + p_m\pi_m.$$

▷ *Proof.** We shall prove this result for $m = 3$, because this index is high enough to illustrate the full complexity of the issue. There is no loss of generality if we assume that $\pi_1 \geq \pi_2 \geq \pi_3$, because if it were otherwise we could relabel the E's and C's. By substitutability and transitivity, ℓ is indifferent to

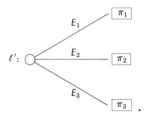

Now consider an auxiliary urn that contains colored balls in the proportions given in Table 5.5, and let lottery ℓ'' depend jointly on whichever E-event occurs and on which ball you draw at random from this auxiliary urn, accord-

---

* You may omit the proof since we have already described the basic ideas of the proof in the previous section.

TABLE 5.5

Proportions of balls	Color of ball drawn from auxiliary urn	Event		
		E_1	E_2	E_3
π_3	Green	W	W	W
$\pi_2 - \pi_3$	Yellow	W	W	L
$\pi_1 - \pi_2$	Orange	W	L	L
$1 - \pi_1$	Blue	L	L	L

ing to the schedule given in Table 5.5. Thus, for example, there is a proportion of $(\pi_2 - \pi_3)$ yellow balls, and if you draw a yellow ball and E_2 occurs, then the consequence is prize W. Note in lottery ℓ'' that if E_1 occurs, then there is a chance

$$\pi_3 + (\pi_2 - \pi_3) + (\pi_1 - \pi_2) = \pi_1$$

at W and a complementary chance at L; if E_2 occurs, then there is a chance

$$\pi_3 + (\pi_2 - \pi_3) = \pi_2$$

at W and a complementary chance at L; and if E_3 occurs, then there is a π_3-chance at W and a complementary chance at L. Thus ℓ'' is equivalent to ℓ'.

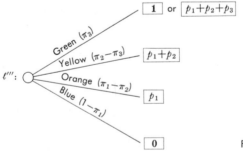

Figure 5.10

Now we can give ℓ'' alternative representation as lottery ℓ'''; this appears in Fig. 5.10. Thus, for example, if you draw a yellow ball you will receive a W-prize if and only if event E_1 *or* E_2 occurs; but this uncertain result is by definition indifferent to a $P^*(E_1 \text{ or } E_2)$-BRLT, and according to the results of the additivity of the P^*-measure (proved in Section 5),

$$P^*(E_1 \text{ or } E_2) = P^*(E_1) + P^*(E_2) = p_1 + p_2.$$

Now lottery ℓ''' is in standard objective form and it is equivalent to a $\bar{\pi}$ basic reference lottery, where

$$\begin{aligned}
\bar{\pi} &= (\pi_3)(p_1 + p_2 + p_3) + (\pi_2 - \pi_3)(p_1 + p_2) + (\pi_1 - \pi_2)(p_1) \\
&\quad + (1 - \pi_1)(0) \\
&= \pi_1 p_1 + \pi_2 p_2 + \pi_3 p_3.
\end{aligned}$$

This is what we wished to prove.   ◁

We are now in the position to prove the assertion that we mentioned at the close of Section 3:

> If the decision maker wishes to behave in a manner that is consistent with the principles of substitutability and transitivity, then his judgmental probability assignment $P^*(E)$ for the event E should not depend on the reference prizes W and L.

What has to be shown. Suppose that for some real-world event E, the decision maker is indifferent between the two lotteries

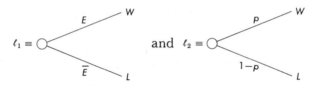

and between the two lotteries

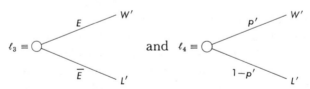

Our task is to prove $p = p'$.

▷ *Proof.* There are several special cases to consider but we shall consider only one, since you can prove the remaining ones in a similar manner. Also, the other proofs do not give us any new insights.

Special Case:

$$L \prec L' \prec W' \prec W \qquad \text{(where "$\prec$" is read "is less preferred than").}$$

Let L and W be reference consequences for BRLT's and let $L' \sim \pi_1$-BRLT, $W' \sim \pi_2$-BRLT. From the result just proved about the reduction of a general lottery, we have

$$\ell_3 \sim \overline{\pi}\text{-BRLT}, \qquad \text{where} \qquad \overline{\pi} = p\pi_1 + (1 - p)\pi_2. \tag{1}$$

From the reduction formula for a standard lottery, we have

$$\ell_4 \sim \overline{\pi}'\text{-BRLT}, \qquad \text{where} \qquad \overline{\pi}' = p'\pi_1 + (1 - p')\pi_2. \tag{2}$$

Since $\ell_3 \sim \ell_4$, we find from (1) and (2) and from the transitivity principle that

$$p\pi_1 + (1 - p)\pi_2 = p'\pi_1 + (1 - p')\pi_2,$$

and by algebra that

$$p(\pi_1 - \pi_2) + \pi_2 = p'(\pi_1 - \pi_2) + \pi_2, \qquad \text{or} \qquad p = p'.$$

This is what we wished to prove.   ◁

8. THE REVISION OF JUDGMENTAL PROBABILITIES

In the preceding sections of this chapter, we have demonstrated that if you wish to be consistent with the principles of substitutability and transitivity you should analyze the e_0-branch of your decision tree just as if your vague judgmental probability $P^*(\theta_1) = .8$ were a coldly objective, firm .8. We are now ready to handle the rest of the tree, but we shall concentrate on the e_1-branch, since our discussion of it will involve all the complexities that are necessary for an analysis of the e_2- and e_s-branches.

It is not at all obvious that you should treat your judgmental probability just as if it were an objective probability. For example, suppose you choose e_1 and draw a red ball. If we assume that the probability of θ_1 is an objective, frequency-based .8 (for example, where the experimenter chooses an urn at random from a collection of 800 θ_1-urns and 200 θ_2-urns), we can calculate the revised probability of θ_1, given the information Red (R), by Bayes' Theorem:

$$P(\theta_1|R) = \frac{P(R|\theta_1)P(\theta_1)}{P(R|\theta_1)P(\theta_1) + P(R|\theta_2)P(\theta_2)} = \frac{(.4)(.8)}{(.4)(.8) + (.9)(.2)} = .64.$$

That is, the objective event R pushed your coldly objective probability for θ_1 from .8 to .64. Now if instead you start with a vague judgmental probability of .8 for θ_1, shouldn't the hard objective evidence of event R push you further? As objective evidence is disclosed, should you not disengage yourself from the weaknesses of your own precarious, initial judgment about θ_1 faster than you would do by using Bayes' Theorem, which was, after all, derived for objective, frequency-based probabilities? I believe we can demonstrate to your satisfaction that you should *not*.

TABLE 5.6

Ball drawn from urn	Type of urn	
	θ_1	θ_2
R	W	L
B	L	L

Consider the lottery ℓ, whose prizes depend on the type of urn the experimenter presents and on the color of the ball you draw from this urn, according to the schedule in Table 5.6. You can give lottery ℓ the two equivalent representations shown in Fig. 5.11. Now follow this argument:

1) Since ℓ yields W if and only if the event (R and θ_1) occurs, but otherwise yields L, then by definition of P^* you have

$$\ell \sim \boxed{P^*(R \text{ and } \theta_1)} . \tag{1}$$

2) Since the events (R and θ_1) and (R and θ_2) are mutually exclusive (that is, one of these events can occur at most), and since you can express the event R as

$$R = [(R \text{ and } \theta_1) \text{ or } (R \text{ and } \theta_2)],$$

by the additivity of P^*-measure which we proved in Section 5 you should conclude that

$$P^*(R) = P^*(R \text{ and } \theta_1) + P^*(R \text{ and } \theta_2). \tag{2}$$

3) In lottery ℓ'' you can substitute a $P(R|\theta_1)$-BRLT for the prize associated with θ_1. Recall that $P(R|\theta_1)$ is the conditional probability that you will draw

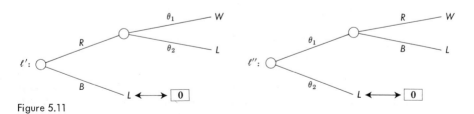

Figure 5.11

a red ball from the unidentified urn *if* this urn happens to be of type θ_1. Observe also that P in this case has no asterisk. We shall carry along the symbol $P(R|\theta_1)$ and substitute its value (.4) at the very end. Hence, from the reduction formula for a general lottery, you should conclude that

$$\ell'' \sim \boxed{P^*(\theta_1) \cdot P(R|\theta_1)} \ . \tag{3}$$

4) From (1) and (3), since $\ell' \sim \ell''$, you should conclude that

$$P^*(R \text{ and } \theta_1) = P^*(\theta_1) \cdot P(R|\theta_1). \tag{4a}$$

But now interchange the roles of θ_1 and θ_2; from symmetry you should also conclude that

$$P^*(R \text{ and } \theta_2) = P^*(\theta_2) \cdot P(R|\theta_2). \tag{4b}$$

5) From (2), (4a), and (4b), you should conclude that

$$P^*(R) = P(R|\theta_1) \cdot P^*(\theta_1) + P(R|\theta_2) \cdot P^*(\theta_2). \tag{5}$$

6) If R occurs in lottery ℓ', then the resulting lottery gives W if θ_1 happens and L if θ_2 happens. This lottery will be indifferent in your judgment to *some* basic reference lottery. Suppose, without committing yourself to a specific number, that you denote this number by $P^*(\theta_1|R)$. Then you get

$$\text{lottery} \quad \ell' \sim \ \begin{array}{c} R \to \boxed{P^*(\theta_1|R)} \\ \\ B \to \boxed{0} \end{array} \quad \sim \boxed{P^*(R) \cdot P^*(\theta_1|R)} \ . \tag{6}$$

7) Since $\ell \sim \ell'$, you should conclude that

$$P^*(R) \cdot P^*(\theta_1|R) = P^*(R \text{ and } \theta_1), \quad \text{or} \quad P^*(\theta_1|R) = \frac{P^*(R \text{ and } \theta_1)}{P^*(R)} . \tag{7}$$

8) From (7), using (4a) and (5), you should conclude that

$$P^*(\theta_1|R) = \frac{P(R|\theta_1) \cdot P^*(\theta_1)}{P(R|\theta_1) \cdot P^*(\theta_1) + P(R|\theta_2) \cdot P^*(\theta_2)},$$

which shows that once you choose values for $P^*(\theta_1)$ and $P^*(\theta_2)$, you are not at liberty to choose arbitrarily a value for $P^*(\theta_1|R)$. Indeed *the formula for*

$P^*(\theta_1|R)$ *is merely Bayes' Theorem, where* $P^*(\theta_1)$ *and* $P^*(\theta_2)$ *are treated in the same fashion as* $P(\theta_1)$ *and* $P(\theta_2)$.

The implications of this demonstration are clear. If you go down the e_1-branch and Chance gives you an R, you should analyze your choice of a_1 or a_2 just as you would analyze this same choice if you had started from a coldly objective, frequency-based $P(\theta_1) = .8$. Working backwards by averaging out in terms of the units on the basic reference lottery tickets, you will come to an analysis at the e_1-fork. Once again you should act just as if your $P^*(R)$- and $P^*(B)$-assessments were objectively based.

This completes the demonstration that you *should* analyze the e_1-branch by using your judgmental assessment $P^*(\theta_1) = .8$ just as if it were an objective assessment $P(\theta_1) = .8$. So far as action is concerned, you should make no allowances for your vagueness. When I say "You *should* conclude so-and-so or *should* behave in such-and-such a manner", I mean that you *must* conclude or behave in that manner *if* you wish to be consistent with your basic preferences and judgments and satisfy the principles of substitutability and transitivity.

9. RECAPITULATION

We have considered the problem faced by a person who on most occasions makes decisions intuitively and more or less inconsistently, but who on some one particular occasion wishes to make one particular decision in a reasoned, deliberate manner. We have assumed he starts by structuring the anatomy of his problem in a decision-flow diagram that depicts the chronological interaction between his decision alternatives at any stage and the information he obtains in the dynamic evolution of his problem. We have shown that if the decision maker adopts two principles of consistent behavior, transitivity of preferences and substitutability of indifferent consequences in a lottery, then he is pretty well fenced in. He should scale his preferences for the consequences at the tips of the decision tree in terms of utility values and scale his judgments about uncertain events in terms of probability assignments at chance moves, and, finally, he should select his best strategy for experimentation and action by the process of averaging out and folding back.

Our conclusions represent the foundations of the so-called "Bayesian" position. Nowhere in our analysis did we refer to the behavior of an "idealized, rational, economic man" who always acts in a perfectly consistent manner as if somehow there were embedded in his very soul coherent utility and probability evaluations for all eventualities. Rather, our approach has been *constructive:* We have prescribed the way in which an individual who is faced with a problem of choice under uncertainty should go about choosing an act that is consistent with his basic judgments and preferences. He must consciously police the consistency of his subjective inputs and *calculate* their implications for action. These lectures do not present a descriptive theory of actual behavior, nor a positive theory of behavior for a fictitious superintelligent being, but rather present an approach designed to help us erring folk to reason and act a bit more systematically—when we choose to do so!

CHAPTER 6

THE NORMAL FORM
OF ANALYSIS

1. INTRODUCTION

Thus far, we have established four principal steps in the analysis of the basic decision problem presented to you in these lectures.

Step 1. Chart the decision-flow diagram.

Step 2. Assign payoffs or utilities at the tips of the branches.

Step 3. Assign probabilities at all chance forks.

Step 4. Average out and fold back.

We call this four-step procedure the *extensive form* of analysis. If for some reason or another you are reluctant to assign some of the judgmental probabilities required in Step 3, you cannot commence the analysis in Step 4. There is another mode of analysis, called the *normal form* of analysis, which does not require (at least at the outset) an assessment of probabilities at all chance forks. This form of analysis goes as far as it possibly can without using judgmental probabilities. These judgmental probabilities can be brought into the analysis, if at all, at the very last step. By using the *normal form* of analysis we shall therefore demonstrate just how far it is possible for you to go without using judgmental probabilities; and we shall also use this analysis to argue once again the merits of judgmental probabilities.

One can argue very persuasively that the weakest link in any chain of argument should not come at the beginning. If you are a bit squeamish about assessing judgmental probabilities, then you may balk at going through the involved averaging-out-and-folding-back procedure of the extensive form of analysis, which uses these judgmental probabilities in a quite pervasive way. You may feel that you have given up control, and that the mathematics could very well grind out nonsensical results and you would not have any way of knowing it. For tactical reasons, it might be better to let you use your judgment at the very end, so that you feel in complete "objective" control. However, if you terminate the normal form of analysis by finally putting in judgmental probabilities (which I shall argue that you ought to do), then by a simple mathematical exercise we can show that you would arrive at the very same solution, barring of course any numerical errors, as you would if you had

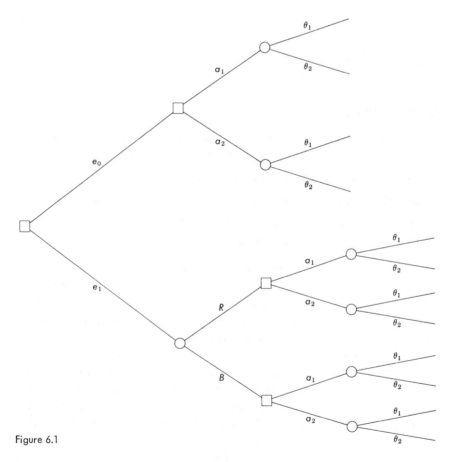

Figure 6.1

assessed these judgmental probabilities at the very beginning and had used the extensive form of analysis.

For your convenience, Fig. 6.1 exhibits the e_0- and e_1-branches of your decision-flow diagram. Observe that in this flow diagram there are seven chance moves, and that the probability assignments at any one of these moves requires, either directly or indirectly, the assignments for $P^*(\theta_1)$ and $P^*(\theta_2)$. The probability assignments $P(R|\theta_1)$, $P(B|\theta_1)$, $P(R|\theta_2)$, and $P(B|\theta_2)$ do not explicitly appear on the decision-flow diagram. In the normal form of analysis we shall use these latter four assignments, which we can think of as falling in the objective domain, but we shall make no use of the assignments $P^*(\theta_1)$ and $P^*(\theta_2)$ until the very last step of the analysis.

Before we begin the formal description of the normal form of analysis, it will be helpful if you turn to Fig. 2.13. In the analysis accompanying that figure, we showed that your best strategy for experimentation and action is to choose experiment e_s, to continue with a second drawing if and only if you have drawn a red ball, to choose not to replace the first ball before drawing a second, and to take a_2 if and only if you have drawn two red balls. Figure 6.2 describes this strategy in a much clearer fashion. This is only one of many possible strategies that you might have employed, but it happens to be the best one for an EMV'er when $P(\theta_1) = .8$.

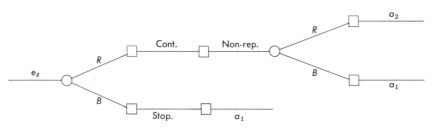

Fig. 6.2 The optimal strategy for an EMV'er.

In the normal form of analysis, we start by considering all possible strategies for experimentation and action. Roughly speaking, a strategy is a decision rule that you can give to your agent, one that unambiguously tells him what to do at any point given any past history up to that time. For each such strategy we shall ask: How good is this strategy if θ_1 happens to be true? If θ_2 happens to be true? If we see that strategy A is better than strategy B when either θ_1 or θ_2 is true, then we shall simply say that A is better than B overall. If A is better than B when θ_1 is true but B is better than A when θ_2 is true, then we shall have a tug of war; we must then worry about *by how much* one strategy is better than the other when θ_1 is true and when θ_2 is true. But in the end we shall see that even after we have done all this analysis we shall not be able to choose a "best" strategy in any objective manner. We shall, however, be able to rule out hosts of strategies as noncontenders. To do more than this, to isolate some one particular strategy as the "best", we shall have to introduce some subjective evaluations.

This chapter is rather long, and since some of the arguments are a bit more involved than those in previous chapters, it is natural to ask whether the concepts introduced are worth the effort. So far all I have said is that

a) the normal form of analysis can do what the extensive form of analysis can do;

b) using the normal form, we can see how far we can push the analysis without introducing judgmental probabilities for the states; and

c) discussing the normal form will give me an opportunity to present a slightly different argument for the introduction of judgmental probabilities.

However, there are other equally compelling reasons for introducing the normal form of analysis, reasons which I can only briefly suggest to you now.

d) With the normal form, we can quite efficiently employ a break-even type of argument, which will put less stringent demands on the numerical codification of your judgment. For example, instead of asking you to assess a specific number for $P^*(\theta_1)$, we shall ask you whether you think the proportion of θ_1's falls in one interval rather than another interval. Corresponding to each interval there will be a best strategy for experimentation and action.

e) Suppose V is the value a decision maker assigns to a new venture or decision problem under uncertainty. An EMV'er, for example, would assign $V = \$31.15$ to your basic decision problem if $P^*(\theta_1) = .8$. The value V will depend on the judgmental probabilities the decision maker assigns to the states of the problem. We shall use the normal form to investigate how sensitive V is to shifts in these probability assignments.

f) In really complicated problems a decision analyst might not be able to make a comprehensive analysis in either the extensive or normal form. Instead he might seek a "good" solution to a problem even if he can't be sure it is the "best" solution. Using the normal form he can often isolate a limited class of potentially good strategies and then choose a best strategy from this class. In Chapter 9, *The Art of Implementation*, I shall also describe how he can use the normal form, together with the extensive form, to attack some rather large problems.

g) In Chapter 8, we shall consider problems in which the decision-making unit is a group of individuals. If these individuals have different judgmental probabilities for the states of the problem, the analyst might choose to work in the normal form so that he may initially process the parts of the problem over which there is no disagreement.

h) In Chapter 10, I shall describe how the approach I have taken in these lectures is related to standard statistical methodology, which for the most part is cast in a normal-form context. The material presented in this chapter will facilitate that discussion.

2. STRATEGIES

Let's once again consider your basic decision problem, for the time being not specifying anything about the specific number of urns of type θ_1 and type θ_2 in the collection of 1000 urns from which the experimenter randomly chooses the urn in question. In the normal form of analysis, we start out by listing all the conceivable* strategies for experimentation and action. In your problem there are 115 such strategies, which we shall label $\sigma_0, \sigma_1, \ldots, \sigma_{114}$. (The symbol σ, read "sigma", is a lower-case Greek "ess", a mnemonic for "strategy".) Each strategy must give a complete description of exactly what you will do in each and every contingency that may arise. We shan't bother with the details, except to mention that there are two strategies with e_0, four with e_1, eight with e_2, and 100 with e_s; these, with the option of not playing, make a total of 115. For example, σ_5 is defined as follows: Pay \$8.00 for e_1, and guess a_2 if you draw a red ball and a_1 if you draw a black ball. Or, σ_{11}: Pay \$12.00 for e_2, and guess a_2 if RR, a_1 if RB or BR or BB. Or, σ_{17}: Pay \$9.00 for e_s. If R_1, stop and take a_1. If B_1, pay \$4.50 and continue with replacement; then if R_2, take a_1, and if B_2, take a_2.

Our next task is to *evaluate* each such strategy *conditional on θ_1 being true and conditional on θ_2 being true.* To make our discussion concrete, let us conditionally evaluate strategy σ_5:

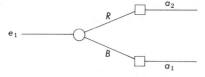

It is instructive to represent the strategic consequences of σ_5 in a decision-flow

---

* Shortcuts exist, but they would only cloud the basic logic.

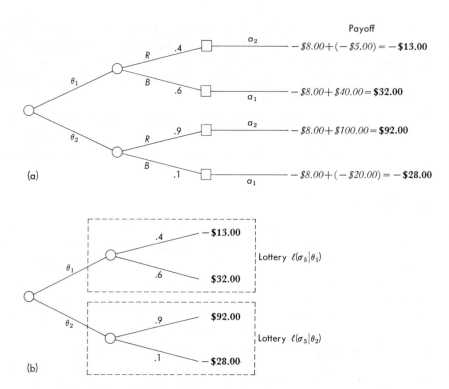

Fig. 6.3(a). The tree representation of strategy σ_5: Choose e_1, and adopt a_2 if R and a_1 if B.
Fig. 6.3(b). The reduced tree representation of strategy σ_5.

diagram, given in Fig. 6.3(a) and reduced in Fig. 6.3(b). We shall say that strategy σ_5, given θ_1, leads to the conditional lottery $\ell(\sigma_5|\theta_1)$, which gives a .4 chance at $-\$13.00$ and a .6 chance at $\$32.00$, and that strategy σ_5, given θ_2, leads to the conditional lottery $\ell(\sigma_5|\theta_2)$, which gives a .9 chance at $\$92.00$ and a .1 chance at $-\$28.00$. It is important for you to observe that the pair of conditional lotteries $\ell(\sigma_5|\theta_1)$ and $\ell(\sigma_5|\theta_2)$ are completely *objective*, in the sense that they do not depend on any judgmental probability assessment of θ_1 or θ_2. In an analogous manner, we can associate the completely objective pair of conditional lotteries $\ell(\sigma_i|\theta_1)$ and $\ell(\sigma_i|\theta_2)$ with any strategy σ_i, for i from 0 to 114.

The analysis of these conditional lotteries will depend on whether the decision maker is an EMV'er or a non-EMV'er. Rather than juggle too many balls at one, however, we shall first consider the analysis for an EMV'er and

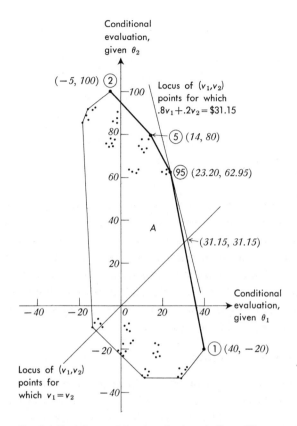

Fig. 6.4 The joint conditional evaluation of all possible strategies for an EMV'er.

then in Section 5 come back to the case of a non-EMV'er to describe briefly the necessary modifications.

We shall use the symbol $V(\sigma_5|\theta_1)$ to denote the EMV of $\ell(\sigma_5|\theta_1)$. Referring to Fig. 6.3(b), we get

$$V(\sigma_5|\theta_1) = (.4)(-\$13.00) + (.6)(\$32.00) = \$14.00$$

and

$$V(\sigma_5|\theta_2) = (.9)(\$92.00) + (.1)(-\$28.00) = \$80.00.$$

We say that for an EMV'er, the *joint conditional evaluation* of σ_5 is given by the pair of numbers (14, 80). In principle, we now can present a table that lists the 115 strategies and the joint conditional evaluation for each strategy:

	Conditional evaluation given	
Strategy	θ_1	θ_2
⋮	⋮	⋮
σ_5	$14.00	$80.00
⋮	⋮	⋮

Rather than present this data in tabular form, we shall plot the joint conditional evaluation for each strategy as a point in 2-space (see Fig. 6.4). Thus, for example, for strategy σ_5, we place a point at coordinate position (14, 80). Less than 115 points appear in this Fig. 6.4 because more than one strategy can have the same joint conditional evaluation. The only strategies we label in this figure are strategies 1, 2, 5, and 95, and these we shall discuss in the next section. For the time being, you should ignore the lines other than the coordinate axes that appear in the figure.

3. RANDOMIZED STRATEGIES

By a simple device we can build new strategies from the ones we already have, and we should consider these new strategies in our evaluations. An example will help get the idea across. Strategy σ_5 has a joint conditional evaluation (14, 80). Strategy σ_2 (take a_2 without experimentation) has a joint conditional evaluation $(-5, 100)$. Now suppose that you were to toss a fair coin—heads you take σ_5 and tails you take σ_2. This *randomized strategy* can be denoted by $(.5\sigma_5, .5\sigma_2)$. (See Fig. 6.5.) What is the evaluation of this randomized strategy if θ_1 is true? If θ_2 is true? Conditional on θ_1 being true, there is a .5 chance of getting $V(\sigma_5|\theta_1) = \$14.00$, and a .5 chance of getting

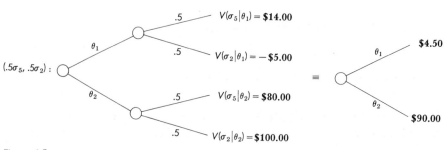

Figure 6.5

$V(\sigma_2|\theta_1) = -\$5.00$, for an expected value of $.5(\$14.00) + .5(-\$5.00) = \$4.50$. Conditional on θ_2 being true, there is a .5 chance of getting $V(\sigma_5|\theta_2) = \$80.00$ and a .5 chance of getting $V(\sigma_2|\theta_2) = \$100.00$, for an expected value of

$$.5(\$80.00) + .5(\$100.00) = \$90.00.$$

Thus the joint conditional evaluation of $(.5\sigma_5, .5\sigma_2)$ is $(4.50, 90)$, which is midway between $(-5, 100)$ and $(14, 80)$. By changing the probability of using strategy σ_5 and the complementary probability of using strategy σ_2, we can

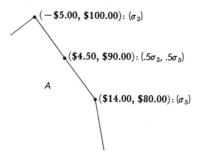

realize any point on the line segment from $(14, 80)$ to $(-5, 100)$ as a joint conditional evaluation of some randomized strategy that uses σ_2 and σ_5 together. If you use randomized or mixed strategies (and nothing prevents you from doing so), then you will considerably enrich the set of achievable or feasible joint conditional evaluations. This set, denoted by A, comprises the boundary and interior of the closed region shown in Fig. 6.4. This set appears as a so-called convex polyhedron, the vertices of which are achievable by non-randomized strategies.

Now the question is, what shall you do with this set once you have it? How shall you choose *your* best strategy, the strategy *you* would employ? We can show that you should confine your deliberations to the darkened northeast boundary of the set as it is shown in Fig. 6.4, the so-called *efficient* or *admissible* set. Just suppose that strategies σ_a and σ_b have joint conditional evaluations as represented by points **a** and **b** in this figure. It doesn't make sense for you

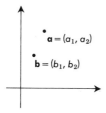

to choose **b**, since **a** is better than **b** if θ_1 is true $(a_1 > b_1)$ and **a** is better than **b** if θ_2 is true $(a_2 > b_2)$; hence point **b** is *inadmissible*. The only points that are admissible lie on the indicated northeast boundary of Fig. 6.4.

The four possible efficient nonrandomized strategies on that boundary are numbers 1, 2, 5, and 95. These numbers are circled in the figure.

Strategy 1. Choose a_1 without experimentation. Obviously this is optimal if you know that the urn is θ_1. Its evaluation is $(40, -20)$.

Strategy 2. Choose a_2 without experimentation. Obviously this is optimal if you know that the urn is θ_2. Its evaluation is $(-5, 100)$.

Strategy 5. Take a sample of one ball for $8.00, and choose a_2 if you draw a red ball and choose a_1 if you draw a black ball. Its evaluation, as we have indicated, is $(14, 80)$.

Strategy 95. Follow the sequential sampling procedure indicated in Fig. 6.2. It will be instructive for you to verify that the joint conditional evaluation of σ_{95} is $(23.20, 62.95)$.

4. CHOICE OF STRATEGY FROM THE EFFICIENT SET WHEN YOU ARE GIVEN $P(\theta_1)$

If you start with an assessment of $P(\theta_1)$, based either on an actual count of the urns or on your judgment, and if you proceed by the extensive form of analysis, then you ought to employ a strategy whose joint conditional evaluation lies in the efficient set. Your next task is to choose a particular strategy from the efficient set. Naturally your choice should depend on your information about the number of θ_1 urns. In this section, we shall consider the completely objective case in which you know there are 800 θ_1's and 200 θ_2's. For example, let's consider strategy σ_5, which has a joint conditional evaluation of $(14, 80)$. You now *know* there is an .8 chance that θ_1 is true and a .2 chance that θ_2 is true, and therefore you can compute the *unconditional* evaluation of σ_5:

$$.8(\$14.00) + .2(\$80.00) = \$27.20,$$

which is the EMV of adopting σ_5. In general, an EMV'er will wish to choose a strategy σ^* that maximizes

$$.8V(\sigma|\theta_1) + .2V(\sigma|\theta_2).$$

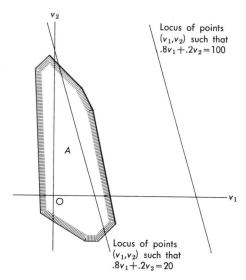

Locus of points (v_1, v_2) such that $.8v_1 + .2v_2 = 100$

A

O

v_2

v_1

Locus of points (v_1, v_2) such that $.8v_1 + .2v_2 = 20$

Figure 6.6

Another way of putting the same thing is to say that you should

1) find the point (v_1^*, v_2^*) in the achievable set A that maximizes

$.8v_1 + .2v_2,$

2) choose the strategy σ^* whose joint conditional evaluation is (v_1^*, v_2^*).

In the v_1v_2-plane consider the locus of (v_1, v_2)-points for which

$.8v_1 + .2v_2 = 20,$

for example. (I have picked the number 20 out of the air for the sake of concreteness, and shortly I shall manipulate this number.) This locus is a straight line (see Fig. 6.6). Can you find a strategy that will give you an expected value of 20 for the game? Is 20 a realizable aspiration level? The answer is "Yes", because this line intersects the achievable set A. Is the value 100 a realizable aspiration level? The answer is "No", because the line

$.8v_1 + .2v_2 = 100$

does not intersect A. The problem reduces to this: Consider the family of parallel straight lines†

$.8v_1 + .2v_2 = k,$

---

† We shall say that the line represented by the equation $.8v_1 + .2v_2 = k$ has *direction numbers* .8 and .2. This line goes through the point (k, k). If k is held fixed and the direction numbers are changed (keeping their sum equal to 1), the line will tilt around the point (k, k).

where k may take on different values, and then select the maximum k whose associated line intersects A. If you refer to Fig. 6.4, you will see that this happens at $k^* = \$31.15$, where the line just touches A at the point (23.20, 62.95). This is of course the joint conditional evaluation of strategy σ_{95}. The conclusion you ought to draw is that σ_{95} is your optimal strategy and the EMV of this strategy is $\$31.15$, a conclusion that agrees with the result we obtained by the extensive form of analysis.

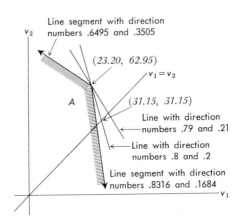

Fig. 6.7 Note that the difference of slopes is amplified and not drawn to scale.

What happens if we reduce $P(\theta_1)$ slightly, say from .80 to .79? Will σ_{95} still be optimal? Observe that the assessment of $P(\theta_1)$ controls the slope of the family of lines considered in Fig. 6.6. Thus when $P(\theta_1) = .79$, the family of lines becomes

$$.79v_1 + .21v_2 = k,$$

and when k is controlled so that the line just touches the achievable set A, the point of contact remains at (23.20, 62.95). (See Fig. 6.7.) Therefore if $P(\theta_1) = .79$, the optimal strategy is still σ_{95} and the EMV is just a bit higher than $\$31.15$, since the tangent or supporting line crosses $v_1 = v_2$ at a slightly higher value. In fact, you can show that σ_{95} *is optimal if* $P(\theta_1)$ *ranges from .6495 to .8316* if you will take the trouble to verify the entries in Table 6.1 by referring to Fig. 6.4.

As $P(\theta_1)$ changes, the optimal strategy stays fixed for a while (this gives you a bit of latitude), but at critical points (in this case, .5128, .6495, .8316) it changes abruptly. But it is comforting to observe that the value of the game

TABLE 6.1

Interval for $P(\theta_1)$			Optimal strategy
.0000	to	.5128	σ_2
.5128	to	.6495	σ_5
.6495	to	.8316	σ_{95}
.8316	to	1.0000	σ_1

does not then change abruptly. For example, if $P(\theta_1) = .66$, the optimal strategy is σ_{95} and yields an expected value of

$$.66(\$23.20) + .34(\$62.95) = \$36.72;$$

if you employ σ_5 by mistake, the expected value is

$$.66(\$14.00) + .34(\$80.00) = \$36.44.$$

Thus when $P(\theta_1) = .66$, the opportunity you lose in employing σ_5 instead of σ_{95} is

$$\$36.72 - \$36.44 = \$0.28;$$

not a very disturbing figure.

Now consider once again your decision problem when you are not told the number of θ_1's but instead have some vague feelings about their possible number. Earlier we suggested that you analyze your feelings and assign a judgmental probability to the event that the unknown urn is a θ_1, granted that this is a hard thing to do. For this particular example, you can simplify your self-analysis considerably by referring to Table 6.1: *To determine your optimal strategy you merely have to assign your judgmental value $P^*(\theta_1)$ to one of the four intervals on the left.*

Suppose you still don't feel comfortable about assigning a judgmental probability to θ_1 even to one of these four intervals. Is there any way you can proceed? We shall continue to discuss this question in the next section.

5.   MODIFICATION FOR A NON-EMV'ER

Before we study the way you ought to choose a best strategy from the efficient set, let us first describe the modifications you would need to make if you carried out the analysis as a non-EMV'er. The notion of a strategy is just as before. There are still 115 of them. If we choose some strategy such as σ_5, we can associate with it a pair of completely objective conditional lotteries $\ell(\sigma_5|\theta_1)$ and $\ell(\sigma_5|\theta_2)$. (See Fig. 6.3.) But now, instead of assigning a monetary value to each of these conditional lotteries as we did for an EMV'er, you can assign a utility value, or, more fundamentally, a π-equilibrating basic reference lottery ticket. As before, suppose $W = \$100.00$ and $L = -\$50.00$, and for the sake of argument let's assume that as far as you are concerned (cf. Fig. 4.13), you are indifferent between

$$-\$13.00 \quad \text{and a} \quad .395\text{-BRLT},$$
$$\$32.00 \quad \text{and a} \quad .72\text{-BRLT},$$
$$\$92.00 \quad \text{and a} \quad .97\text{-BRLT},$$
$$-\$28.00 \quad \text{and a} \quad .26\text{-BRLT}.$$

From this and from Fig. 6.3(b), you ought to be able to understand the implications that strategy σ_5 has for you. These implications are represented in Fig. 6.8.

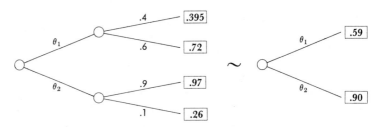

Fig. 6.8 The reduced tree representation of strategy σ_5 for a non-EMV'er.

We shall use the symbol $\pi(\sigma_5|\theta_1)$ to denote the π-equilibrating value for $\ell(\sigma_5|\theta_1)$; that is, you are indifferent between

lottery $\ell(\sigma_5|\theta_1)$ and a $\pi(\sigma_5|\theta_1)$-BRLT,

and between

lottery $\ell(\sigma_5|\theta_2)$ and a $\pi(\sigma_5|\theta_2)$-BRLT.

We define *the joint conditional π-evaluation* of any strategy σ_i to be the pair of numbers $(\pi(\sigma_i|\theta_1), \pi(\sigma_i|\theta_2))$. In particular, the joint π-evaluation of σ_5 is (.59, .90), which is plotted in Fig. 6.9 as a point in the $\pi_1\pi_2$-plane. We

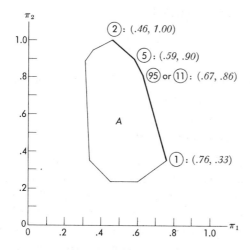

Fig. 6.9 Joint conditional π-evaluations of all possible strategies. Note that the (dark) northeast boundary represents the efficient set.

could plot the associated joint π-evaluations of all 115 strategies in an analogous manner.

Note that the results of randomization are just as before in the case of the EMV'er. For example, suppose you use the randomized strategy that adopts σ_2 with probability .5 and σ_5 with probability .5. Figure 6.10 shows the implications of this randomized strategy: It has a joint conditional π-evaluation which lies at the point midway between the evaluation points for σ_2 and for σ_5. If we consider the randomized strategy $\left(p\sigma_2, (1 - p)\sigma_5\right)$, then we can generate any point on the line segment connecting (.46, 1.00) and (.59, .90), and by using randomized strategies we can achieve any point in the region A, Fig. 6.9. As before, the efficient points lie on the northeast boundary of A, and we can achieve the vertices of A by nonrandomized strategies.

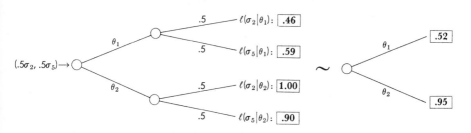

Fig. 6.10 Analysis of the randomized strategy $(.5\sigma_2, .5\sigma_5)$ for a non-EMV'er.

6. INDIFFERENCE-CURVE ANALYSIS

The normal form of analysis which we have discussed has so far been broken down into two major steps.

Step 1. Objective Achievability or Feasibility. Find the set of joint conditional π-evaluations that are achievable.

Step 2. Subjective Preference. Use your judgment or some other criterion to choose a best point from the efficient set.

One can interchange the order of these two steps, achievability and preference. As is commonly done in classical economic theory, we could initially forget about the set of achievable values and prepare a set of indifference curves that completely order the set of (π_1, π_2)-points, *whether they are achievable or not*. We should then construe any two points that lie on the same indifference curve (see Fig. 6.11) as equally desirable from the point of view of the decision maker. For example, consider the two points $(.43, .86)$ and $(.75, .39)$; you would find these two points indifferent if you found the following two prospects equally desirable, given your present vague information about the proportion of θ_1's.

Prospect 1. Obtain $\boxed{.43}$ if θ_1 is true, and $\boxed{.86}$ if θ_2 is true.

Prospect 2. Obtain $\boxed{.75}$ if θ_1 is true, and $\boxed{.39}$ if θ_2 is true.

You can pick off your best strategy from your set of indifference curves and the achievable set A. In Fig. 6.12, for example, although (π_1, π_2)-pairs on

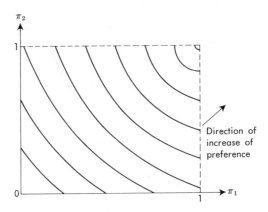

Fig. 6.11 The family of indifference curves ordering (π_1, π_2)-points according to preference.

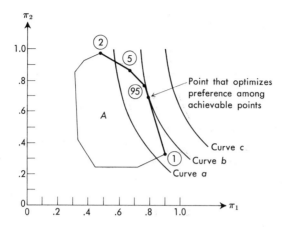

Fig. 6.12   Use of indifference curves to choose the "best" of the achievable strategies.

indifference curve c are preferable to (π_1, π_2)-pairs on indifference curves a or b, none of the points on c is achievable. It is possible to achieve some of the points on indifference curve a, but it is not optimal to do so. The aim, of course, is to choose the point in A that lies on the highest indifference curve. This is accomplished at the point marked with a dot in Fig. 6.12. At this point indifference curve b just touches the achievable set A. In the figure, this point of tangency does not occur at a vertex of the efficient set and therefore it would be necessary to randomize between choice of σ_{95} and σ_1. From the figure it looks as though it would be appropriate to select σ_{95} with a chance of roughly .85 and σ_1 with a chance of .15.

In the next section I shall try to convince you that your indifference curves ought to be parallel straight lines. If you are convinced, then we shall show that the point of the achievable set A that lies on your highest indifference curve is a vertex of the set A and that you therefore can achieve it by a non-randomized strategy.

7.   THE PRINCIPLE OF SUBSTITUTION FOR STRATEGIES

Imagine that the experimenter has not told you the proportion of θ_1-urns, but that you have some vague information on the subject. Suppose you draw a set of indifference curves that seems reasonable to you. First, if you will agree to adopt a certain variation of the substitution principle we have considered before, we can show that your indifference curves ought to be parallel straight lines. Second, we can show that for all practical purposes you would then be

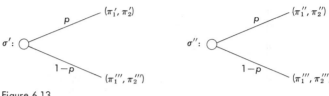

Figure 6.13

acting *as if* you were assigning a weight w between zero and one to θ_1 and assigning the complement of this weight, $1 - w$, to θ_2. It will follow that you should choose the (v_1^*, v_2^*)-point of A to maximize $wv_1 + (1 - w)v_2$. Then all that will remain is the semantic question: Do we wish to call this weighting factor w a "probability"?

Let σ' and σ'' be the two mixed† strategies shown in Fig. 6.13. Strategy σ' leads to the payoff (π_1', π_2') with probability p and to the payoff (π_1''', π_2''') with probability $(1 - p)$. Strategy σ'' is a modification of σ' that we obtain by substituting (π_1'', π_2'') for (π_1', π_2'). [Recall that any payoff of the form (π_1, π_2) means that you will receive a π_1-BRLT if θ_1 is the true state and a π_2-BRLT if θ_2 is the true state.] We now state the

> **Principle of Substitutability.**† If you are indifferent between (π_1', π_2') and (π_1'', π_2''), then you should be indifferent between mixed strategies σ' and σ''.

Figure 6.14 depicts the Principle of Substitutability graphically. If points (π_1', π_2') and (π_1'', π_2'') are indifferent (that is, if they lie on the same indifference curve), then the point A, which lies a proportion $1 - p$ of the distance from (π_1', π_2') to (π_1''', π_2'''), is indifferent to the point marked B, which lies a proportion $1 - p$ of the distance from (π_1'', π_2'') to (π_1''', π_2''').

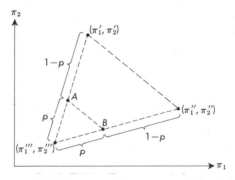

Fig. 6.14 The geometric interpretation of the Substitution Principle.

---

† The terms "mixed strategy" and "randomized strategy" are used interchangeably; ditto for "Principle of Substitutability" and "Substitution Principle".

An important special case of this substitution principle occurs if we let (π_1''', π_2''') and (π_1', π_2') be identical. In this special case, σ' would simply yield the payoff (π_1', π_2') and the Principle of Substitutability would assert:

> If you are indifferent between (π_1', π_2') and (π_1'', π_2''), then you should be indifferent between (π_1', π_2') and the mixed strategy that yields (π_1'', π_2'') with probability p and (π_1', π_2') with probability $(1 - p)$.

But this means that if two points (π_1', π_2') and (π_1'', π_2'') are indifferent, then these points are indifferent to every point on the line segment connecting them (since p is chosen arbitrarily between zero and one). Figure 6.15 illustrates this fact. This figure ought to convince you that any indifference curve must be a straight line; and it should be clear from Fig. 6.14 that these straight lines must be parallel.

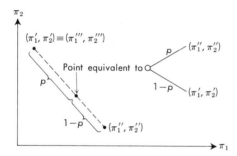

Fig. 6.15 The geometric interpretation of a special case of the Substitution Principle.

The crux of the matter is whether you think the version of the Substitution Principle we have used in this section is compelling. Let us examine the special case of this principle. If, for *you*, $(\pi_1', \pi_2') \sim (\pi_1'', \pi_2'')$, this certainly means that if you were offered one of these points you couldn't care less which one you choose. Presumably this also means you wouldn't care if some disinterested party were to make the choice for you. But in particular, this certainly means that you would not mind if the particular choice were made on the basis of a random drawing. Well, this is all that the special case of the Substitution Principle says, no more and no less.

At this point you may be worried that by some trickery or other, we have proved too much. "Haven't we proved," you may say, "that *all* indifference curves in economic analyses must be parallel straight lines? This is patently ridiculous!" But our argument does not say that in other contexts indifference curves should be straight lines. For example, a housewife might want to make either an apple pie or a peach pie, and therefore she might be indifferent between the combination of six apples and zero peaches [that is, (6, 0)] and the combination of zero apples and six peaches [that is, (0, 6)]. If she is truly indifferent between (6, 0) and (0, 6), then she should not object if someone chooses one of these alternatives for her by the toss of a fair coin: Heads she gets (6, 0) and tails she gets (0, 6). So far, so good. *But this does not imply that the lottery*

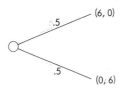

is indifferent to (3, 3). With only three apples and three peaches, she might be forced to end up with a fruit salad, which her children perhaps don't consider an appropriate dessert. We therefore cannot conclude that indifference curves in apple-peach space are straight lines.

Now let's contrast this homely situation with the case in which with heads you get the payoff (π_1', π_2') and with tails you get the payoff (π_1'', π_2''). What does this mean? In this case, according to Table 6.2, your payoff depends on the toss of the coin and the true state. We can represent this lottery in turn as the tree in Fig. 6.16(a), which appears in reduced form in Fig. 6.16(b). The important point to observe is that in this example the values interpreted in π-units are probabilities, and a .5 chance at a π_1'-BRLT (that is, at a π_1' chance at W) plus a .5 chance at a π_1''-BRLT is identical to a $(.5\pi_1' + .5\pi_2'')$-BRLT. However, a .5 chance at six apples and a .5 chance at zero apples is not necessarily indifferent to three apples for certain. *All we have proved is that when indifference curves are drawn in a 2-space in which the units of measurement on both axes are interpreted as probabilities or utilities (surrogates for break-even probabilities), then the indifference curves should be parallel straight lines.*

TABLE 6.2
Payoffs for a mixed strategy

Outcome of toss	State	
	θ_1	θ_2
H	π_1'	π_2'
T	π_1''	π_2''

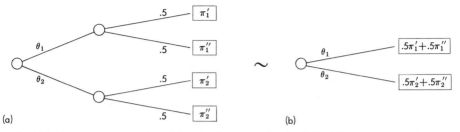

Fig. 6.16 The tree representation of the mixed strategy given in Table 6.2.

Enough of this!—let's go on to the next phase of the analysis. Let's assume that your indifference curves are parallel straight lines. A typical equation for one of these lines might be

$$6\pi_1 + 9\pi_2 = 30.$$

The coefficients of π_1 and π_2 must both have the same sign, since the indifference lines slope downward from northwest to southeast. Dividing both sides of the above equation by $6 + 9$, or 15, we get

$$\tfrac{6}{15}\pi_1 + \tfrac{9}{15}\pi_2 = \tfrac{30}{15}, \qquad \text{or} \qquad .4\pi_1 + .6\pi_2 = 2.$$

In other words, there is no loss of generality if we express the equations of the indifference lines in the form

$$w_1\pi_1 + w_2\pi_2 = k,$$

where

$$w_1 \geq 0, \qquad \text{and} \qquad w_2 \geq 0,$$

and

$$w_1 + w_2 = 1.$$

We can conceive the numbers w_1 and w_2 as weights that determine the slope of the family of indifference lines. The constant k varies from line to line, and with increasing k the lines move up in preference (see Fig. 6.17).

Let's defer to the next section any discussion of how you might go about determining weights w_1 and w_2 that are appropriate for you to use. Given the slope of your indifference curves, your task now is to choose a point (π_1, π_2) that is achievable and that lies on the highest possible indifference line (see

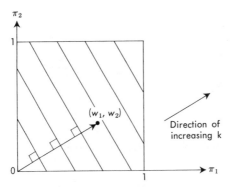

Fig. 6.17 The family of indifference lines for weights (w_1, w_2). The equation of the typical indifference line is $w_1\pi_1 + w_2\pi_2 = k$.

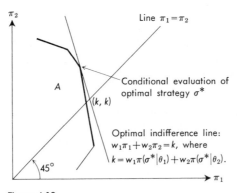

Figure 6.18

Fig. 6.18). But any such point must lie on a vertex on the achievable set A, and must therefore be the evaluation of a nonrandomized strategy.† Hence, your problem is to choose a nonrandomized strategy σ that maximizes the expression

$$w_1\pi(\sigma|\theta_1) + w_2\pi(\sigma|\theta_2);$$

that is, you must choose a σ that maximizes the weighted average of the conditional π-evaluations, where the weights are w_1 and w_2. If σ^* is the optimal strategy, then the indifference line tangent to A intersects the 45° line $\pi_1 = \pi_2$ at the point (k, k) at which $k = w_1\pi(\sigma^*|\theta_1) + w_2\pi(\sigma^*|\theta_2)$.

---

† It is, of course, possible that the highest achievable indifference line might coincide with a flat boundary of the efficient set. In this case all points on this flat will be optimal. It will be true, however, that the extreme points of this flat segment are vertices.

8.   CHOICE OF WEIGHTS

Suppose you have agreed to these points.

1) For any strategy σ, you are willing to assign π-equilibrating basic lottery tickets to the objective lotteries $\ell(\sigma|\theta_1)$ and $\ell(\sigma|\theta_2)$.

2) You want to satisfy the Substitution Principle we described in the last section.

Then all that remains for you to do is to choose your weights w_1 and w_2. There is no way to get out of this! To begin with, you must force yourself to think about the trade-offs between π_1- and π_2-values: For a decrease of Δ_1 in π_1, what is the compensating increase Δ_2 in π_2? I can suggest one way to think about the problem.

Find the point (π, π) that you would take to be indifferent to the point $(1, 0)$. At first sight, this suggestion does not seem very natural or easy to follow, but let's investigate it further. First, the point (π, π) is a representation of the lottery

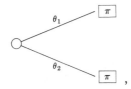

which is clearly indifferent to getting a π-BRLT outright. Second, the point $(1, 0)$ is a representation of the lottery

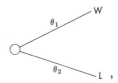

where W and L are the reference prizes of the basic reference lottery tickets. Hence, in comparing (π, π) and $(1, 0)$, you are comparing a π-BRLT with the lottery that gives W if θ_1 and L if θ_2. *But this is a comparison you have met before. By definition,* the equilibrating value is your judgmental probability of θ_1, written $P^*(\theta_1)$. In Fig. 6.19, therefore, the points $(1, 0)$ and $\big(P^*(\theta_1), P^*(\theta_1)\big)$ lie on the same indifference line. A typical point (π_1, π_2) on this line must satisfy the condition

$$\frac{\pi_2 - 0}{\pi_1 - 1} = \frac{\pi_2 - P^*(\theta_1)}{\pi_1 - P^*(\theta_1)},$$

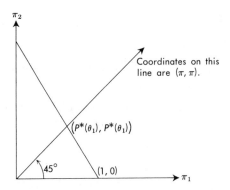

Fig. 6.19 A construction to help you determine the weights (w_1, w_2).

which reduces to

$$P^*(\theta_1)\pi_1 + [1 - P^*(\theta_1)]\pi_2 = P^*(\theta_1)$$

after cross-multiplication. Thus we have demonstrated that the equations of the indifference lines are of the form

$$P^*(\theta_1)\pi_1 + P^*(\theta_2)\pi_2 = k,$$

where $P^*(\theta_2)$ is $1 - P^*(\theta_1)$ by definition and k is arbitrary. In other words, *we have identified the weights w_1 and w_2 with our old friends $P^*(\theta_1)$ and $P^*(\theta_2)$.*

To summarize: If you proceed by a normal form of analysis, you can avoid making your judgmental probability assessments of θ_1 and θ_2 until the very last step. But there is no escaping it. If you want to satisfy the Substitution Principle, then your indifference curves must be parallel straight lines, and the slopes of these lines will implicitly determine your assessment of $P^*(\theta_1)$. We can also show that the strategy you would finally select using a normal-form analysis is identical with the strategy you would select by an extensive-form analysis that averages out and folds back in the decision-flow diagram. In the extensive-form analysis, you must commit yourself to judgmental probabilities of θ_1 and θ_2 to be able to start the averaging-out-and-folding-back process.

9. GENERALIZATIONS†

Let's suppose that you are faced with a given decision problem under uncertainty, and that you wish to make a reasoned, logical analysis of your choices among various courses of experimentation and action. Suppose that the

---

† This section requires a bit more mathematical sophistication than the previous ones. Skip to Section 10 if you are struggling.

consequence of any course of action depends on the as-yet unknown, true "state of the world". Let's denote the set of possible states by θ_1, θ_2, . . . , θ_m, where m may be a very large number, and suppose that with any strategy for experimentation and action σ, and for any state θ_i, there is associated a complex lottery $\ell(\sigma|\theta_i)$ that terminates in one of several consequences with known objective chances. Let's also assume that we can systematically analyze your preferences for these consequences so that we can associate a π-equilibrating basic lottery ticket with each objective lottery $\ell(\sigma|\theta_i)$. We shall choose our notation so that you are symbolically indifferent between getting the lottery $\ell(\sigma|\theta_i)$ and a $\pi(\sigma|\theta_i)$-BRLT. Then we shall be in a position to associate with this strategy σ a joint conditional π-evaluation for σ; this will be a sequence of m numbers π_1, π_2, . . . , π_m, where

$$\pi_1 = \pi(\sigma|\theta_1), \qquad \pi_2 = \pi(\sigma|\theta_2), \qquad \ldots, \qquad \pi_m = \pi(\sigma|\theta_m).$$

The set of possible strategies may be monstrously large (although that's not a real concern in a conceptual development). It is nonetheless possible to introduce the notion of a randomized strategy, which is a scheme for choosing one of a prescribed set of nonrandomized strategies with prescribed probabilities. Just as before, when we discussed the case in which $m = 2$, there is no conceptual difficulty in obtaining the joint conditional π-evaluation for a randomized strategy. Furthermore we can consider the set A of $(\pi_1, \pi_2, \ldots, \pi_m)$-sequences,† which we shall suggestively call "points" in m-space, that we can achieve by nonrandomized and randomized strategies. Your task is now to choose a point (or sequence) in A which you deem "best". The crux of your problem is the way you *ought* to order various π-sequences (that is, points in m-space) according to your preferences.

In essence, the Substitution Principle states that if for some reason or other you consider a π'-sequence indifferent to a π''-sequence, then these are substitutable in a lottery. If you agree to adopt the Substitution Principle, we shall then be able to show that there exists a set of weights w_1, w_2, . . . , w_m, where

$$w_1 \geq 0, \quad \ldots, \quad w_m \geq 0, \qquad \text{and} \qquad w_1 + w_2 + \cdots + w_m = 1,$$

such that you *ought* to choose a nonrandomized strategy σ that maximizes the index

$$w_1\,\pi(\sigma|\theta_1) + w_2\,\pi(\sigma|\theta_2) + \cdots + w_m\,\pi(\sigma|\theta_m).$$

Your next problem concerns the interpretation and selection of weights. We shall find it helpful to simplify a bit by supposing that $m = 5$, say. We can,

---

† For the sake of brevity, we shall refer to such sequences as π-sequences.

for example, ask that you choose a π-value so that you are indifferent between

$$(1, 1, 1, 0, 0) \qquad \text{and} \qquad (\pi, \pi, \pi, \pi, \pi).$$

This means that you must choose a π so that you are indifferent between

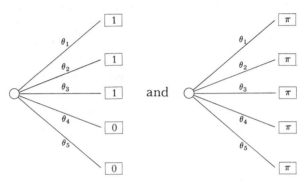

and therefore between

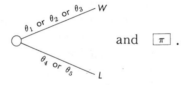

But now the equilibrating π-value is, by definition, your judgmental probability of the event "θ_1 *or* θ_2 *or* θ_3", which has been labeled $P^*(\theta_1$ or θ_2 or $\theta_3)$. In this situation, it follows that

$$P^*(\theta_1 \text{ or } \theta_2 \text{ or } \theta_3) = w_1 + w_2 + w_3.$$

In principle it is possible to use such an analysis as the one we have just presented to get a set of equations by means of which we can determine values for $w_1, w_2, \ldots, w_m$. In general, w_i is equal to $P^*(\theta_i)$, but for purposes of assessment it might *not* be practical to find w_i by asking questions directly about $P^*(\theta_i)$; this is true in particular if the number m of states is large. In the next chapter, we shall discuss this assessment problem in a concrete situation.

10. THE QUEST FOR OBJECTIVE PROCEDURES

The question is often raised, "Can the decision maker, in some way or another, avoid making these purely subjective and often agonizing assignments of judgmental probabilities to the states θ_1 and θ_2? Is there any objective solution to this problem that uses mathematics or logic rather than psychology?"

To simplify our answer let us suppose that you, as the decision maker, are an EMV'er so that you can use Fig. 6.4 in your analysis.

One objective mathematical procedure is this: Find the pair (v_1, v_2) on the efficient set for which the smaller of the two components is as large as possible. In other words, choose (v_1^*, v_2^*) in A to maximize the minimum of (v_1, v_2). In your particular problem, this maximin point occurs at the point where the line $v_1 = v_2$ pierces the efficient set. (Check this!) From Fig. 6.4, you can see that this occurs at $(30, 30)$, and you can achieve this joint conditional evaluation by a randomized strategy using σ_{95} and σ_1. Let's denote this randomized strategy by σ^*. Note that σ^* would be an optimal strategy if it were known that $P(\theta_1)$ were .8316; indeed, in this case, σ_{95}, σ_1, and any mixture of these would also be optimal strategies.

Suppose that both you and I are observing a decision maker, an EMV'er, who has some vague information about the number of θ_1's (say, he has seen the 1000 urns strewn around the floor) but who prefers to suppress his subjective, imprecise, and all-too-vague feelings and to select σ^*. Before he implements σ^*, that is, before he uses a randomized device to decide on σ_1 or σ_{95}, let's ask him this question: "If, on the basis of the knowledge you now have, you *must* guess whether the urn on the table before you is a θ_1 or a θ_2, and if your entire fortune depends on a correct guess, would you say θ_1 or θ_2?" He may respond, "This is a terribly hard question to answer. I am confused. If I were forced to choose, I would say θ_2, but I am often wrong in my guesses."

Do you think he should use σ^* in this situation? Is he being "objective", in the sense that he is using *all* the evidence and information at hand? From his response, we could argue that he believes $P^*(\theta_1) < .5$ and that according to Table 6.1 he should therefore use σ_2. Furthermore, suppose he decides on the randomized strategy σ^* and the randomization happens to come out σ_1, which prescribes a_1 without sampling. Would he not be foolish indeed at that point to choose σ_1 with joint conditional payoff $(40, -20)$ rather than σ_2 with joint conditional payoff $(-5, 100)$? Remember, if he were *forced* to guess, he would choose θ_2 over θ_1!

Perhaps one may argue at this point that this particular objective mathematical criterion (the maximin criterion) is *not* the answer to such problems—perhaps there is another, more appealing, objective procedure. Personally I feel that this quest for a "scientific" and "mathematically objective" rule is all wrong! When there is a paucity of objective evidence at hand, we require a methodology that brings information, however vague and imprecise, into the analysis, rather than a methodology that suppresses information in the name of scientific objectivity. We must be wary of objective panaceas that grind out answers by throwing away information that is not easily quantified. Rather than accept these, we might reasonably argue, we should limit formal analysis to the characterization and determination of the efficient set and let unaided, intuitive judgment take over from there.

One cogent objection to this prescription is that in most decision problems the efficient set is too complicated to think about. This is not so for the simple example we have been analyzing, but suppose that instead of two types of urns, θ_1 and θ_2, we were to start with five, $\theta_1, \theta_2, \ldots, \theta_5$. Then the joint conditional evaluation for any strategy would be a quintuple

$$[V(\sigma|\theta_1), \ V(\sigma|\theta_2), \ V(\sigma|\theta_3), \ V(\sigma|\theta_4), \ V(\sigma|\theta_5)].$$

We could not so easily graph the set of joint conditional evaluations that are achievable, and the efficient set is horrendous to think about. Yet in a real problem five may be a modest number of alternatives, and therefore the objection is not academic. We might also grant that it is much more difficult to assign prior judgmental probabilities to the five possibilities $\theta_1, \theta_2, \ldots, \theta_5$ than to assign them to the two possibilities θ_1 and θ_2, but we should still maintain that it is easier to think *systematically* about assigning these probabilities than to think directly about which strategy for experimentation and action is appropriate.

11. PROJECT

Analyze the oil drilling problem in normal form, using the data of Section 9 , Chapter 2. Exhibit all the nonrandomized strategies, describe the efficient boundary, and use the objective probabilities of θ_1, θ_2, and θ_3 to choose among the efficient nonrandomized strategies.

CHAPTER 7

MORE ABOUT
THE ECONOMICS OF SAMPLING

1. INTRODUCTION

At the beginning of Chapter 5, I suggested the following complication of your basic decision problem. Suppose you know at the outset that the true proportion of θ_1 urns in the collection of 1000 urns is either .7 or .9, each possibility being equally likely. From this collection the experimenter selects an urn at random, removes its label, and sets it before you on the table. Because the probability of state θ_1 is $.5 \times .7 + .5 \times .9 = .8$, I argued that you should analyze your decision problem just as if you had been told in the first place that the true proportion of θ_1's is exactly .8; you should make no allowance for the fact that one .8 is a little fuzzier than another .8. I emphasized and reemphasized the point that if you have vague information about the proportion of θ_1 urns, and if your judgmental probability of state θ_1 is .8 (that is, if you are indifferent between getting prize W if θ_1 and L if θ_2 and getting a .8-BRLT), then you should analyze your decision problem just as if this .8 probability had been given objectively, in a crystal-clear manner. It is an entirely different story, however, if you can purchase, at a cost, *perfect* information about the true proportion of θ_1's. We saw that it is worth $3.41 to an EMV'er to learn whether the true proportion of θ_1 urns in the collection is .7 or .9. In this chapter, we shall investigate the value of getting *imperfect* sample information about the true proportion of θ_1 urns when you have only vague judgmental information about this proportion.

We shall add two sorts of complication to your basic problem.

Modification 1: Purchase of Perfect Information. You have seen the 1000 urns strewn about in the hall and this has given you some impression of the proportion p of θ_1's. Suppose you can find out the *exact* proportion p of θ_1's in the collection before the experimenter selects an urn at random, and thus establish the state θ_1 or θ_2 of your basic problem; suppose also that this perfect information costs \$5.00. Would you buy this perfect information about p? After we discuss this question I shall ask you to consider

Modification 2: Purchase of Imperfect Information. You have the same vague impression about the true proportion of θ_1's as in Modification 1. However, your purchase option is for *imperfect* sample information about p. Specifically, by random sampling with replacement you can inspect the labels of as many urns in the collection as you like for a price of \$0.05 per label. After you complete this inspection the experimenter will select an urn at random and remove its label, and your basic decision problem will begin. Would you sample labels? If so, how many?

These problems are not easy; we shall have to spend a little effort on them. In fact, if you were to assign a cost to your effort of analysis, your best bet at these prices might be to proceed without any formal analysis in Modification 1 and simply pay the \$5.00. If all payoffs and costs were increased a thousand-fold, however, the cost of analysis would be insignificant in comparison with the stakes involved. We shall proceed without taking into account the cost of analysis. To keep the analysis as uncomplicated as possible, let us assume throughout this chapter that you are an EMV'er. The generalizations for a non-EMV'er are not conceptually difficult.

The methodological issues that we are about to consider have very broad applicability. In your basic problem there is a true proportion, let us say p, of θ_1 urns, and if you knew this proportion you could use this information to plan your future action. Instead of the proportion p of θ_1 urns, a decision maker might be interested in the proportion p of

1) individuals in a given population who have attribute x,

2) patients with symptom s who have disease d,

3) students who learn more by educational process a than by b,

4) defective electronic components in a shipment of n components,

5) potential customers who will buy new product q at price π, etc.

In analyzing the two modifications of your basic problem, we shall introduce some concepts and techniques that play a central role in the analysis of all sampling problems dealing with an unknown population proportion p. This class of problems is prototypical of a wide variety of practical statistical problems.

2.   IS IT WORTH $5.00 TO LEARN THE TRUE PROPORTION p?

The Start of the Analysis

Should you spend $5.00 to obtain the exact proportion of θ_1 urns? The fact is, most people are willing to pay excessive amounts of money to get rid of vagueness. Perhaps this is because they don't know how to cope with it rationally or purposively or perhaps the explanation is more purely emotional; the specific reasons are immaterial.

Is the $5.00 toll excessive? Let's look at the partial decision-flow diagram shown in Fig. 7.1.

Note that if you request the true proportion, then the potential responses at the next fork can range anywhere from 0.0 to 1.0. If the true proportion were .721, say, then the remaining analysis, although tedious, would be routine. You would assign $P(\theta_1) = .721$ and calculate the other relevant assignments, for example, $P(R)$ and $P(\theta_1|R)$. For each possible value p you could, at least conceptually, calculate the expected monetary or utility value of playing the

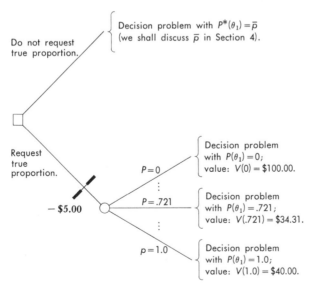

Fig. 7.1 Decision-flow diagram for analyzing whether you should pay $5.00 to get the true proportion of θ_1 urns.

game from the certain knowledge that $P(\theta_1) = p$. This value depends on p; let's denote it by $V(p)$. How de we find the value of this function?

Table 6.1 gives the optimal strategy for each p. Thus, for example, we know that strategy σ_2 is optimal for p in the interval .0000 to .5128. But since the joint conditional evaluation of σ_2 is $(-5, 100)$, we know that

$$V(p) = -5p + 100(1 - p) \qquad \text{for} \qquad .0000 \leq p \leq .5128.$$

Making use of Table 6.1 and the joint conditional evaluations of strategies $\sigma_2, \sigma_5, \sigma_{95}$, and σ_1, we get

$$V(p) = \begin{cases} -5p + 100(1 - p) & \text{for} & .0000 \leq p \leq .5128 & (\text{use } \sigma_2), \\ 14p + 80(1 - p) & \text{for} & .5128 < p \leq .6495 & (\text{use } \sigma_5), \\ 23.20p + 62.95(1 - p) & \text{for} & .6495 < p \leq .8316 & (\text{use } \sigma_{95}), \\ 40p - 20(1 - p) & \text{for} & .8316 < p \leq 1.000 & (\text{use } \sigma_1). \end{cases}$$

Figure 7.2 shows V plotted against p.

Now if you were to pay your \$5.00 toll and go down the *Request true propor-tion* path, you would perceive ahead of you the many-forked lottery whose values are given in Fig. 7.2. But what kind of move is this? Clearly it is not a

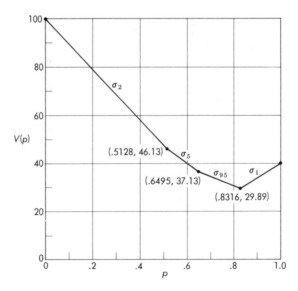

Fig. 7.2 The value V that an EMV'er assigns to the basic problem as a function of the known proportion p of θ_1 urns.

decision fork. Many argue that is not a chance fork either. They assert that there is a *true p* and that it is meaningless to assign probability measures to such events as "$p = .721$" and "$p \leq .9$"; the state is true or not true, and that's all there is to it. But in Chapters 5 and 6, we saw that if you want to be consistent with the behavioral principles of transitivity and substitutability, you should assign judgmental probabilities to the 1001 events

$$(p = 0), \quad (p = .001), \quad \ldots, \quad (p = .999), \quad (p = 1.000).$$

The expected monetary value of being perched at the 1001-forked lottery would then be the weighted average of the values $V(0)$, $V(.001)$, ..., $V(.999)$, $V(1.000)$, where the weights are

$$P^*(p = 0), \quad P^*(p = .001), \quad \ldots, \quad P^*(p = .999), \quad P^*(p = 1.000),$$

respectively. A term such as $P^*(p = .721)$ is the judgmental probability you assign to the event "there are 721 urns of type θ_1". Specifically, then, this expected monetary value is

$$\overline{V} = P^*(p = 0)V(0) + P^*(p = .001)V(.001) + \cdots$$
$$+ P^*(p = .999)V(.999) + P^*(p = 1.000)V(1.000).$$

In this computer age a thousand and one multiplications and a thousand additions shouldn't faze us, but how in heaven's name could you probe your inner self for the 1001 required numbers $P^*(p = 0)$, $P^*(p = .001)$, ..., $P^*(p = .999)$, $P^*(p = 1.000)$? The next section suggests one method you might use.

3. ASSESSMENT OF A JUDGMENTAL DISTRIBUTION FOR AN UNCERTAIN PROPORTION

The following dialogue illustrates how to obtain a judgmental probability distribution for an unknown population proportion p. With this as background, I hope you will see how you might generate your own judgmental distribution for the proportion p of θ_1 urns from the vague impression suggested in Modification 1. The persons of the dialogue are a decision analyst and his client or subject, who takes the part of the decision maker or an expert agent delegated by the decision maker.

Analyst. I should like to show you how you can obtain a judgmental probability distribution for some unknown proportion p. I want to choose a context that is sufficiently meaningful to you, because

I want to probe into *your* judgments rather than into someone else's. Let's consider the population of medical doctors in the U.S. who are nonteetotalers. Now suppose we let p be the proportion of these imbibers who consumed more scotch than bourbon in the past year. Incidentally, do you know much about the drinking pattern of doctors?

Subject. Not much. The usual, I suppose. I know three or four doctors personally, but I imagine doctors are not much different from lawyers or dentists or engineers. The trouble is that I would not know how to answer your question for any of those groups. I don't have the foggiest notion what p is.

Analyst. Good. I wanted to take just such an example.

Subject. I suppose you want me to give a best guess at p. I don't know if I could even do that.

Analyst. No, I don't want you to do that. In fact, I don't think it's very meaningful to talk about a 'best' guess. Best for what? Let me start off with some warming-up questions. Do you think it's more likely that p is less than .10 or above .10?

Subject. That's easy! Above.

Analyst. Is it more likely that p is above .90 or below?

Subject. Below.

Analyst. Those were easy. See, you do know something about p. Now I want you to think hard about the next one. Give me a value such that it would be extremely hard for you to make up your mind to choose above it or below it. In other words, I want you to give me a value such that you will think it equally likely that p falls below or above it.

Subject. (After some thought.) I would say .60. But, boy, am I vague about this. I *think* more doctors prefer scotch. You know, the upwardly mobile group and all that sort of thing.

Analyst. Don't fret about this too much; if you want to change your mind later on, that's all right with me. You have now told me that you think it is equally likely that p is less than .60 or more than .60.

Subject. That's right. But don't ask me to define what 'equally likely' means.

Analyst. By 'equally likely' in this context I mean that you are indifferent between receiving a very desirable prize conditional on p being below .60 and receiving this identical prize conditional on p being above

.60. Or, more dramatically, if your life depended on it, you would just as soon opt for $p \leq .60$ as $p \geq .60$. Are you with me?

Subject. So far, so good.

Analyst. Essentially you have now told me, *and* yourself, that .60 divides the interval from zero to 1.0 into two judgmentally equally likely parts. Now I am going to ask you to repeat this process of judgmentally subdividing different intervals into two equally likely parts. For example, do you think it is more likely that p is less than .20 or is between .20 and .60?

Subject. Between .20 and .60.

Analyst. Between zero and .58 or between .58 and .60?

Subject. Between zero and .58.

Analyst. All right, now give me a number such that you think it is judgmentally equally likely that p is between zero and that number or between that number and .60.

Subject. What happens if p is greater than .60?

Analyst. As things stand now, you lose. Look, if you tell me the number is p^*, then this means that you think your chances of winning the prize are just as good if you choose the interval zero to p^* as they are if you choose the interval p^* to .60. If p is greater than .60, you would not get the prize no matter which side of p^* you choose because p would not be in either interval.

Subject. All right, let's see. I'll say that .50 divides the interval zero to .60 into two equally likely parts.

Analyst. Once you had given me the number .60, would it have been easier for you if I had posed my last request this way: 'Look, suppose I tell you that p is less than .60. Knowing this, how would you divide the interval zero to .60 into two equally likely parts?'

Subject. Are these the same questions?

Analyst. I think so. Think about it.

Subject. I suppose they are the same. The second way seems easier, but second ways always seem easier to me.

Analyst. Let's go on. Suppose I tell you that p is greater than .60. Then how would you divide the interval .60 to 1.00 into two equally likely parts?

Subject. Hmm—.70. From .60 to .70 is just as likely as above .70. But I really feel uncomfortable about the .50 and .70 because the .60 is so shaky. I feel I'm building on a sponge. I hope you realize these numbers are mighty shaky.

Analyst. I hope you realize that I realize that. You are doing fine. You have now given me three numbers, .60, .50, and .70. Let me draw an interval from zero to 1.00 and place these points on it:

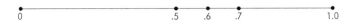

0   .5   .6   .7   1.0

Now you have told me that so far as you are concerned, you believe it is just as likely that p lies in any one of the four intervals [0 to .50], [.50 to .60], [.60 to .70], and [.70 to 1.00].

Subject. I guess I said that.

Analyst. Now I am just checking up. I don't want to catch you and it certainly is not my intention to embarrass you, but it is important to look at these things from many different angles. For example, would you rather bet that p lies in the interval [.50 to .70], or outside this interval?

Subject. I think I would bet that it lies inside the interval. But now I'm being inconsistent, am I not?

Analyst. Yes, you are, but almost everyone else is too. I want you to think about it more. It will help if you try consciously to be consistent.

Subject. Well, I don't want to change the .60. I feel shakiest about the .70. I suppose I'd be willing to live with .68. So far as I'm concerned, it's a 50-50 bet that p lies in the interval [.50 to .68].

Analyst. Would you be willing to say that it is equally likely that p lies in the interval [.60 to .68] as in the interval [.68 to 1.00]?

Subject. All right, I'll go along with this. But if we did it all over again and if I erased this conversation from my memory, I can imagine that instead of ending up with the numbers .50, .60, and .68, I could have ended up with numbers like .52, .64, and .74.

Analyst. Well, these are in the same ballpark. Could you imagine ending up with numbers like .20, .40, and .55?

Subject. No. Not really. But what would you do if I said 'Yes'?

Analyst. I would push you further and use some averaging process that would pull the three numbers you have given me further apart. But let's go on. I'll refer to the number .60 as your judgmental .50-fractile, the number .50 as your judgmental .25-fractile, and the number .68 as your judgmental .75-fractile.
Aside to the reader. Symbolically I shall write this as

$$p_{.25} = .50, \qquad p_{.50} = .60, \qquad p_{.75} = .68.$$

A few more numbers will help me. How would you divide the interval [0 to .50] into two equally likely parts?

Subject. .42.

Analyst. *Aside.* This means $p_{.125} = .42$.
Now divide the interval [.00 to .42].

Subject. You are pushing me pretty far.

Analyst. Well, suppose I told you that p is less than .42. Would you rather bet on [.00 to .21] or on [.21 to .42]?

Subject. On the latter, of course. All right, use .36.

Analyst. *Aside.* This means $p_{.0625} = .36$.
Now let's pass quickly to the high end. Divide [.68 to 1.00].

Subject. Use .75.

Analyst. *Aside.* This means $p_{.875} = .75$.
All right, divide [.75 to 1.00].

Subject. Use .80.

Analyst. *Aside.* This means $p_{.9375} = .80$.
Let's summarize your judgmental responses in a table:

TABLE 7.1

Fractile k	Judgmental fractile value p_k
.0625	.36
.125	.42
.25	.50
.50	.60
.75	.68
.875	.75
.9375	.80

Now let's break off this dialogue and show how we can manipulate this data and represent it in two different graphical displays. A word about notation first: The expression $p_{.125} = .42$, for example, indicates that the subject's judgmental probability of the event $(p \leq .42)$ is .125; that is, the subject attaches a $\frac{1}{8}$ probability to the event "among physicians choosing whiskeys, 42% or less prefer scotch to bourbon". Symbolically we write

$P^*(p \leq .42) = .125.$

[There is some question whether the endpoints of intervals are included or not. This is really a minor issue because we can always interpret the endpoints of intervals as being exact numbers and the probability that would be assigned to an event such as $(p = .4200 \ldots)$ is minuscule and can be ignored.]

Figure 7.3 shows the points of Table 7.1 with a smooth curve drawn through them. For any value x on the horizontal axis, the smoothed curve gives the subject's judgmental probability that the proportion p of doctors who consume more scotch than bourbon is less than or equal to x. This is called the *left-tail cumulative judgmental probability distribution* for the unknown proportion p. If one of the original data points (the dots on the curve) did not line up nicely with the others, the analyst would have asked the subject to alter his assessments slightly to make his data points line up better. It is important to remember that the vaguer the subject is, the more pliable are his answers and the easier it is for the analyst to get a pattern of consistent answers. I have taken poetic license in extending the tails of the distribution below $x = .36$ and above

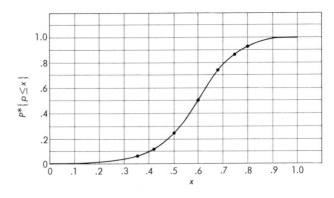

Fig. 7.3   The left-tail cumulative judgmental probability distribution for the proportion p of doctors who consumed more scotch than bourbon. The points marked on the curve correspond to the data given in Table 7.1. I have "smoothed" the curve through these points.

$x = .80$. If the problem we are trying to analyze is very sensitive to the shapes in the tails, it would be appropriate to ask the subject to subdivide the interval [0 to .36] into two equally likely parts, and so on, until we have enough data points for our purposes. This would be especially important if we were studying the probability of rare events such as power surges that black out cities or whole regions of the nation.

From Fig. 7.3 we can easily obtain this subject's judgmental probability that p lies in a particular interval. For example, suppose we want his P^*-value for the event $(.40 < p \le .50)$. We would then have

$$P^*(.40 < p \le .50) = P^*(p \le .50) - P^*(p \le .40)$$
$$= .25 - .10 = .15.$$

Figure 7.4 shows a histogram that gives the probability that p falls in the ten successive intervals [0 to .10], [.10 to .20], ..., [.90 to 1.00]. Thus the height of the flat portion of the histogram is .15 over the interval from .40 to .50. I have drawn in by eye a smooth curve through the flat levels of the histogram. This smooth curve approximates what we can call the subject's judgmental *density function* for the unknown proportion p. We interpret this density function

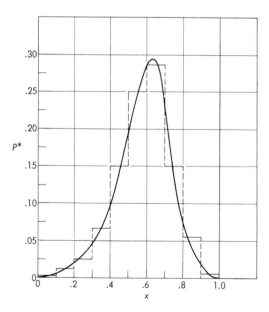

Fig. 7.4 A histogram showing the judgmental probability P^* that the proportion p of doctors who consumed more bourbon than scotch lies in successive intervals of length .1.

as follows: The area under the histogram or under the density curve as I have drawn it is less than one; —actually it is approximately .1. Suppose we now imagine the vertical scale is changed so that the area under the density curve is equal to one. Then for any interval, the subject's judgmental P^*-value for this interval is the area under the curve within this interval. Thus, for example, $P^*(.35 < p \leq .60)$ is the area under the density curve from .35 to .60 on the x-axis. We shall use this density function in the next section.

4. IS IT WORTH $5.00 TO LEARN THE TRUE PROPORTION p?

The End of the Analysis

Now we turn back to the urns and to your decision problem. After getting a quick glance at the labels of the urns strewn around the adjoining hall, suppose you now assess your judgmental distribution for this unknown proportion p in the manner we described in the previous section. You would ask yourself for a number $p_{.50}$ such that you think it just as likely that the true proportion is below or above the number $p_{.50}$. This number $p_{.50}$ will divide the interval into two judgmentally equally likely parts. Next you would ask yourself to subdivide each of the intervals $[0$ to $p_{.50}]$ and $[p_{.50}$ to $1]$ into two equally likely parts; and so on. Eventually you would obtain a curve similar to the one shown in Fig. 7.3, and after some calculation you could reexpress your judgments about the uncertain proportion p of θ_1 urns in terms of a histogram and a density function. For the sake of concreteness, suppose this process results in the assessment indicated in Fig. 7.5.

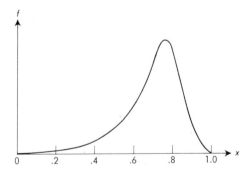

Fig. 7.5 Your alleged judgmental density function for the unknown proportion p of θ_1 urns. The area under the curve between any two points a and b, $0 \leq a \leq b \leq 1$, gives $P^*\{a \leq p \leq b\}$. The area under the whole curve is equal to 1. For any x, the height is labeled $f(x)$.

Suppose once again that you have gone down the *Request true proportion* path in Fig. 7.1, and paid your $5.00 toll. What is it worth to you to be perched at the 1001-forked juncture? As we have indicated before, we must evaluate

$$P^*(p = 0)V(0) + \cdots + P^*(p = .721)V(.721)$$
$$+ \cdots + P^*(p = 1.000)V(1.000). \quad (1)$$

Now let's look at a typical term $P^*(p = .721)$. We can think of this probability as the area under the density curve over the interval $[(.721 - .0005)$ to $(.721 + .0005)]$. But to a very good approximation, this area is clearly the height of the density function at .721, or $f(.721)$, multiplied by the length of the interval, namely .001. Hence we get

$$P^*(p = .721) = .001f(.721).$$

We can now restate expression (1) as

$$\overline{V} = .001[f(0)V(0) + f(.001)V(.001) + \cdots$$
$$+ f(.721)V(.721) + \cdots + f(1.000)V(1.000)]. \quad (2)$$

I think we have now squeezed all the conceptual juice out of this problem. All that remains is a routine computing job.† I have done this computation, and the sum comes out to be $39.57. At the end of this section we shall briefly describe an approximate procedure for obtaining $\overline{V}$ that is suitable for hand calculation.

Now let's back up and go down the *Do not request* path. To see how we should analyze this branch, we take a cue from the discussion given in Section 2, Chapter 5. In that section I introduced the case in which you know at the outset that p is either .7 or .9, and you are told that those two possibilities are equally likely:

$$P(p = .7) = P(p = .9) = .5.$$

In that section we argued that if you could not obtain any further information about which of these two situations prevails, then the probability you ought to assign to state θ_1 is

$$.7P(p = .7) + .9P(p = .9) = .8.$$

The .8-value that you worked with is the average of the two numbers .7 and .9.

---

† For the mathematical reader: The sum to be evaluated is approximately equal to $\int_0^1 V(x)f(x)\,dx$.

If you go down the *Do not request* path, then so far as you are concerned p can be any value from zero to 1. If p were .721, say, then you could assign $P(\theta_1) = .721$. By analogy with what went before, we see that consistency requires us to compute $P^*(\theta_1)$ from the equation

$$P^*(\theta_1) = .000P^*(p = 0) + .001P^*(p = .001) + \cdots$$
$$+ .721P^*(p = .721) + \cdots + 1.000P^*(p = 1.000);$$

this gives the *mean* or expected value of your judgmental distribution for p. Now I have used your alleged judgmental density function for the uncertain proportion p (see Fig. 7.5) to compute its expected value $\bar{p}$, and this turns out to be .75. Therefore you should use $P^*(\theta_1) = \bar{p} = .75$ to evaluate the *Do not request* path of Fig. 7.1, and Fig. 7.2 tells us that this evaluation is $V(.75) = \$33.11$.

This discussion raises an interesting point. Back in Chapter 5 we asked you to assess $P^*(\theta_1)$. At that time you did not make any specific attempt to formally develop your insight into the true proportion p of θ_1 urns, and indeed there was no need to assess a whole distribution for p just to analyze the decision-flow diagram; all we needed at that time was a "best guess" at p. But this best guess ought to have been your assessment of the mean of your judgmental distribution of p. This is not an easy number to give, and in Chapter 5 it was not worth our trouble to derive it—we had enough difficulties to contend with. Suppose, however, that your snap judgment of $P^*(\theta_1)$ is .8 and that you compute the mean of your judgmental distribution of p to be .75. This represents an inconsistency in your judgments, to be sure, but no one would expect you to be consistent in such complicated assessments. Don't be unduly concerned about such inconsistencies. In our example, as it happens, the same strategy is optimal for $P^*(\theta_1) = .75$ and for $P^*(\theta_1) = .80$. Even if the optimal strategies were different, however, you ought not to worry too much because these strategies would have approximately the same expected payoffs for $P^*(\theta_1)$-values that are this close together. Nevertheless when we uncover an inconsistency we shall follow our usual practice and reconcile values. You could perhaps compromise by modifying your assessed distribution (Fig. 7.5) so that its mean $\bar{p}$ is pushed up from .75 to .77, say, and letting $P^*(\theta_1) = .77$, but it's easier and simpler just to change your assessed probability for θ_1 from .8 to .75 and leave Fig. 7.5 intact. If you were to change Fig. 7.5, you would also have to redo the analysis of the *Request true proportion* path (Fig. 7.1).

Now let's return to the main line of development and complete our analysis of Fig. 7.1. The results we have obtained thus far are shown in Fig. 7.6. This

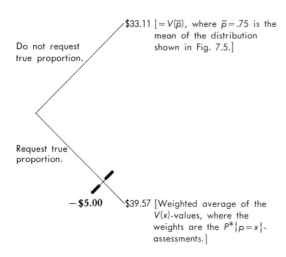

Fig. 7.6 The reduction of the decision-flow diagram shown in Fig. 7.1.

figure makes it clear that you ought to pay $5.00 to learn the exact proportion p. Indeed the expected value of this piece of perfect information† is worth $39.57 − $33.11 = $6.46. Once you purchase this information, your subsequent optimal strategy for experimentation and action depends on what you are told the true p is. See Table 6.1 for details.

An approximate computational procedure for hand calculation. We can obtain an approximation to the weighted average $\overline{V}$ of the $V(x)$-values, where the weights are the $P^*(p = x)$-assessments, by this simple computational procedure.

1) Obtain your judgmental fractiles of p as described in the dialogue. Use these values to plot your left-tail cumulative judgmental probability distribution for p, as shown in Fig. 7.3. From this curve read off the ten numbers on the x-axis that correspond to the numbers .05, .15, .25, .35, .45, .55, .65, .75, .85, .95 on the vertical axis, and label them $p_{.05}, p_{.15}, \ldots, p_{.85}, p_{.95}$. For example, if you were using Fig. 7.3, you would get $p_{.35} = .545$.

---

† For the mathematically sophisticated reader: If we let E be the expectation operator and treat p as a random variable, then the expected value of perfect information about p is

$$EV(p) - V(Ep).$$

This is always nonnegative since V is a convex function.

2) Use Fig. 7.2 to obtain the numbers $V(p_{.05})$, $V(p_{.15})$, . . . , $V(p_{.85})$, $V(p_{.95})$.

3) Then obtain the weighted average $\bar{V}$ from the approximate formula

$$\bar{V} \approx \tfrac{1}{10}[V(p_{.05}) + V(p_{.15}) + \cdots + V(p_{.85}) + V(p_{.95})].$$

You can use the same technique to get $\bar{p}$, the mean of the distribution of p. In this case you would use the approximate formula

$$\bar{p} \approx \tfrac{1}{10}[p_{.05} + p_{.15} + \cdots + p_{.85} + p_{.95}].$$

Essentially this procedure replaces the chance fork of 1001 branches in Fig. 7.1 by one having just ten branches, where each of the branches has probability assignment .1.

If we use this approximate procedure to obtain $\bar{V}$ and $\bar{p}$, we don't need to obtain the density function f. This density function will play a more crucial role in the next sections.

5.   SHOULD YOU SAMPLE TO OBTAIN INFORMATION ABOUT p?

The Start of the Analysis

You have now seen that it is worth $5.00 to get perfect information about the proportion p. It might be preferable to get relevant but imperfect information about p at a much cheaper cost. If you could take a random sample of the 1000 urns, would you sample at $0.05 an urn? If so, how much? If, for example, you were to decide to take a sample of 50, then you would have to pay $50 \times \$0.05 = \$2.50$. Next, suppose that the vagaries of the sample are such that 28 of these 50 urns turn out to be θ_1's and 22 turn out to be θ_2's. After you have obtained your information, the experimenter will select an urn at random and remove its identifying label, and once again you will be confronted with your basic decision problem: Should you choose e_0, e_1, e_2, or e_3, and so forth? In this situation you would not know $P(\theta_1)$ but you would have a vague impression from your quick look at the urns strewn about in haphazard fashion on the floor, plus the hard objective fact that a random sample of 50 of these urns yielded 28 of type θ_1. Of course, the sample outcome could yield any number of θ_1 urns from zero to 50.

Figure 7.7 displays the strategic structure of your present decision problem in a decision-flow diagram. Let n denote the sample size (so that $n = 0$ means no sample is taken, for example) and let r denote the number of θ_1 urns in the sample. At the first move you must choose a value for n. Note that the figure

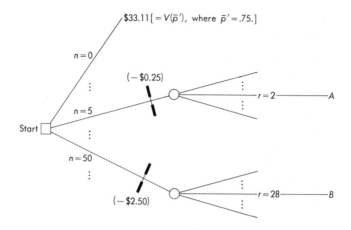

Fig. 7.7 Decision-flow diagram for analyzing whether you should sample, and if so, how much.

presents only three of the many possible branches. At the second move, Chance selects the particular outcome of the random drawing (assuming $n > 0$). For example, if you choose $n = 5$ and pay a \$0.25 toll, then Chance, so to speak, can choose the number r of θ_1's in this sample, r ranging from zero to five. Note that the figure shows only the branch $r = 2$; you are to imagine the five remaining branches. Again, if you choose $n = 50$, Chance has the choice of r from zero to 50 and once again you are to imagine that all branches are present, although the figure shows only $r = 28$.

We must now discuss two major tasks. First, how should you evaluate your CME, given that you are located at a point such as A or B and assuming that you will behave optimally thereafter? Second, how should you assign probabilities to the branches of your second move, which is controlled by Chance? For example, how should you assign a probability to the event ($r = 2$) when $n = 5$?

You will be delighted to learn that there is no need for you to furnish any more judgmental information. All our subsequent operations will build from your judgmental density function, shown in Fig. 7.5, and will be purely mechanical. I am sure that you will also be delighted to know that it will not be necessary to develop any new theory; all we need do is apply results already discussed. For convenience, let's continue to assume that you are an EMV'er. If we did not make this assumption, then we should simply have to work with π-equilibrating basic reference lottery tickets instead of working with monetary values; but you already know how to handle that sort of complication.

6. REVISION OF YOUR PRIOR DISTRIBUTION OF *p* IN LIGHT OF SAMPLE EVIDENCE

How does your problem change if you select $n = 50$, for example, and observe $r = 28$? With this added information you should presumably no longer feel that the density function given in Fig. 7.5 describes your judgments about the unknown, true proportion p of θ_1 urns. Figure 7.5 displays the judgments you made about p before you received any experimental sample evidence. Now that you know that a random sample of 50 urns yielded 28 urns of type θ_1, it seems reasonable that your judgments about p should change. For example, you should reduce your P^*-value for the event $(p > .8)$. We shall employ the symbols $f^{(b)}$ and $f^{(a)}$ to distinguish between your density function **before** (or prior to) the sample and **after** (or posterior to) the sample. Also, to indicate the dependence of $f^{(a)}$ on the results of experimentation, we shall write $f^{(a)}_{28,50}$ to designate the density function for the unknown proportion p *after* a sample of size 50 has resulted in 28 urns of type θ_1. Figure 7.8 exhibits the shifts from $f^{(b)}$ to $f^{(a)}$ that occur after one sample results in $(r = 28, n = 50)$ and another results in $(r = 2, n = 5)$. Note that $f^{(a)}_{28,50}$ is quite a way from $f^{(b)}$, whereas $f^{(a)}_{2,5}$ is considerably closer. Furthermore, note that $f^{(a)}_{28,50}$ is quite steep, or *tightly distributed*, and thus values of p below .4 or above .8 do not get much weight. These results should seem intuitively plausible to you; however, since these operations of revision are a bit technical, and since this subject matter can be meaningfully isolated as a comprehensible unit, I shall defer its development to an appendix. My aim in the appendix will not be to give a brief course in how one should update a prior distribution to get a posterior distribution, but rather to dispel some of the conceptual mystery that surrounds these operations.

7. SHOULD YOU SAMPLE TO OBTAIN INFORMATION ABOUT *p*?

The End of the Analysis

Let us again consider Fig. 7.7. We are now in a position to say something about what your EMV should be at points A and B. Suppose you choose $n = 5$ and pay your $0.25 toll, and then Chance gives you $r = 2$. At the end of Section 4 of this chapter we described how to analyze such a situation. To recapitulate: Since p is still unknown at this point and since you do not have the opportunity to gather any further information about p, you should proceed by assigning to $P^*(\theta_1)$ the mean of your current judgmental distribution† of p.

---

† It is not always true that the mean of a probability distribution is the relevant, effective summarization of the entire distribution. It happens to be so in the problem discussed here, but beware of drawing unwarranted conclusions for other contexts.

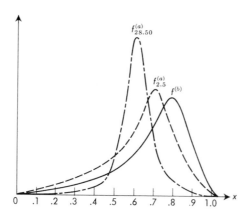

Fig. 7.8 Density functions for p before and after sampling.

At the point A, the function $f_{2,5}^{(a)}$ shown in Fig. 7.8 gives your current probability judgments about p, and you should assign the mean of this distribution to $P^*(\theta_1)$. However, it is not possible to read the mean of this distribution from those graphs; instead one must compute it from the formula†

$$.001[.000 f_{2,5}^{(a)}(.000) + .001 f_{2,5}^{(a)}(.001) + \cdots$$
$$+ .999 f_{2,5}^{(a)}(.999) + 1.000 f_{2,5}^{(a)}(1.000)],$$

which we shall suggestively label $\bar{p}_{2,5}^{(a)}$. Carrying out the calculations, we get $\bar{p}_{2,5}^{(a)} = .68$. Hence, from Fig. 7.2, the value of being at position A is $V(.68) = \$35.92$. Arguing in an analogous fashion, we find that the EMV at position B is $V(\bar{p}_{28,50}^{(a)})$, where $\bar{p}_{28,50}^{(a)}$ is the mean of the distribution $f_{28,50}^{(a)}$; we compute this mean to be .60 and hence from Fig. 7.2, the value of being at position B is $V(.60) = \$40.35$. In general, in Fig. 7.7, if you draw a sample of size n at the first fork and Chance responds at the second fork with r, then the value of being at the resulting juncture is $V(\bar{p}_{r,n}^{(a)})$, where $\bar{p}_{r,n}^{(a)}$ is the mean of the distribution $f_{r,n}^{(a)}$.

Our next task is to fold back the analysis one more step. What is the value, for example, of being at the fork that comes immediately after you have chosen $n = 5$ and paid the $0.25 toll? At this juncture we see the lottery described in Fig. 7.9. To find the EMV of this lottery, which we shall denote by $\bar{V}(5)$, we multiply each of the payoffs $V(\bar{p}_{0,5}^{(a)}), \ldots, V(\bar{p}_{5,5}^{(a)})$ by the probability that

---

† The mean of the distribution $f_{2,5}^{(a)}$ is

$$\bar{p}_{2,5}^{(a)} \equiv \int_0^1 x f_{2,5}^{(a)}(x)\, dx.$$

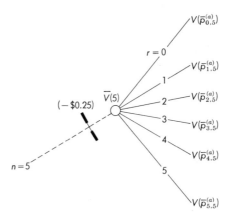

Fig. 7.9 Lottery at the second fork following choice of $n = 5$ at the first fork.

Chance will select the branch in question and then add the results. In the appendix to this Chapter I have noted a procedure for calculating these probabilities. Except for a few details the procedure is the same as the one we discussed in Chapter 2 when we obtained the probability of red (R) and black (B) on the e_1-branch.

We can compute $\overline{V}(n)$ for values $n = 1, 2, 3, \ldots$ in a similar manner. Since the expected value of perfect information about the true proportion p is

$$\$39.57 - \$33.11 = \$6.46$$

(see Fig. 7.6), it would certainly not be worthwhile to let n exceed $\$6.46/\$0.05 \approx 129$; for $n = 130$ the cost of sampling would exceed $\$6.46$, and a sample of 130, while giving extremely valuable information, would not give perfect information about the true proportion p of θ_1 urns. The EVPI thus sets an upper limit to the reasonable values of n.

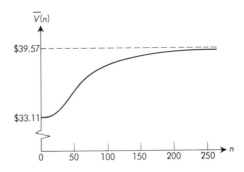

Fig. 7.10 The EMV of being at the fork that follows a choice of n at the first fork and after paying a toll of ($.05)$n$. The EMV is plotted as a function of n.

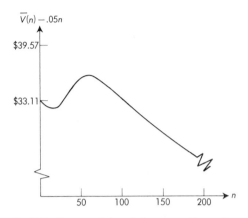

Fig. 7.11 The EMV of the whole venture if you choose a sample of size *n* at the first fork. The EMV is plotted as a function of *n*.

Figure 7.10 shows the shape of the $\overline{V}(n)$-function. Note that the curve starts at $\overline{V}(0) = \$33.11$ and increases to the value $39.57. Observe also that there is no increase in $\overline{V}(n)$ for very small values of *n*. To see why this is so, let $n = 2$, for example; then no matter whether $r = 0$, 1, or 2, the mean $\overline{p}_{r,2}^{(a)}$ will fall within the interval [.6495 to .8316] (see Fig. 7.2 and Table 6.1), and therefore you would use the same subsequent strategy (that is, σ_{95}) for experimentation and action. In other words, small samples, regardless of how they may come out, may not be powerful enough to change subsequent behavior and as such are not of any value.

To find the *optimal* sample size *n* we must subtract the cost of sampling from $\overline{V}(n)$; see Fig. 7.11. This figure shows that the optimal sample size lies in the neighborhood of $n = 50$.

It might appear that this analysis requires a frightening amount of computational work. Although this is true of the computational procedure described above, there are several analytical shortcuts that we can take, and if we use these in conjunction with a digital computer the analysis takes less than a second to execute. Of course, this remark does not take into account the fixed costs that go into developing analytical machinery and the considerable amount of time that is required to write a computer program. But these costs should not be solely allocated to the solution of a single problem. Sections or modules of this effort can be used with little or no modification for other problems, and libraries of computer programs are being developed to facilitate this interchange. There is an economy of scale here that often brings the per-unit cost of a given analysis down to the point at which it becomes economically feasible. We shall say more about this topic in Chapter 9, *Art of Implementation*.

8. GENERALIZATIONS

In this section, I should like to indicate how we may generalize the concepts developed in this chapter and how we might apply them in less frivolous, real-world contexts.

First, consider a businessman who has several viable production and distribution alternatives for a new product. Suppose he clearly understands the economics of his problem, but he is uncertain about the proportion p of customers who would purchase his product (at a price already determined) if it were generally available. If he were to use the methodology of these lectures to analyze his problem, he would first assess a judgmental distribution for the unknown p. He would presumably base this distribution on his intimate knowledge of the product, his experience with the market on products similar to the one he is presently concerned with, and any informal sampling he may have already taken. On the basis of this distribution he would determine the best action to take if he were not going to gain further information about p, and he would obtain a monetary evaluation of this action. Next he might investigate the expected value of perfect information about p, and if this amount were large in comparison with the cost of certain experiments that would give him relevant but imperfect information about p, then he might decide to evaluate some of these experimental options in a formal manner. Let us single out one of the many possible experimental plans and let us call it Q. If our businessman were to conduct Q, then he would obtain some particular information, I^*, say, and on the basis of I^* he would revise his distribution of p. After observing that Q yields I^*, then, he might shift his optimal choice of a terminal action (for example, how much to produce and how to distribute his production), and at this point he would calculate a new monetary evaluation of his prospects. Remember that these prospects are still uncertain since information I^* does not *pinpoint* the value of p; it only influences the man's distribution of p. We refer to the part of the analysis that deals with the optimal choice and evaluation of an action subsequent to all experimentation as "terminal analysis" or "posterior analysis". In discussing terminal analysis we shall use the function $V(Q, I^*)$, which gives the decision maker's CME of his prospects after he learns that experiment Q results in information I^*. (See Fig. 7.12.)

The businessman's immediate problem is to decide whether or not to experiment, and if he decides to experiment, to choose an experimental plan. To analyze this phase of his problem systematically, he would like to know what it's worth to him to go down the Q-path as evaluated *before* he has learned the particular results of the experiment. He knows that if Q results in I^*, then his subsequent evaluation will be $\overline{V}(Q, I^*)$. But since he does not know that I^*

will obtain, he must assign probabilities to each of the manifold possibilities and average out (in monetary units if he is an EMV'er and in utilities if he is a non-EMV'er) and fold back to get an evaluation at Q. Let us denote the value of being at Q, with all the possible I^* averaged out, by $\overline{\overline{V}}(Q)$, where the second superior bar designates another averaging process. As you well know by now, the next task is to fold back yet another move and choose the experimental plan that maximizes $\overline{\overline{V}}(Q)$. The part of the analysis in which we average out the $\overline{V}(Q, I^*)$-entries to get $\overline{\overline{V}}(Q)$ and then maximize $\overline{\overline{V}}(Q)$ by our choice of Q is called "preposterior analysis", since it makes prior or "pre"-analysis of the posterior evaluations $\overline{V}(Q, I^*)$. Notwithstanding the fact that this phase of the folding back procedure is called the "preposterous" phase, pejoratively by some and affectionately by others, it is possible to execute this part of the analysis efficiently in important classes of problems. Also, although it may not be possible to implement the full details of the analysis in other classes of problems, the spirit of the approach may help to guide intuitive reasoning.

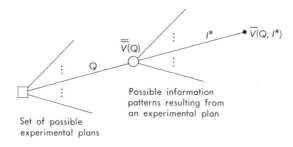

Fig. 7.12 Note the juncture marked with the black dot. At this juncture the businessman must take the distribution he assigns to *p after* he sees that Q results in *I** and use it to decide his problem. We let $\overline{V}(Q, I^*)$ represent the CME of his prospects as he views them from this juncture.

Now let's go through another round of generalizations. Instead of talking about the businessman, we could easily change the context and talk about the medical practitioner who is concerned with the proportion p of patients who will benefit from some new chemical treatment; or we could talk about the educator who is concerned with the proportion of children who will learn better by instructional procedure A than they will by B; and so on.

Furthermore, at least at our present level of conceptualization, we can easily extend our horizons by considering other summary measures of a population than the simple proportion p. For example, a marketing man might be interested in the average amount A of a given product that a target population of customers will purchase in a given year; an agronomist might be interested in the average incremental yield per plant that a newly developed seed will produce; and so on. Instead of starting with a prior distribution of p that we then modify on the basis of experimental results, we could start with a prior distribution of the uncertain average response A of a population of elements and see how we would modify this distribution with the accumulation of experimental data. Indeed, instead of p or A, we could consider *any* numerical characteristic C of a population, provided that C is a characteristic that we should know with certainty if we could just examine each element of the population. With only minor modifications, we could talk about prior and posterior distributions of C and about decision problems whose payoffs partly depend on this uncertain quantity.

We could go further. Why only one summary measure C of a population? There may be two or several uncertain quantities, A, B, C, and D, say, whose values affect the payoffs to a decision maker. He would start with some knowledge of the joint behavior of these uncertain quantities and by experimenting modify his prior judgments.

Although it's easy to generalize in conceptual terms, there is an engineering or technological aspect that we cannot ignore. As the complexity of the problem increases, the measurement data become more unmanageable and the volume of analysis rapidly gets out of hand, *unless* we employ specialized shortcut analytical procedures. It's my personal opinion that decision theory does not suffer from any lack of an adequate philosophical or conceptual base but rather from a lack of specialized techniques, which are not being developed rapidly enough for us to realize the full potential of the theory. It's as if there were loads of theoretical physicists but only a few engineers.

9. PROJECT

1) Find your left-tail cumulative judgmental distribution function and corresponding density function for each of the following proportions:

a) the proportion of people who are lefthanded,

b) the proportion of undergraduate college males who have beards,

c) the proportion of secretaries who drink their coffee black at morning coffee breaks.

Also try getting distributions of these uncertain proportions from a friend of yours who knows very little or nothing about the subject area of these lectures. Be sure to pose questions without any technical jargon.

2) Here's a variation of your basic problem that you should be able to analyze.

Tomorrow morning at about 11:30 a.m. I shall choose at random a secretary at Harvard and ask her if she had coffee this morning at her coffee break and, if so, if she drank it black. (If she did not have any coffee I'll try another secretary, and another if necessary.) If she says she took it black, then I'll place a θ_2 urn on the table; if she says she used cream or milk, I'll place a θ_1 urn on the table. The particular outcome will not be disclosed to you. Tomorrow afternoon *you* will play your basic decision problem with this unknown urn.

Given your present information about the coffee-drinking patterns of Harvard secretaries, how much would you pay to learn the true proportion of secretaries who drink their coffee black? (Use EMV-analysis, and use the approximate method described at the end of Section 4.)

APPENDIX: PRIOR-TO-POSTERIOR ANALYSIS FOR A POPULATION PROPORTION *p*

Consider a population in which a proportion p of the elements possess a given attribute. For example, the population might be U.S. residents of voting age, in which $100p$ percent are currently registered voters. In your basic decision problem, the population is 1000 urns, $1000p$ of which are of type θ_1. You can surely think of a thousand other examples.

Let's suppose that you do not know the proportion p with certainty, although you may possess some more or less vague (prior) information concerning it. We shall assume that you are able to establish a probability betting distribution on p on the basis of your prior information. We shall assume that in some way or other you have established an initial or prior probability density function for p, denoted by $f^{(b)}(\cdot)$, that represents your cumulative present knowledge about p. This present knowledge might be based on loads of objective data you have collected in the past or it might, at the other extreme, be a codification of your vague judgments. Recall that for any pair of numbers such as .015 and .324, say, your prior probability that $.015 \leq p \leq .324$ is the area under the curve $f^{(b)}$ from .015 to .324. (If p is measured to the nearest one-thousandth, then, strictly speaking, it is more appropriate to take the area from .0145 to .3245, but this is of minor importance.) In this appendix, we shall think of p as taking on any one of the 1001 values .000, .001, . . . , .999, 1.000.

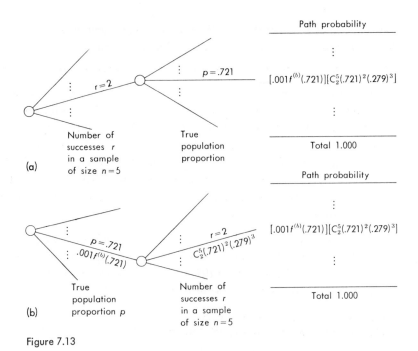

Figure 7.13

The probability that p takes on the value .721, say, we shall write† as $P^*(p = .721)$. Note that

$$P^*(p = .721) = .001f^{(b)}(.721).$$

Suppose we now consider an experiment in which you draw five elements at random from the population. If the population size is large, then it is not critical to the analysis whether each element is replaced or not before the next drawing. Since the analysis will be a bit easier to explain if you make the drawings with replacement, this will be our working assumption. To analyze the decision problem of this chapter, we need probability assignments for the branches of Fig. 7.13(a). We shall obtain these probabilities by making assignments to the branches of Fig. 7.13(b) and flipping the trees.

Let's first examine the assignments in Fig. 7.13(b). Of the 1001 possibilities for p, the figure represents only the branch for $(p = .721)$. The probability assignment for this branch is $.001f^{(b)}(.721)$. At the next fork, Chance selects

† In some respects it would have been analytically a little cleaner if we had chosen exactly 1000 possible values: .0005, .0015, .0025, . . . , .9985, .9995. With the 1001 values, there is some confusion about $P^*(p = .000)$ and $P^*(p = 1.000)$. We shall assume that these values are $.001f^{(b)}(.000)$ and $.001f^{(b)}(1.000)$.

the number of successes S and failures F in a random sample of $n = 5$ drawings with replacement. (In the context of your problem, S stands for drawing a θ_1 and F for drawing a θ_2.) If $p = .721$, then the probability of getting a sample such as $SFFSF$ is $(.721)^2(1 - .721)^3$. But since several different sequences can give rise to two S's and three F's, we must multiply $(.721)^2(.279)^3$ by the number of ways that two S's can appear in five positions. We write this number as a combination, C_2^5; it is equal to ten. (The value C_2^5 will not play a critical role in what follows, so let's not get bogged down in any further explanation of combinations and permutations.) From these assignments we can get a probability assignment for the path $(p = .721, r = 2)$. We assign this same probability to the corresponding path in Fig. 7.13(a). Our next task is to compute an assignment for the branch $(r = 2)$ in Fig. 7.13(a). But we know how to do this: We merely add up the 1001 path-probability assignments that emanate from the $(r = 2)$-branch. In symbols, after factoring out common terms, we get

$$P^*(r = 2) = .001C_2^5[f^{(b)}(.000)(.000)^2(1.000)^3 + \cdots$$
$$+ f^{(b)}(.721)(.721)^2(.279)^3 + \cdots$$
$$+ f^{(b)}(1.000)(1.000)^2(.000)^3].$$

In the rest of this appendix, we shall be concerned with the problem of assigning a probability to a branch such as $(p = .721)$ after learning that a sample $n = 5$ has resulted in the event $(r = 2)$. We shall try to get some intuitive feel for the qualitative changes that take place when we go from a prior distribution to a posterior distribution via a sample.

Noting Fig. 7.13(a), we get the probability assignment for $(p = .721)$ after $(r = 2)$ by dividing the path probability by $P^*(r = 2)$. In symbols, we have

$$P^*(p = .721|r = 2, n = 5) = \frac{.001C_2^5[(.721)^2(.279)^3]f^{(b)}(.721)}{P^*(r = 2)}. \quad (1)$$

In this chapter, we have introduced the notation $f_{r,n}^{(a)}(x)$ to denote the density function at x for the unknown proportion of S's in the population *after* a sample of size n has yielded r successes. If we recall that

$$P^*(p = .721|r = 2, n = 5) = .001f_{2,5}^{(a)}(.721),$$

then we can substitute to get

$$f_{2,5}^{(a)}(.721) = k[C_2^5(.721)^2(.279)^3]f^{(b)}(.721), \quad (2)$$

where $k = 1/P^*(r = 2)$.

Now let's see what happens when r and n remain fixed and p changes from .721. For p equal to any arbitrary x-value, $x = .000, .001, \ldots, .999$, 1.000, we get

$$f_{2,5}^{(a)}(x) = k[C_2^5 x^2 (1 - x)^3] f^{(b)}(x). \tag{3}$$

First let's consider only the expression in square brackets in (3), namely, the probability that $r = 2$ given $n = 5$ and $p = x$:

$$P(r = 2 | n = 5, p = x).$$

Note that this probability statement is in the public domain; it is an objective, frequency-based statement and does not depend on your judgment. We shall find a new notation helpful in investigating how this expression changes as the number x changes. We shall define the symbol $L(x|2, 5)$ by

$$L(x|2, 5) = P(r = 2 | n = 5, p = x), \qquad \text{or} \qquad L(x|2, 5) = C_2^5 x^2 (1 - x)^3, \tag{4}$$

and in this notation we have

$$f_{2,5}^{(a)}(x) = k \cdot L(x|2, 5) f^{(b)}(x). \tag{5}$$

It is important at this point to keep in mind that the value of k does not depend on the value of x. Shortly we shall find that we can think of k merely as a

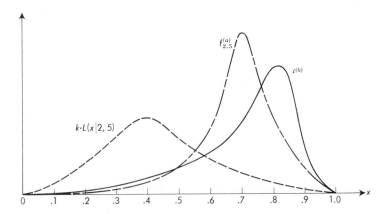

Fig. 7.14 The vertical scale is such that the area under each of the curves $k \cdot L$, $f_{2,5}^{(a)}$, and $f^{(b)}$ is equal to 1. We multiply $f^{(b)}$ and $L(x|2, 5)$ and then rescale to get $f_{2,5}^{(a)}$.

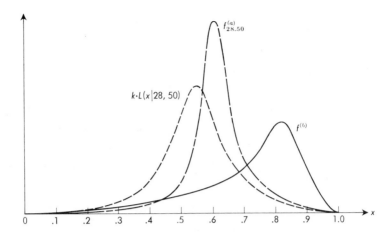

Fig. 7.15 The vertical scale is such that the area under each of the curves $k \cdot L$, $f^{(a)}_{28,\,25}$, and $f^{(b)}$ is equal to 1. We multiply $f^{(b)}$ and $L(x|28, 50)$ and then rescale to get $f^{(a)}_{28,\,50}$.

scaling factor that ensures that the area under the product of L and $f^{(b)}$ is unity. Note that the shape of $f^{(a)}_{2,5}$ therefore depends only on the shapes of L and $f^{(b)}$, and we can ignore the factor k.

We shall refer to $L(x|2, 5)$ as the *likelihood* value at x corresponding to an observed sample of $r = 2$, $n = 5$. Figure 7.14 shows the likelihood function L plotted against x-values for $x = .000, .001, \ldots, .999, 1.000$. As you look at the figure, remember that the graph of the L-function is not a connected curve but a series of 1001 points, and keep in mind that the true population proportion p is located somewhere on the x-axis in the interval from 0 to 1 but that *you* don't know where it is.

Let's take the next step and see what happens when we follow (5) and we multiply $L(x|2, 5)$ and $f^{(b)}(x)$ to get $f^{(a)}_{2,5}(x)$. Figure 7.14 shows the result of this multiplication. I have chosen the vertical scale so that the area under $f^{(b)}$ is 1; next, I have drawn $k \cdot L(x|2, 5)$ instead of $L(x|2, 5)$, where k is chosen so that the area under the $k \cdot L$ curve is 1. If we now multiply $L(x|2, 5)$ and $f^{(b)}(x)$ together for each x, then this product, as a function of x, gives the shape of $f^{(a)}_{2,5}$. However, we must once again rescale this product so that the area under $f^{(a)}_{2,5}$ is equal to 1. Figure 7.15 shows this same procedure repeated for the sample $r = 28$, $n = 50$. In this case

$$L(x|28, 50) = C^{50}_{28} x^{28} (1 - x)^{22}.$$

A few general observations are in order.

1) If $f^{(b)}$ is flat, then $f^{(a)} = k \cdot L$.

2) If $f^{(b)}$ is relatively flat over the portion where L is relatively steep (as is the case in Fig. 7.15), then $f^{(a)}$ is very close to $k \cdot L$.

3) As n increases, L is more and more concentrated around the sample mean r/n, and therefore as n increases, the shape of $f^{(a)}$ is dictated more and more by L and less and less by $f^{(b)}$. Contrast Figs. 7.14 and 7.15.

4) If $f^{(b)}$ is very steep and if n is very small so that L is broad, then $f^{(a)}$ will be shaped like $f^{(b)}$.

A Technical Digression. I shall now sketch one analytical approach to the problem we are considering in this appendix, which both simplifies the analysis considerably and also generalizes nicely to other situations. We assumed for the sake of concreteness that you assessed the density function $f^{(b)}$ shown in Fig. 7.14 on the basis of your vague impressions about the proportion p of θ_1 urns, and before you have obtained any objective sample evidence. We now pose the following question: Does there exist a pair of numbers (r_0, n_0) such that $L(x|r_0, n_0)$ is shaped like $f^{(b)}(x)$? For the density shown in Fig. 7.5 the answer is "Yes", and we can show that

$$k \cdot L(x|14,\, 18) \approx f^{(b)}(x),$$

where $\approx$ means "approximately equal to", and k is a proportionality factor that is introduced to make the area under kL equal to 1. Now here is the reason why this result is of interest. We can *imagine* that you started out initially with a flat density function $f^{(i)}$ (here i is mnemonic for "initially") and that you subsequently took a (purely fictitious) sample of 18 urns and observed that 14 of these were θ_1's. In this case you would have modified your initial density $f^{(i)}$ by multiplying it by $L(x|14,\, 18)$. But since $f^{(i)}$ is flat, this product is shaped like $L(x|14,\, 18)$. We therefore conclude that we can view your density function $f^{(b)}$ as being posterior to a (fictitious) sample $(14, 18)$ where you have started from an initial flat distribution $f^{(i)}$.

Now if you subsequently obtain a real sample $(28, 50)$, you can think of your current position in two ways:

1) starting from $f^{(b)}$, you observe $(28, 50)$, or

2) starting from $f^{(i)}$, you observe first the (fictitious) sample $(14, 18)$ and second the (real) sample $(28, 50)$. You can interpret this as saying that you start with $f^{(i)}$ and get a composite (fictitious plus real) sample of $(42, 68)$.

It therefore follows that

$$f^{(a)}_{28,50}(x) \approx kL(x|42, 68).$$

In general,

$$f^{(a)}_{r,n}(x) \approx kL(x|r_0 + r, n_0 + n),$$

where (r_0, n_0) is such that

$$f^{(b)}(x) \approx kL(x|r_0, n_0).$$

(The factor k is chosen differently in each expression to make the area under kL equal to 1.)

Furthermore, it can be shown that the mean* of a density function in the form $kL(x|a, b)$ is merely $(a + 1)/(b + 2)$. Hence for the analysis of Section 7 we get

$$\bar{p}^{(a)}_{r,n} = \text{mean of } f^{(a)}_{r,n}(x)$$

$$= \text{mean of } k \cdot L(x|r_0 + r, n_0 + n) = \frac{r_0 + r + 1}{n_0 + n + 2}.$$

In particular we have

$$\bar{p}^{(a)}_{28,50} = \frac{14 + 28 + 1}{18 + 50 + 2} = \frac{43}{70} = .614$$

and

$$\bar{p}^{(a)}_{2,5} = \frac{14 + 2 + 1}{18 + 5 + 2} = \frac{17}{25} = .68.$$

---

* The mode (or maximum value) of the density function of the form $kL(x|a, b)$ is a/b.

CHAPTER 8

RISK SHARING AND
GROUP DECISIONS

PART ONE: RISK SHARING

This Chapter is divided into two parts. *Part One: Risk Sharing*, comprises Sections 1 through 9, and *Part Two: Group Decisions*, comprises Sections 10 through 14. There is a brief introduction to *Part Two* in Section 10. This chapter is somewhat more sophisticated, mathematically speaking, than the previous ones, and it uses more symbolism. Since the material in Chapters 9 and 10 is completely independent of the material in this chapter, you can skip directly to Chapter 9 if you wish to do so.

1. INTRODUCTION TO PART ONE

Would you pay $300.00 for a 50-50 chance at $0.00 or $1000.00? Perhaps your answer is "No", but certainly you would change your mind if you knew that Mr. X would buy your option for $400.00. Of, if you knew that Mr. Y would pay you $200.00 for a half-share of your option, then you might have second thoughts about refusing this venture. Would you strike a bargain with X or with Y? Suppose that you and others were jointly offered this option; as a group, would you accept it? If so, how would you go about dividing the option? These are some of the types of questions we shall consider in this chapter.

Let us consider a variation of your basic problem. Suppose your past industriousness has earned you the exclusive rights to a business venture which, when analyzed, leads to a decision-flow diagram identical to the one shown in Fig. 2.13, with the sole exception that all payoffs and experimental costs are multiplied by 1000. That is, for example, to go down the e_s-path in this venture, you must pay a toll of $9000.00 instead of $9.00. Although the EMV of this venture is now worth $31,150.00 instead of $31.15, you might be reluctant to accept it exclusively for yourself if you could not strike a bargain that would enable you to limit some of your potential losses. You might do this in several ways.

For example, you might offer **Mr. X** this option: Mr. X will pay $12,000 to conduct experiment e_2. If e_2 results in an outcome analogous to RR or BB in Fig. 2.13, then Mr. X gets $\frac{1}{4}$ of the remaining deal and you take $\frac{3}{4}$. If it results in RB or BR, Mr. X gets full rights to the remaining deal. Or, you may wish to incorporate and divide the venture into shares. For example, suppose you tentatively decide it would be nice to follow the strategy for experimentation and action that would be optimal for an EMV'er: that is, pay $9000.00 to go down the e_s-path; if B, stop experimenting and take a_1; if R_1 pay $4500.00 for another drawing and then take a_2 if R_2 and a_1 if B_2. (We have labeled this strategy σ_{95} and displayed it in Fig. 6.2.) Now the worst thing that could happen is that you would draw an R_1, then a B_2, and then have θ_2 be true; this would involve a loss of $33,500.00 (that is, $9000.00 + $4500.00 + $20,000.00). Keeping this possible loss in mind, suppose you decide to put $8500.00 of your own money into the corporation, divide the venture into 1000 shares, keep 500 shares for yourself and sell 500 shares at $50.00 per share. Mr. Y might agree to give you $25,000.00 for these 500 shares, and then turn around and sell them at $53.00 a share. After you sell the shares to Y, the corporation has $33,500.00 available. Table 8.1 exhibits the possible eventualities, their probabilities, and the financial results to the corporation from

TABLE 8.1

Possible outcome	Probability	Total value of corporation
$R_1 R_2 \theta_1$	.1067	$15,000
$R_1 R_2 \theta_2$	.1600	$120,000
$R_1 B_2 \theta_1$	.2133	$60,000
$R_1 B_2 \theta_2$	.0200	$0
$B_1 \theta_1$	.4800	$64,500
$B_1 \theta_2$	.0200	$4,500
	1.0000	

using strategy σ_{95}. For example, the probability of R_1 on the first drawing, B_2 on the second and θ_1 next is

$$P(R_1, B_2, \theta_1) = P(\theta_1)P(R_1|\theta_1)P(B_2|\theta_1, R_1)$$
$$= \tfrac{8}{10} \times \tfrac{4}{10} \times \tfrac{6}{9} = .2133.$$

If you use strategy σ_{95} and event (R_1, B_2, θ_1) occurs, then you can compute the total value of the corporation thus:

Original assets	$33,500
Cost of drawing first ball	− $9,000
Cost of drawing second ball	− $4,500
Payoff from a_1 when θ_1 is true	$40,000
Total	$60,000

In this situation each share would pay off $60.00 and you, who own 500 shares, would get a payment of $30,000.

Suppose that you borrow $3000.00 to put up your initial $8500.00 and that $R_1 B_2$ occurs. You realize you would be in a terrible mess if θ_2 turns out to be true, so you might approach Mr. Z with this proposition: He (Mr. Z) will give you $3000.00 with the understanding that he will get back $3500.00 if θ_1 is true, and nothing otherwise. (Observe that the chance of getting a θ_1 after $R_1 B_2$ is $\tfrac{64}{70}$, or .914.) This kind of "wheeling and dealing" is not uncommon in financial management, and it is this ability to share risk that makes our corporate society aggressive and dynamic.

2. A SIMPLE EXAMPLE OF RISK SHARING

Several years ago I conducted an experiment on risk sharing with a class of business school students who were taking an elementary course in decision theory. At the first meeting of the class, I told them that in a few days I just might choose a student at random and offer him the opportunity to accept or reject a lottery that would give him an equal chance of winning $x or losing $y, viz.:

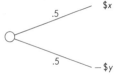

Thus, for example, if x were 100 and y were 1, this would be a very favorable gamble; whereas if x were 50 and y were 60, this would be a poor bet. I in-

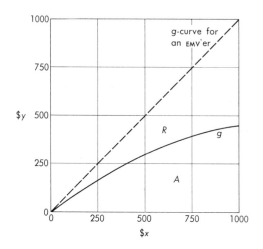

Fig. 8.1 The lottery that pays off x and −y with equal chances is acceptable if (x, y) falls below g. It is not acceptable if (x, y) falls above g.

formed the class that *x* would be somewhere between 0 and 1000. As an assignment, I asked each of them to think about the problem, keeping his own finances in mind, and to prepare a set of instructions such that an agent, acting in his behalf, could determine whether any (*x, y*)-lottery is acceptable or not. I suggested that they communicate these instructions in the form of a graph that divided (*x, y*)-points in the plane into an *acceptance* set and a *rejection* set. Figure 8.1 shows a typical curve that divides the set of (*x, y*)-points into an acceptance set and a rejection set. A lottery such as

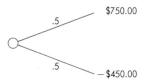

would be rejected because the point (750, 450) falls above the curve *g* and thus is in the rejection set *R*; whereas the lottery

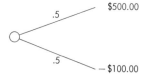

would be accepted because the point (500, 100) falls below the curve *g* and thus is in the acceptance set *A*. The value $g(x)$ would be the maximum that the individual student would be willing to lose to get an equal chance at winning $x.* Well, I never did carry out the experiment but I did collect their graphs, and, as you might suspect, they were wildly different. The *g*-values for $x = 1000$ ranged from $25.00 to $800.00.

Digression. We can easily find a subject's *g*-curve from his utility curve for money. If we let $u(0) = 0$, then an (x, y)-lottery is acceptable if and only if

$$\frac{u(x) + u(-y)}{2} \geq u(0) = 0, \qquad \text{or} \qquad u(x) \geq -u(-y).$$

Hence *g* is such that

$$u(x) = -u[-g(x)].$$

The *g*-curve merely relates the *u*-function for positive amounts to the *u*-function for negative amounts.

Group Acceptance and Rejection Sets

I later asked a group of students whether *collectively* they would ever accept an (x, y)-proposal that was *not in any one of their acceptance sets*. This question led them to the problem of defining a group acceptance set as a function of their individual acceptance sets. I should like to take up this problem now.

Let's consider a group of two individuals, unimaginatively labeled "individual 1" and "individual 2", whose *g*-curves, acceptance sets, and rejections sets are labeled g_1 and g_2, A_1 and A_2, R_1 and R_2, respectively. Now suppose g_1 and g_2 are as shown in Fig. 8.2, and the two individuals are asked whether or not they wish to accept collectively a lottery that gives a .5 chance at $1000.00 and a .5 chance at $-$500.00. This lottery, which has the designation (1000, 500), is not acceptable to either individual. Now suppose the individuals are allowed to share the lottery; that is, individual 1 takes a proportional share ρ_1 and individual 2 takes a proportional share ρ_2, where $\rho_1 + \rho_2 = 1$. For example, if $\rho_1 = \frac{3}{4}$ and $\rho_2 = \frac{1}{4}$, then 1 and 2 are confronted with the lotteries (750, 375) and (250, 125), respectively. Note that this is acceptable to individual 2 but not to individual 1. The dashed line in Fig. 8.2 connecting (0, 0) and (1000, 500) is the locus of all lotteries that can result

---

* In the rest of this chapter, we shall drop the dollar sign from such indefinite payoffs as $x, and simply write *x*.

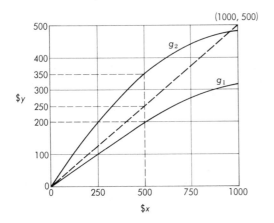

Fig. 8.2 An example that illustrates the case in which a lottery is not acceptable to either player singly, but is acceptable to them jointly.

from taking a proportional share of the lottery (1000, 500), and this dashed line intersects A_2 (that is, 2's acceptance set) but not A_1. Hence there is no proportional share of the lottery (1000, 500) that is acceptable to 1. Nevertheless the individuals ought to accept the lottery (1000, 500). One possibility is that we decompose the lottery *nonproportionally*, by giving individual 1 the lottery (500, 175), for example, and individual 2 the lottery (500, 325). Both these lotteries fall in the respective acceptance sets of the individuals and as such are preferable to the status quo. We should exclude the alternative of not accepting the lottery, obviously, since we have been able to construct a sharing rule for the lottery that is acceptable to each of the individuals. I do not wish to assert that the particular sharing rule just mentioned is the "best" one; that's another story, which we shall discuss eventually.

In the next sections, we shall consider more general versions of this sharing problem. To help the notational transition, it will be helpful if we represent the above lottery in the format of Table 8.2. On the left we display the lottery

TABLE 8.2

Lottery			Typical partition	
State	Probability	Payoff	1	2
S_1	.5	$1000.00	$500.00	$500.00
S_2	.5	−$500.00	−$175.00	−$325.00

under consideration and on the right we display the partition we just mentioned, which is acceptable to both individuals.

We can look at this partition in another fashion. Suppose 2 gives $50.00 to 1 at the outset and then 1 and 2 share the lottery in proportions .45 and .55, respectively. From Table 8.3, we observe that this sharing rule results in the same partition shown in Table 8.2.

TABLE 8.3

State	1's share	2's share
S_1	$+\$50.00 + .45(\$1000.00) = \$500.00$	$-\$50.00 + .55(\$1000.00) = \$500.00$
S_2	$+\$50.00 + .45(-\$500.00) = -\$175.00$	$-\$50.00 + .55(-\$500.00) = -\$325.00$

Digression. It is a simple algebraic exercise to show that we can represent *any* partition of a lottery that gives a p_1 chance at amount x_1 and a p_2 chance at amount x_2 in terms of an initial side payment between the players plus a proportional sharing of the lottery.

At this point you may feel that the partition shown in Table 8.2 is not quite fair to individual 2, but we can easily mention contexts in which this would be an eminently fair division from 2's viewpoint. Imagine, for example, that the lottery has been offered exclusively to 1, or that the existence of this lottery has become available because of the business acumen and industriousness of 1. Here the lottery, if kept intact, is not acceptable to 1 by himself; but it would be reasonable for him to request a prepayment of $50.00 from 2 for a .55 proportional share of it.

We now have enough background material to set and solve the following problem. We shall state the problem for two individuals, but we can easily generalize it for any number.

Problem. Let individuals 1 and 2 have curves g_1 and g_2. Describe the set of lotteries that are jointly acceptable in the sense that there is a partition of the lottery (that is, a sharing of the risk) that is acceptable to each of the individuals.

Let us define the set of lotteries that the players should jointly accept by A^* and the set they should jointly reject by R^*; and let the curve g^* divide the A^*- and R^*-sets. Our problem is to find g^*, given g_1 and g_2. For example, if g_1 and g_2 are as shown in Fig. 8.2, then the point (1000, 500) belongs to A^* and is below g^*.

Mathematically we can characterize the acceptance set A^* or curve g^* as follows: A point or lottery (x^0, y^0) belongs to A^* if and only if there exists a pair of lotteries (x_1, y_1) and (x_2, y_2) such that

a) $x_1 + x_2 = x^0$,

b) $y_1 + y_2 = y^0$,

c) (x_1, y_1) belongs to A_1, or equivalently, $y_1 \leq g_1(x_1)$,

d) (x_2, y_2) belongs to A_2, or equivalently, $y_2 \leq g_2(x_2)$.

Hence if $x_1 + x_2 = x^0$, then

$$g^*(x^0) \geq g_1(x_1) + g_2(x_2),$$

and the equality will hold for some breakdown of x^0 into shares x_1 and x_2. Mathematically this says that for any x^0,

$$g^*(x^0) = \text{maximum of all values } [g_1(x_1) + g_2(x_2)],$$
$$\text{where} \quad x_1 + x_2 = x^0, \quad x_1 \geq 0, \quad x_2 \geq 0. \tag{1}$$

Thus, for example, to find $g^*(600)$, we could make a list of the form

$$g_1(0) + g_2(600),$$
$$g_1(1) + g_2(599),$$
$$g_1(2) + g_2(598),$$
$$\vdots$$
$$g_1(600) + g_2(0),$$

and choose the largest sum in this list. (This would not be quite accurate, since x_1 and x_2 need not necessarily be integers.)

[**Mathematical digression.** If g_1 and g_2 are differentiable, and if the maximum for expression (1) occurs where $x_1 > 0$ and $x_2 > 0$, then at the maximum we have $g_1'(x_1) = g_2'(x_2)$, where the prime denotes the derivative function. We can see this by forming the Lagrange function, or, more simply, by noting that if $x_1 > 0$, $x_2 > 0$ and if $g_1'(x_1) \neq g_2'(x_2)$, then it is possible to find a small number Δ such that

$$g_1(x_1 + \Delta) + g_2(x_2 - \Delta) > g_1(x_1) + g_2(x_2).$$

Furthermore we can show that if the individuals' utility (or π-indifference) functions are concave (that is, if both players are risk-averse), then their g-functions are also concave, and in this case $g_1(z) + g_2(x^0 - z)$, treated as a function of z, has a unique local maximum point.]

Before we generalize these concepts to more involved lotteries, let us summarize the main points of this section. For the special class of lotteries that yield payoffs x and $-y$ with equal chance, it is possible for any individual i to construct a function g_i that separates these lotteries into an acceptance set (A_i) and a rejection set (R_i). Even though a lottery falls in the rejection sets of two (or more) individuals, the lottery may be made jointly acceptable to them by partitioning the lottery in such a manner that the share of the lottery belonging to any individual i falls in his acceptance set A_i. This partitioning may involve more than merely giving each individual a proportional share of the lottery. Finally, given the g_i-functions of two (or more) individuals, it is meaningful to talk about a group g^*-function that separates those lotteries which are *jointly* acceptable from those which are not, and it is mathematically possible to describe this g^*-function in terms of the individual g_i-functions. A lottery may be divided in many ways to make it acceptable; we have not yet considered choosing the "best" division.

3.   FORMULATION OF A MORE GENERAL PROBLEM OF RISK SHARING

Next we shall generalize the case to several individuals in the group and to lotteries having more than two outcomes. Let ℓ be a lottery that pays off x_1 if state S_1 occurs, . . . , x_k if state S_k occurs, . . . , and x_m if state S_m occurs. Let the states $S_1, \ldots, S_k, \ldots, S_m$ have known objective probabilities $p_1, \ldots, p_k, \ldots, p_m$, respectively. Denote the n members of a group by $1, \ldots, i, \ldots, n$. A *partition* of the lottery ℓ describes for state S_k how the joint payoff x_k will be split between the individuals:

x_{k1} is paid to 1, . . . , x_{ki} is paid to i, . . . , x_{kn} is paid to n,

where

$$x_{k1} + \cdots + x_{ki} + \cdots + x_{kn} = x_k \qquad \text{for all } k. \tag{2}$$

Table 8.4 exhibits this notation.

Thus we can describe a partition of ℓ by an $m \times n$ array of numbers, where the sum of the entries in row k is x_k for $k = 1, 2, \ldots, m$. We shall refer to this array by the symbol X. The ith column of X is the share that goes to individual i, and it is equivalent to a lottery that pays off x_{1i} in state $S_1, \ldots, x_{ki}$ in state $S_k, \ldots,$ and x_{mi} in state S_m. We shall refer to this lottery as $\ell_X^{(i)}$. Thus the partition of ℓ described by array X decomposes lottery ℓ into the n lotteries

$$\ell_X^{(1)}, \ldots, \ell_X^{(i)}, \ldots, \ell_X^{(n)}.$$

TABLE 8.4

	Lottery ℓ			Partition of ℓ	
States	Probabilities	Payoffs	1 $\cdots$	i	$\cdots$ n
S_1	p_1	x_1	$x_{11} \cdots$	$x_{1i} \cdots$	x_{1n}
$\vdots$	$\vdots$	$\vdots$	$\vdots$	$\vdots$	$\vdots$
S_k	p_k	x_k	$x_{k1} \cdots$	$x_{ki} \cdots$	x_{kn}
$\vdots$	$\vdots$	$\vdots$	$\vdots$	$\vdots$	$\vdots$
S_m	p_m	x_m	$x_{m1} \cdots$	$x_{mi} \cdots$	x_{mn}

Even though it is possible to continue this discussion for an arbitrary number n of individuals, it will be easier to follow if we set $n = 2$. The mathematically sophisticated reader should have no difficulty generalizing the results for the case of arbitrary n.

We shall assume that individuals 1 and 2 have utility functions (that is, π-indifference functions with a change of scale) labeled u_1 and u_2, respectively, where the scales are so chosen that $u_1(0) = 0$ and $u_2(0) = 0$. With any partition X of lottery ℓ, we can now associate a pair of numbers $(\bar{u}_1, \bar{u}_2)$, where

$$\bar{u}_1 = p_1 u_1(x_{11}) + p_2 u_1(x_{21}) + \cdots + p_m u_1(x_{m1}) \tag{3a}$$

is the expected utility value of individual 1 for lottery $\ell_X^{(1)}$, and where

$$\bar{u}_2 = p_1 u_2(x_{12}) + p_2 u_2(x_{22}) + \cdots + p_m u_2(x_{m2}) \tag{3b}$$

is the expected utility value of individual 2 for lottery $\ell_X^{(2)}$. We shall call the pair $(\bar{u}_1, \bar{u}_2)$ the *joint utility evaluation of the partition X of ℓ*. If we keep ℓ fixed, then we can associate with each partition X a point $(\bar{u}_1, \bar{u}_2)$ that we can plot as a point in 2-space, as in Fig. 8.3. We shall denote the set of all possible joint utility evaluations by A.

The northeast boundary of A (along a, b, c, d, e, f) may have local dips in it; note the curve from b to c to d in Fig. 8.3. By randomization, however, we can fill in these dips. For example, suppose one partition X_b leads to point b and another, X_d, leads to point d. We could then toss a coin: Heads, we take X_b, and tails, we take X_d. This randomized procedure has a joint utility evaluation at the point h midway on the chord joining b and d. By changing the probability of using X_b and X_d, we can get any point on this chord.

If the achievable set A is as shown in Fig. 8.3, then it is desirable for the individuals to accept ℓ. This result follows because there are partitions X with

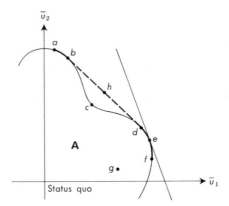

Fig. 8.3 The set of all joint utility evaluations arising from partitions of a given lottery ℓ. The tangent line at e has the equation $\lambda_1 \bar{u}_1 + \lambda_2 \bar{u}_2 = k^*$, where $\lambda_1 + \lambda_2 = 1$.

associated joint evaluations $(\bar{u}_1, \bar{u}_2)$ that fall in the northeast quadrant, which means that there is some partition with a joint $(\bar{u}_1, \bar{u}_2)$-evaluation such that $\bar{u}_1 > 0$ and $\bar{u}_2 > 0$; and this indicates that *both* individuals would prefer their respective shares from this partition to the status quo. [Recall that we set $u_1(0) = 0$ and $u_2(0) = 0$.] It is important to realize that it is possible to get points in the northeast quadrant even though the partition that gives the entire lottery to 1 has an evaluation $(\bar{u}_1, 0)$ with $\bar{u}_1 < 0$, and the partition that gives the entire lottery to 2 has an evaluation $(0, \bar{u}_2)$ with $\bar{u}_2 < 0$; in other words, as we demonstrated in the last section, it is possible to have a lottery that in its entirety is not acceptable to either individual but that admits a jointly acceptable partition. It is also possible, of course, that A does not contain any points in the northeast quadrant, as suggested by Fig. 8.4.

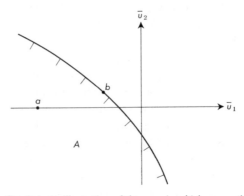

Fig. 8.4 An illustration of the case in which no partition of a lottery ℓ is jointly acceptable.

4. PARETO OPTIMALITY

In the situation represented by Fig. 8.3 it would *not* be reasonable for the individuals to choose a partition leading to point *g*, since there are other partitions (such as the one leading to point *e*) that both individuals prefer. We say that a joint action (in this case a partition) is *Pareto-optimal,** or *efficient,* or *admissible,* if there does *not* exist an alternative action that is at least as acceptable to all and definitely preferred by some. Stated slightly differently, a joint action is Pareto-optimal if it is not possible to make one individual better off without making another individual worse off. In Fig. 8.3, the partition leading to point *g* is *not* Pareto-optimal, but a partition leading to any point on the darkened boundary of the achievable region *A* (where the dips have been filled in by randomization) is Pareto-optimal. In this section, we shall describe or characterize those partitions which are Pareto-optimal, that is, those partitions which lead to joint utility evaluations on the northeast boundary of the set *A* that are not in local dips.

To characterize the Pareto-optimal boundary of *A*, we first observe from Fig. 8.3 that for any point *e* on this boundary (not in a local dip) there is some supporting tangent line. Let the equation of this line be given by

$$\lambda_1 \bar{u}_1 + \lambda_2 \bar{u}_2 = k^*, \qquad \text{where} \qquad \lambda_1 + \lambda_2 = 1. \tag{4}$$

Now we can reverse our orientation and state the following problem: For the same λ_1, λ_2 given in expression (4), find the point in *A* that maximizes the expression

$$\lambda_1 \bar{u}_1 + \lambda_2 \bar{u}_2. \tag{5}$$

It is not difficult to see that the answer to this problem leads us back to the point *e*. Thus we see that we can establish a correspondence between a point *e* on the northeast boundary and a pair of positive numbers λ_1 and λ_2, where $\lambda_1 + \lambda_2 = 1$. Note that as the point *e* moves to the right on the boundary of *A* the tangent line tilts, and λ_1 increases toward 1 and λ_2 decreases toward zero. If we assume $\lambda_1 + \lambda_2 = 1$, therefore, we can generate the entire northeast boundary of *A* by allowing λ_1 and λ_2 to range (reciprocally) over the entire interval between zero and 1 and by associating with each pair of numbers (λ_1, λ_2) the point(s)† of *A* that maximize expression (5).

---

* From V. Pareto, *Manuel d'économie politique,* 2nd edition, Paris, M. Giard, 1927.

† There is a pair of values (λ_1, λ_2) for which both points *b* and *d* simultaneously maximize (5). In this case, we shall consider that the points on the chord between *b* and *d* also maximize (5).

We now wish to find out how to choose a partition X that maximizes (5) for a *given* (λ_1, λ_2). Once again, we use $(\bar{u}_1, \bar{u}_2)$ to denote the joint utility evaluation of partition X. The method we seek is rather straightforward.

Rule. If S_k occurs, divide the total amount x_k between the two individuals so as to maximize

$$\lambda_1 u_1(x_{k1}) + \lambda_2 u_2(x_{k2}) \tag{6a}$$

where

$$x_{k1} + x_{k2} = x_k. \tag{6b}$$

(Observe that the partition of x_k does *not* depend on p_k or on the p or the x for states other than S_k. We must emphasize once again that this assumes λ_1 and λ_2 have been chosen; we have not yet discussed how we are to make the choice.)

▷ *Proof.* Consider any partition X that gives x_{k1} to individual 1 and x_{k2} to individual 2. For this X, we have

$$
\begin{aligned}
\lambda_1 \bar{u}_1 + \lambda_2 \bar{u}_2 &= \lambda_1[p_1 u_1(x_{11}) + \cdots + p_k u_1(x_{k1}) + \cdots + p_m u_1(x_{m1})] \\
&\quad + \lambda_2[p_1 u_2(x_{12}) + \cdots + p_k u_2(x_{k2}) + \cdots + p_m u_2(x_{m2})] \\
&= p_1[\lambda_1 u_1(x_{11}) + \lambda_2 u_2(x_{12})] + \cdots \\
&\quad + p_k[\lambda_1 u_1(x_{k1}) + \lambda_2 u_2(x_{k2})] + \cdots \\
&\quad + p_m[\lambda_1 u_1(x_{m1}) + \lambda_2 u_2(x_{m2})]. \tag{7}
\end{aligned}
$$

Now we wish to choose the partition X that maximizes the expression (7). But from (7) it is clear for any state S_k we should choose x_{k1} and x_{k2} to maximize expression (6a) subject to the constraint (6b).   ◁

Mathematical Digression. The maximization required in expression (6) is similar to that required in expression (1), Section 2. By an argument analogous to the one in the Mathematical Digression following (1), Section 2, we can determine that the appropriate (x_{k1}, x_{k2})-pair for (6) must be such that

$$\lambda_1 u_1'(x_{k1}) = \lambda_2 u_2'(x_{k2}), \qquad \text{where} \qquad x_{k1} + x_{k2} = x_k, \tag{8}$$

and where once again the prime denotes the derivative function.

If u_1 and u_2 are both risk-averse, then it follows from (8) that each of the individual's optimal share of x_k increases as x_k increases. To see this, suppose the contrary is true, specifically that x_{k1} decreases as x_k increases. This implies that as x_k increases,

1) $\lambda_1 u_1'(x_{k1})$ *increases*, since u_1 is concave,

2) x_{k2} increases, since $x_{k1} + x_{k2} = x_k$, and

3) $\lambda_2 u_2'(x_{k2})$ decreases, since u_2 is concave.

But if the left-hand side of (8) increases and the right-hand side decreases, a balance cannot be maintained. Hence x_{k1} cannot decrease as x_k increases.

Special Case. In Section 11, Chapter 4, we introduced the very special, but important, exponential utility function

$$u(x) = 1 - e^{-x/c}.$$

This utility function has the property that if we add a constant amount Δ to each of the prizes of a lottery, then we merely have to add Δ to the CME of the original lottery to get the CME of the modified lottery. For this utility function, furthermore, the buying price and the selling price of any lottery are the same. The only other utility function that enjoys these properties is the linear one; that is, the one where the EMV is an appropriate index to maximize. The constant c here determines the decision maker's aversion to risk. Figure 8.5 shows the g-function plotted with various c-values. Thus, for example, if $c = 1000$, then $g(1000) = 490$, which indicates that a lottery giving a .5 chance at

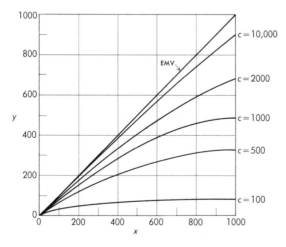

Fig. 8.5 This figure shows g-curves for utility functions $u(x) = 1 - e^{-x/c}$.

$1000.00 and a .5 chance at $-\$490.00$ is just acceptable. If c is 500, then $g(1000) = 310$, which indicates that a lottery giving a .5 chance at $1000.00 and a .5 chance at $-\$310.00$ is just acceptable. (The π-curve drawn in Fig. 4.13 roughly corresponds to $c = 1000$.)

Now suppose that our two individuals have exponential utility curves with constants c_1 and c_2, respectively, and suppose $c_1 > c_2$. In this case we can show that the *only* Pareto-optimal partitions of a lottery ℓ take the following form: One individual makes an initial side payment to the other and then they take proportional shares of the lottery in the ratio c_1 to c_2; in other words, individual 1's proportional share of the lottery is $\rho_1 = c_1/(c_1 + c_2)$. The side payment determines the position of the partition on the Pareto-optimal boundary. However,

> *no matter what Pareto-optimal point is chosen, the individuals 1 and 2 still take the same proportional shares.*

This is a surprising result, but it derives directly from the specific utility functions chosen. The result generalizes in a natural way to the case where there are n individuals with parameters $c_1, c_2, \ldots, c_n$. Here there are initial side payments between the individuals and then the ith individual receives the proportional share

$$\rho_i = \frac{c_i}{c_1 + c_2 + \cdots + c_n}.$$

▷ *Proof.* To prove these results we use expression (8), which gives, in this special case,

$$\frac{\lambda_1}{c_1} e^{-x_{k1}/c_1} = \frac{\lambda_2}{c_2} e^{-x_{k2}/c_2}, \quad \text{or} \quad e^{-x_{k1}/c_1} = \frac{\lambda_2 c_1}{\lambda_1 c_2} e^{-x_{k2}/c_2}.$$

Taking logs (to base e) of both sides, we obtain

$$-\frac{x_{k1}}{c_1} = -\frac{x_{k2}}{c_2} + \log \frac{\lambda_2 c_1}{\lambda_1 c_2}.$$

Now substituting $x_k - x_{k1}$ for x_{k2} and reducing, we obtain

$$x_{k1} = \frac{c_1}{c_1 + c_2} x_k - \frac{c_1 c_2}{c_1 + c_2} \log \frac{\lambda_2 c_1}{\lambda_1 c_2}.$$

Thus we see that individual 1 gets the proportion $c_1/(c_1 + c_2)$ of the amount x_k (and this does not depend on λ_1 or λ_2) and that he makes a side payment to individual 2 of the amount

$$\frac{c_1 c_2}{c_1 + c_2} \log \frac{\lambda_2 c_1}{\lambda_1 c_2} .$$

This last quantity is positive if $\lambda_2 c_1 > \lambda_1 c_2$, zero if $\lambda_2 c_1 = \lambda_1 c_2$, and negative if $\lambda_2 c_1 < \lambda_1 c_2$. A negative quantity indicates that 1 will *receive* a side payment from 2. ◁

We shall say that we have used a *linear* sharing rule to partition a lottery whenever we can interpret the partition as proportional sharing after an initial side payment; that is, whenever there is a proportion ρ and a payment b such that we have

$$x_{k1} = \rho x_k + b \qquad \text{and} \qquad x_{k2} = (1 - \rho)x_k - b \tag{9}$$

for any state S_k.

The Pareto-optimal sharing rules usually are *not* linear for any two utility functions u_1 and u_2. There are of course exceptions* as we have seen, and important ones at that. Indeed, it is not difficult to give examples for which *any* linear sharing rule is poor or "inoptimal" in the sense that there are nonlinear sharing rules which both individuals would prefer.

5. THE CHOICE OF A PARETO-OPTIMAL POINT

Before we plunge ahead, let's once again take stock of where we are. Suppose that two individuals wish to partition a lottery ℓ. We have found that we can associate a joint utility evaluation $(\bar{u}_1, \bar{u}_2)$ with each partition X of this lottery. If we plot the evaluations for all partitions (nonrandomized and randomized ones), then the resulting set of achievable evaluations comprises a region A. The individuals should confine their deliberations to the evaluations on the northeast boundary of A, the so-called Pareto-optimal points. For

---

* There are other pairs of utility functions that work nicely together. For example, if $u_1(x) = u_2(x) = \sqrt{x}$, then for any λ_1 and λ_2 we can show that the partition that maximizes $\lambda_1 \bar{u}_1 + \lambda_2 \bar{u}_2$ is such that the individuals share the lottery in proportional amounts without any side payments; but in this case the proportions depend on λ_1 and λ_2. For further detail about sharing rules, see Robert Wilson, "On the theory of syndicates", Working Paper No. 71, Graduate School of Business, Stanford University, 1965.

any choice of (λ_1, λ_2), where $\lambda_1 + \lambda_2 = 1$, $\lambda_1 \geq 0$, $\lambda_2 \geq 0$, we indicated that any $(\bar{u}_1, \bar{u}_2)$-achievable evaluation that maximizes the expression

$$\lambda_1 \bar{u}_1 + \lambda_2 \bar{u}_2$$

necessarily lies on this northeast boundary and is therefore Pareto-optimal. Furthermore, if we vary λ_1 and λ_2, the associated optimal $(\bar{u}_1, \bar{u}_2)$-pairs sweep out the entire Pareto-optimal set.

We now wish to investigate just how the individuals should choose a point on this Pareto-optimal set. We shall see that this largely depends on the context of the problem. We shall consider problems in two contexts: the *bargaining* problem and the *syndicate* problem.

The Bargaining Problem

Suppose lottery ℓ is offered jointly to individuals 1 and 2. If they cannot come to any agreement, they forfeit the lottery. If Fig. 8.4 applies in this particular case, the individuals will of course forfeit ℓ immediately. If Fig. 8.3 applies, on the other hand, then there is strong motivation for them to arrive at some sort of agreement. If individual 1 is solely interested in his own monetary returns, say, he would naturally like to end up at a boundary point near f. If individual 2 feels the same way about things, he would like to end up at a point near a. Now our two individuals might not be so callous; they might actually prefer to get a slightly smaller amount if this means the other fellow would receive a substantially larger amount. Hence 1 might actually prefer point e to f and 2 might prefer b to a. To incorporate this feature into a formal analysis is tricky; we should have to go up to a so-called second-stage utility analysis to accomodate the fact that each individual will choose a preference or utility function for partitions that reflects not only what he would get but what the other fellow would get. An even more sophisticated analysis might go on to higher-stage utility analyses. But notwithstanding all this, there might very well come a time when individual 1 threatens, "I won't move above e," and individual 2 says, "I won't move below b." In situations of this kind, the individuals might remain so adamant that they forfeit accepting lottery ℓ, thus ending up in the position $\bar{u}_1 = 0$, $\bar{u}_2 = 0$, which is surely not Pareto-optimal.

These kinds of bargaining situations have been extensively analyzed in the literature and it would be inappropriate for me to repeat here what I have already written elsewhere on this subject. For a full discussion of the bargaining problem, see my book with Luce entitled *Games and Decisions*, Wiley, 1957, pp. 114–154. I shall briefly summarize, however, some of the salient features of that discussion.

So far in these lectures I have been concerned with the development of techniques which might be of some assistance to you (in your role as a decision maker) in your analysis of a complex decision problem under uncertainty. To be consistent with this approach, we can imagine that you are individual 1, say, and you are engaged in a bargaining problem with 2. Suppose you wish to get him to agree to a point such as *e* and he wants you to move to *b*. What this calls for is an asymmetric form of analysis that will determine how you *ought* to behave in the light of your analysis of how your antagonist *might* behave. This analysis will be asymmetric because it involves a descriptive analysis of his behavior and a prescriptive or normative analysis of your behavior. As you analyze your problem, you may find it wise to keep in mind that he is also thinking how you are thinking, and so forth. We shall discuss this reflexive type of analysis further in Chapter 10, Section 3.

In *Games and Decisions*, Luce and I concentrate on another approach to the bargaining problem, which we can call *externally normative*. Suppose that the individuals in a bargaining situation cannot, or choose not to, resolve their problem, and they submit their problem for arbitration. What is the standard for "fair" or "ethical" principles that an arbiter may follow to help resolve the conflict? We discuss at length a set of guiding principles that lead to the following arbitrated solution, commonly referred to as the "Nash solution": Choose a point $(\bar{u}_1^0, \bar{u}_2^0)$, where $\bar{u}_1^0 > 0$ and $\bar{u}_2^0 > 0$, that maximizes the product $\bar{u}_1 \cdot \bar{u}_2$. (We must understand in this case that the utility functions of the individuals are normalized, so that $u_1(0) = u_2(0) = 0$.) This procedure seems a bit *ad hoc* as stated, but Nash proves that this is the procedure that must be followed if the individuals want to satisfy certain behavioral assumptions. Luce and I discuss this point at length in *Games and Decisions*.

Another arbitrated solution calls for choosing $(\bar{u}_1^0, \bar{u}_2^0)$ such that $\bar{u}_1^0 > 0$ and $\bar{u}_2^0 > 0$, $(\bar{u}_1^0, \bar{u}_2^0)$ lies on the northeast boundary of A, and the CME's corresponding to $\bar{u}_1^0$ and $\bar{u}_2^0$ are equal (that is, both individuals benefit equally, in terms of their CME's).

I think I have said enough to indicate that there are many methods one can use to arbitrate a bargaining controversy. And as you might suspect, no single way seems to be universally applauded. I must break off the discussion at this point, or I shall do what I said I wouldn't—repeat material from *Games and Decisions* at length.

The Syndicate Problem

Suppose individual 1 owns lottery ℓ. He may want to sell or share some part of this lottery with individual 2. If he does, and if he is an analytical sort, he may say to himself, "I must find a partition X that maximizes $\bar{u}_1$ subject to the condition that $\bar{u}_2 \geq \Delta$, where Δ is some positive quantity that will entice 2 into an agreement with me." Now you might say that this context is not very different from the first context, since individual 2 may bargain with 1 over what is an acceptable Δ. This may be true if there is only one potential buyer 2. But suppose 1 plans to negotiate with several different individuals: He could fix on a value of Δ and offer it to 2, and if 2 did not accept it he could offer to individual 3, 4, and so on, until he finds a buyer. Presumably there may be some sort of market mechanism that determines the value of an acceptable Δ, more or less. A few thumbnail sketches of real examples may help to illustrate the syndicate problem.

1) A company wishes to raise capital through the sale of securities. It usually happens that groups of investment banking firms form in a syndicate for the express purpose of bidding on the issue. The investment banking firm that organizes the group, the so-called syndicate leader, tries to partition the issue to maximize the expected utility value of its own share, subject to the constraint that the shares offered to the other syndicate members be attractive enough for them to accept. For a detailed analysis of this problem, see Christenson, C., *Strategic Aspects of Competitive Bidding for Corporate Debt Securities*, Division of Research, Harvard Business School, 1965.

2) An oil wildcatter decides that a particular venture is worth drilling; however, he wants to invite others to join him in this venture to help share the risk. There is a fascinating chapter devoted to this topic in Grayson's book, *Decisions Under Uncertainty: Drilling Decisions by Oil and Gas Operators*, Division of Research, Harvard Business School, 1960. In a chapter titled "Trading", Grayson describes a multitude of different trading devices an oil wildcatter might use to help him maximize his own expected utility; and essentially the wildcatter does this by partitioning a venture into parts that others will accept.

3) The field of insurance provides another example of risk sharing. For instance, take the highly simplified situation in which an individual 1 wishes to insure an article worth \$100,000 against damage in shipping with an insurance company 2. Let S_1 be the state *No damage* and S_2 the state *Complete destruction*. Table 8.5 illustrates this situation. If 1 does not insure the article, the resulting $(\bar{u}_1, \bar{u}_2)$-evaluation might be at point a in Fig. 8.4. If, however,

TABLE 8.5

	Lottery		Partition	
State	Probability	Payoff	1	2
S_1	.9999	$0	$-\$100$	$\$100$
S_2	.0001	$-\$100,000$	$-\$100$	$-\$99,900$

1 insures the article for a $100.00 premium, the resulting partition might have a joint utility evaluation at point *b* in that figure. The insurance company might in turn wish to reinsure itself against this high loss and offer another company a share of the risk.

6. CHOICE BETWEEN LOTTERIES WHEN SHARING IS PERMISSIBLE

In preceding chapters we have discussed at length how a decision maker should choose the best of a set of available lotteries. We shall now discuss how a group of individuals should choose amongst lotteries when they have the option of partitioning any lottery for risk-sharing purposes. At this point I do not want to commit the discussion either to the bargaining context, in which the individuals are jointly offered the lotteries, or to the syndicate context, where individual 1 is offered the choice and can partition it to his own liking, provided the shares he gives to the other individuals meet a prescribed minimum return.

To be concrete, let's suppose two individuals must choose between lotteries ℓ' and ℓ''. Figure 8.6(a, b, c) shows three different situations that might arise. I have plotted the sets of joint utility evaluations for partitions of ℓ' and ℓ''

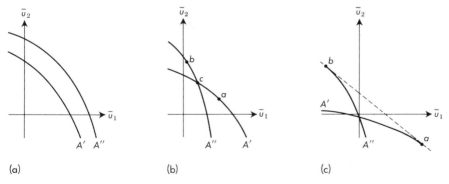

Fig. 8.6 Cases to be considered when choosing between two lotteries where risk sharing is permitted.

for each of these situations. The two curves labeled A' and A'' are the Pareto-optimal boundaries for partitions of ℓ' and ℓ'', respectively. Figure 8.6(a) makes it clear that ℓ'' is better than ℓ', because given any partition of ℓ' there is a partition of ℓ'' that both individuals prefer. From Fig. 8.6(b) we cannot tell which lottery is better: Note that in this case, if individual 1 makes the selection with the option of offering a share to 2 (the syndicate context), then he might choose ℓ' and partition it so as to achieve point a; if, however, 2 is the principal decision maker, he might choose ℓ'' and partition it so as to achieve point b. Observe that point c can be achieved by a Pareto-optimal partition of ℓ' or ℓ''; however, if both ℓ' and ℓ'' are available, it is *not* Pareto-optimal to select c. It is preferable, for example, to toss a coin: If heads, select ℓ'' and partition it to get b; if tails, select ℓ' and partition it to get a. This randomized procedure has a joint evaluation midway between a and b, and therefore both individuals will prefer this randomized procedure to point c. Finally, turning to Fig. 8.6(c), we see that if the individuals have a choice between ℓ' and ℓ'', and if we recall that the status quo is $\bar{u}_1 = \bar{u}_2 = 0$, in accordance with our convention in this chapter, then there are no jointly acceptable partitions of ℓ' or ℓ''; however, by randomizing between point a and b in the manner just described in connection with Fig. 8.6(b), it is possible to get a jointly acceptable partition using ℓ' and ℓ''. We shall now illustrate these cases and discuss them further.

7. CHOICE WITH SHARING WHEN INDIVIDUALS HAVE EXPONENTIAL UTILITY FUNCTIONS

Let's assume the exponential utility functions

$$u_1(x) = 1 - e^{-x/c_1} \quad \text{and} \quad u_2(x) = 1 - e^{-x/c_2}.$$

In Section 4, we showed that the Pareto-optimal partitions for any lottery ℓ involve a side payment of b dollars by 1 to 2 (b may be positive, zero, or negative) and a partition of the lottery into proportional shares

$$\rho_1 = \frac{c_1}{c_1 + c_2} \quad \text{and} \quad \rho_2 = \frac{c_2}{c_1 + c_2}.$$

Let $\rho_1 \cdot \ell$ and $\rho_2 \cdot \ell$ designate the shares of the lottery ℓ given to individuals 1 and 2 respectively. Then

individual 1 will get $[-b + \text{lottery } \rho_1 \cdot \ell]$, and

individual 2 will get $[+b + \text{lottery } \rho_2 \cdot \ell]$.

Now because of *the special nature of exponential utility*, we can conclude that 1's

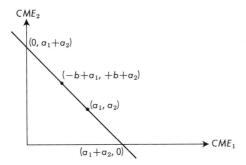

Fig. 8.7 The set of pairs of CME's corresponding to Pareto-optimal partitions of a lottery ℓ.

CME for $[- b + \text{lottery } \rho_1 \cdot \ell]$ is $- b + a_1$, where a_1 is 1's CME for $\rho_1 \cdot \ell$; and that 2's CME for $[+ b + \text{lottery } \rho_2 \cdot \ell]$ is $+ b + a_2$, where a_2 is 2's CME for $\rho_2 \cdot \ell$. Thus the pair of CME's for this partition is $[- b + a_1, + b + a_2]$. In Fig. 8.7, we have plotted the set of pairs of CME's for all Pareto-optimal partitions of a given lottery ℓ. Since we can choose b arbitrarily, the point $(- b + a_1, b + a_2)$ sweeps out an entire line.

Now suppose the individuals have a choice between lottery ℓ' and ℓ''. Let

a_1' and a_1'' be 1's CME's for $\rho_1 \cdot \ell'$ and $\rho_1 \cdot \ell''$, respectively,

a_2' and a_2'' be 2's CME's for $\rho_2 \cdot \ell'$ and $\rho_2 \cdot \ell''$, respectively.

Hence we can achieve any pair of CME's on the line L' in Fig. 8.8 by a

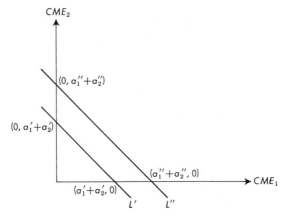

Fig. 8.8 The set of pairs of CME's corresponding to Pareto-optimal partitions of lotteries ℓ' and ℓ''.

Pareto-optimal partition of ℓ'; and similarly for L''. In this particular situation it is clearly never optimal to choose a partition of ℓ' if ℓ'' is available.

For any lottery ℓ, let us designate 1's CME for $\rho_1 \cdot \ell$ by $\text{CME}_1(\rho_1 \cdot \ell)$ and 2's CME for $\rho_2 \cdot \ell$ by $\text{CME}_2(\rho_2 \cdot \ell)$. Then from Fig. 8.8 we can conclude that *if we have a choice between lotteries, then we ought to choose ℓ to maximize the index*

$$\text{CME}_1(\rho_1 \cdot \ell) + \text{CME}_2(\rho_2 \cdot \ell).$$

But now we can demonstrate this important result: for any ℓ,

$$\text{CME}_1(\rho_1 \cdot \ell) + \text{CME}_2(\rho_2 \cdot \ell) = \text{CME}_*(\ell),$$

where $\text{CME}_*(\ell)$ is the CME of ℓ determined from the utility function

$$u_*(x) = 1 - e^{-x/c_*}, \qquad c_* = c_1 + c_2. \tag{9}$$

Conclusion. In other words, if risk sharing is permissible and if individuals 1 and 2 have exponential utility functions with parameters c_1 and c_2, respectively, then it is appropriate to choose between lotteries by using the (group) exponential utility function u_* with parameter $c_* = c_1 + c_2$.

This result does not depend on whether we view the problem in the bargaining or syndicate context, nor on the choice of the (λ_1, λ_2)-pair. Furthermore this result generalizes in a natural manner to more individuals than two. For example, if ten individuals each have an exponential utility with common parameter $c = 1000$ (see Fig. 8.5), then they should collectively behave like a single individual having an exponential utility with parameter $c_* = 10,000$. In Fig. 8.5, note that as c increases, the g-curves approach the EMV-curve.

▷ *Proof.*† Let ℓ be a lottery whose uncertain payoff $\tilde{x}$ is considered a random variable.‡ We shall first prove that if

$$u(x) = 1 - e^{-x/c},$$

then the CME of the lottery $\rho \cdot \ell$, which pays off ρx, is

$$\text{CME}(\rho \cdot \ell) = -c \log E(e^{-\rho \tilde{x}/c}), \tag{10}$$

---

† This argument uses basic notions covered in a first course in probability with a calculus prerequisite.

‡ We distinguish between the random variable and the typical value the random variable can assume by placing a tilde over the letter that represents the random variable. Thus we can talk about the event that the random variable $\tilde{x}$ assumes the value x.

where E is the operator for expected value. To see this, let $\text{CME}(\rho \cdot \ell) = d$; then by definition we have

$$1 - e^{-d/c} = E(1 - e^{-\rho \tilde{x}/c}),$$

and the rest follows easily. Using (10), and the observation that

$$\rho_1/c_1 = \rho_2/c_2 = 1/(c_1 + c_2) = 1/c_*, \qquad \text{where} \qquad c_* = c_1 + c_2,$$

we get

$$\text{CME}_1(\rho_1 \cdot \ell) = -c_1 \log E(e^{-\rho_1 \tilde{x}/c_1}) = -c_1 \log E(e^{-\tilde{x}/c_*})$$

and

$$\text{CME}_2(\rho_2 \cdot \ell) = -c_2 \log E(e^{-\rho_2 \tilde{x}/c_2}) = -c_2 \log E(e^{-\tilde{x}/c_*}).$$

Adding, we get

$$\text{CME}_1(\rho_1 \cdot \ell) + \text{CME}_2(\rho_2 \cdot \ell) = -c_* \log E(e^{-\tilde{x}/c_*}), \tag{11}$$

and the right-hand side of (11), because of (10), is $\text{CME}_*(\ell)$.   ◁

Digression. In the special case in which the lottery ℓ gives an unknown payoff that is normally distributed with mean μ and standard deviation σ, we can show that the CME of $\rho \cdot \ell$ for an exponential utility function with parameter c is

$$\text{CME}(\rho \cdot \ell) = \rho\mu - (\rho\sigma)^2/2c.$$

Hence

$$\text{CME}_1(\rho_1 \cdot \ell) + \text{CME}_2(\rho_2 \cdot \ell) = [\rho_1\mu - (\rho_1\sigma)^2/2c_1] + [\rho_2\mu - (\rho_2\sigma)^2/2c_2]$$
$$= \mu - \sigma^2/2c_*.$$

8. AN EXAMPLE SHOWING NONEXISTENCE OF A GROUP UTILITY FUNCTION

In the previous section, we showed that if each member of a group has an exponential utility function, the group, in its *external* behavior, should choose between lotteries by using a group utility function u_*, also of the exponential type. The function u_* depends only on u_1 and u_2 and *not* on the particular lotteries at hand. In this section we shall discuss an ingenious example, due to John Pratt, which shows that when risk sharing is possible, it is not always true that some group utility function u_* exists that depends only on the indivi-

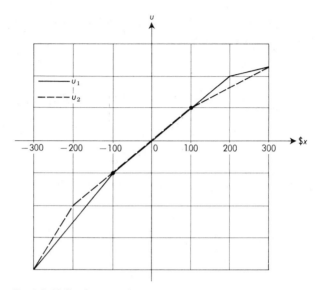

Fig. 8.9 Utility functions for individuals 1 and 2.

dual utility functions and that appropriately guides the group's external behavior. We shall then modify Pratt's example to illustrate the point raised in cases (b) and (c), Fig. 8.6; namely, it is possible to have a situation in which it is best to toss a coin to decide which of two lotteries to accept.

Let individuals 1 and 2 have the utility functions shown in Fig. 8.9. Observe that 1 is linear in the region from $-\$100.00$ to $+\$200.00$, whereas 2 is linear from $-\$200.00$ to $+\$100.00$. Now consider the lottery ℓ described in Table 8.6. The EMV of ℓ is zero. Since both individuals are risk-averse, the CME of ℓ is negative for each individual. Table 8.6 describes a partition of ℓ for which $\bar{u}_1 = 0$, $\bar{u}_2 = 0$. Since the EMV of the lottery is zero, it is *not* possible to partition ℓ in a manner that allows both $\bar{u}_1 > 0$ and $\bar{u}_2 > 0$.

TABLE 8.6

	Lottery ℓ		Partition of ℓ	
State	Probability	Payoff	1	2
S_1	.25	$-\$300.00$	$-\$100.00$	$-\$200.00$
S_2	.25	$-\$100.00$	$-\$100.00$	$\$0.00$
S_3	.25	$+\$100.00$	$\$0.00$	$+\$100.00$
S_4	.25	$+\$300.00$	$+\$200.00$	$+\$100.00$

Now we are ready to show that if the members of a group are free to partition the lotteries they select, then for the pair of utilities (u_1, u_2) given in Fig. 8.9 there is *no* group utility function u_* the group can use to choose between lotteries. Pratt's argument goes as follows: Suppose the contrary is true and that u_* is an appropriate group utility function; then since the lottery ℓ in Table 8.6 is just acceptable, we must have

$$\tfrac{1}{4}u_*(-\$300.00) + \tfrac{1}{4}u_*(-\$100.00) + \tfrac{1}{4}u_*(\$100.00) + \tfrac{1}{4}u_*(\$300.00) = 0,$$

(12)

where it is understood that we have arbitrarily let $u_*(0) = 0$. Now the lottery that gives a .5 chance at $-\$100.00$ and a .5 chance at $+\$100.00$ is just acceptable to either of the individuals; but on the other hand, there is no partition of the lottery that the group members would strictly prefer to zero. Hence it follows that

$$.5u_*(-\$100.00) + .5u_*(+\$100.00) = 0.$$

(13)

But from (12) and (13) it follows that

$$.5u_*(-\$300.00) + .5u_*(+\$300.00) = 0,$$

(14)

which implies that the lottery ℓ^+ that gives a .5 chance at $-\$300.00$ and a .5 chance at $+\$300.00$ is also just barely acceptable. All this follows from the assumed existence of a group u_*. Now comes the trouble. How can lottery ℓ^+ be partitioned into acceptable shares? It cannot be done!

[**Verification.** Consider the partition of this lottery described in Table 8.7. We must have:

1) $x_{11} + x_{12} = -\$300.00,$
2) $x_{21} + x_{22} = +\$300.00,$
3) $x_{11} + x_{21} \geq \$0.00$ for 1's share to be acceptable,
4) $x_{12} + x_{22} \geq \$0.00$ for 2's share to be acceptable.

TABLE 8.7

Lottery ℓ^+		Partition	
Probability	Payoff	1	2
.5	$-\$300.00$	x_{11}	x_{12}
.5	$+\$300.00$	x_{21}	x_{22}

Adding the first two equations, we obtain

$$(x_{11} + x_{21}) + (x_{12} + x_{22}) = 0,$$

which implies that the equality signs must hold in equations (3) and (4). This implies that if 1's share is to be acceptable, then x_{11} and x_{21} must fall within one of the linear segments of 1's utility function; and similarly, x_{12} and x_{22} must fall within one of the linear segments of 2's utility function. Now we cannot choose x_{11} below $-\$100.00$, or else 1's share will fall outside the linear portion of u_1. Therefore x_{12} must be $-\$200.00$ or less. But this means that x_{22} must be $\$200.00$ or more, and this finally implies that if x_{11} is in 1's linear portion, then x_{22} cannot be in 2's linear portion. The inescapable conclusion is that ℓ^+ is not jointly acceptable, which contradicts (14) and establishes the stated assertion that *no group u_* can exist*.]

In summary, we *cannot* always conclude that if the members of a group are free to partition any lottery they accept, the group's internal and external behavior should be so coordinated that it is appropriate for the group to choose the lottery that maximizes an expected u_*-index, where u_* is some function of the individual u_i. This is a bitter pill for us Bayesians to swallow—it would have been much nicer if we had found that there always is an appropriate group utility. Before we attempt to rationalize this negative conclusion, let us first investigate some other disturbing results.

Suppose individuals 1 and 2 have the utility functions shown in Fig. 8.9, and suppose they are offered a choice between lotteries ℓ' and ℓ'', where

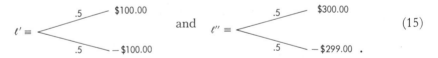

$$\text{(15)}$$

Lottery ℓ'' is sufficiently close to the lottery ℓ^+ described in Table 8.7 for us to conclude that there is no jointly acceptable partition of ℓ''. Since ℓ' is barely acceptable to each individual, we conclude that ℓ' is jointly preferred to ℓ''. Now let us investigate this strategy:

a) Toss a fair coin. If heads, proceed to (b) below, and if tails, proceed to (c) below.

b) *Heads.* Choose ℓ'. If ℓ' results in $\$100.00$, give it all to individual 2. If ℓ' results in $-\$100.00$, make 1 responsible for all the loss.

c) *Tails.* Choose ℓ''. If ℓ'' results in $-\$299.00$, give $-\$199.50$ to 2 and $-\$99.50$ to 1. If ℓ'' results in $\$300.00$, give $\$200.00$ to 1 and $\$100.00$ to 2.

This randomization procedure results in the lottery ℓ^* described in Table 8.8. Let's compare Tables 8.8 and 8.6. Since the partition of ℓ in Table 8.6 is just barely acceptable, the partition of ℓ^* in Table 8.8 should have some slight, but nevertheless positive, joint appeal. We therefore conclude that *tossing the coin to choose between ℓ' and ℓ'' is jointly preferred to ℓ'*, which in turn is jointly preferred to ℓ''.

TABLE 8.8

Lottery ℓ^*		Partition	
Probability	Payoff	1	2
.25	−$299.00	−$99.50	−$199.50
.25	−$100.00	−$100.00	$0.00
.25	+$100.00	$0.00	+$100.00
.25	+$300.00	+$200.00	+$100.00

Let's take a further look at what happens if the group decides to use the partition in Table 8.8 and the coin comes up heads, leading to acceptance of ℓ'. If ℓ' leads to $100.00, then 2 gets this full amount; if ℓ' leads to −$100.00, then 1 must bear the full brunt of this penalty. How unfair to 1! If the coin comes up heads, why doesn't 1 immediately change his mind and call for a different decision rule for acceptance and partition? The answer, of course, is that the individuals entered into a contract that favors 2 if heads and favors 1 if tails. Furthermore, the payoffs are so balanced that the overall procedure is acceptable to each individual *before* the coin is tossed. It is not fair for one individual to back out of his contract with the other *after* the coin is tossed.

With respect to randomization, there is a striking qualitative difference between the external behavior of a group and that of an individual. If an individual prefers ℓ' to ℓ'', it does not make much sense for him to toss a coin to decide.† Suppose he were to do so. Then if tails were to appear, calling for ℓ'', he could always decide at that point to change his mind and opt for ℓ'. As we have seen, however, the group might profitably choose to randomize, in contrast with the individual.

---

† In game contexts it may be desirable to randomize for secrecy purposes. See the discussion in *Games and Decisions*, pp. 74–76, 291–292. Chernoff, in his article "Rational selection of decision functions" (*Econometrica*, **22,** 1954, pp. 422–443) discusses some administrative reasons why a decision maker might choose to use a randomized decision rule.

Once the possibility of randomization is opened, we can obtain still more striking results. For example, suppose individuals 1 and 2 have different judgmental probabilities for an uncertain event A, which has nothing to do with lotteries ℓ' and ℓ''. Suppose 1 thinks A is more likely to occur than *Not A*, and 2 thinks otherwise. Then instead of tossing a fair coin to choose between ℓ' and ℓ'', the individuals might decide to choose ℓ' if A occurs and ℓ'' if *Not A* occurs. But this situation brings us to the question of how groups make decisions when the group members have differing judgmental probability assessments of states, and this question opens up a whole new subject matter rich with new complexities. I shall nibble at the corners of this vast field in Part Two of this chapter and at that time I shall also try to isolate the reason why it is not always possible to find an appropriate group u_*.

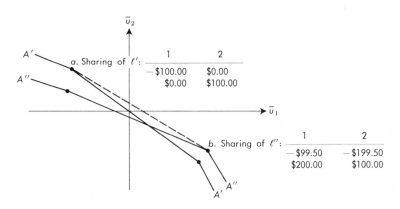

Fig. 8.10 An illustration of the case in which no sharing of either ℓ' or ℓ'' is jointly desirable, but in which a randomized rule using ℓ' and ℓ'' is jointly desirable.

My remaining task in this section is to relate our discussion of the lotteries ℓ' and ℓ'' in (15) with Fig. 8.6(b) and (c). In Fig. 8.10, the Pareto-optimal sets of ℓ' and ℓ'' are labeled A' and A'', respectively. Observe that A' touches the origin $(0, 0)$ but never passes into the northeast quadrant and that A'' is bounded away from the northeast quadrant. Nevertheless, if ℓ' is shared to give point a and ℓ'' is shared to give point b, then tossing a coin to decide between ℓ' and ℓ'' will give a joint utility evaluation midway between the points a and b and this will fall in the *interior* of the northeast quadrant. True, the example is exploiting piddling amounts, but the message should be clear: Because of examples such as this one, it is hopeless to try to assert that a group utility function will always exist.

9.   ANALYSIS OF A DECISION TREE WITH RISK SHARING

Let's now turn our attention to the case in which you, the decision maker, have a complex decision problem which you can diagram as a tree like the one in Fig. 2.13 (or perhaps even a more complicated one), and let's suppose you wish to investigate the merits of sharing your risk with someone else. For example, suppose that the optimal strategy for an EMV'er yields a positive expected return, but for you, a non-EMV'er, the CME of your optimal strategy is negative. Such a situation suggests that you might wish to invite others to participate in this venture. As another example, consider a case in which the CME of your optimal strategy is positive but you wish to increase your CME by sharing the risk. How should you analyze your problem in this wider context of risk sharing?

Let's start by assuming that you and a partner of yours have structured a decision problem and you both agree on the anatomy of the decision-flow diagram; furthermore, suppose that both of you have identical probability assessments at all chance forks, that your utility function for money is u_1 and his is u_2, and that everything is quite open and frank, so that each of you has full information. If u_1 and u_2 are both exponential, then, as we saw in Section 7, your analysis is simple—the two of you will have a group u_* that is appropriate for your joint *external* behavior. You would use this u_* to determine your optimum strategy, σ_* say, by averaging out and folding back in the extensive form of analysis. Corresponding to this strategy σ_* there is a lottery ℓ_* of possible payoffs to your group, and each of you could then find his own CME for his appropriate share. You would then have to determine through some bargaining process a side payment to be paid by one of you to the other. This would constitute your *internal* problem. Finally you would share the proceeds in the ratio of your c-values.

There are other (u_1, u_2)-combinations† that also result in a group u_*. But, as we saw in the previous section, a group u_* will not always exist, and when it doesn't you cannot solve your external choice problem without getting at least partly involved with your internal sharing problem. I should like to examine this problem in some detail. We shall not assume that u_1 or u_2 has any special analytic form, and hence the problem reduces to this form: How should you and your partner jointly choose a strategy for experimentation and action (the external problem) and then how should you share the resulting lottery (the internal problem)?

---

† Two examples are

$$u_1(x) = \log (x + b_1), \qquad u_2(x) = \log (x + b_2);$$
$$u_1(x) = (x + b_1)^c, \qquad u_2(x) = (x + b_2)^c, \qquad \text{for} \quad 0 < c < 1.$$

To analyze this combined problem we must generalize what we did in Section 3. There you did not have to worry about choosing a strategy or lottery, but just about sharing a lottery you already had. In the combined problem, we can evaluate each possible strategy choice together with a possible sharing rule, by a $(\bar{u}_1, \bar{u}_2)$-pair; if we then plot all such pairs, we shall once again come up with an achievable set such as **A** in Fig. 8.3. But now **A** is the set of all joint utility evaluations arising from partitions of *many different lotteries*.

A Method for Computing the Pareto-Optimal Set of A. A Pareto-optimal point of the set **A** will maximize $\lambda_1\bar{u}_1 + \lambda_2\bar{u}_2$ for some $\lambda_1 \geq 0$, $\lambda_2 \geq 0$, where $\lambda_1 + \lambda_2 = 1$. In this case $(\bar{u}_1, \bar{u}_2)$ depends on the strategy choice and on the partition. But if we review the argument in Section 3 that leads to Eqs. (6) and (7), we still can conclude that regardless of the strategy choice, if a lottery leads to payoff x_k, you and your partner should divide x_k into shares x_{k1} and x_{k2} so as to maximize $\lambda_1 u_1(x_{k1}) + \lambda_2 u_2(x_{k2})$. Since this is true for any number x_k, let's drop the subscript k and consider the payoff x. First, to clean up the notation a bit before we push on, let's use λ to refer to the pair (λ_1, λ_2), use $s_1^\lambda(x)$ to denote 1's optimal share of x, which depends on λ, and $s_2^\lambda(x)$ to denote 2's optimal share of x. Remember you are 1 and your partner is 2. Finally let's define

$$u_*^\lambda(x) \equiv \lambda_1 u_1[s_1^\lambda(x)] + \lambda_2 u_2[s_2^\lambda(x)],$$

which we shall call the *group conditional utility value for x given* λ. If it is necessary, it is not difficult to obtain the functions u_*^λ, s_1^λ, and s_2^λ for a given λ by numerical means.

Digression. In the special case in which

$$u_1(x) = 1 - e^{-x/c_1} \qquad \text{and} \qquad u_2(x) = 1 - e^{-x/c_2},$$

we already have shown that

$$u_*^\lambda(x) = 1 - e^{-x/c_*}, \qquad \text{where} \qquad c_* = c_1 + c_2,$$

and this is true for all λ. Furthermore the sharing rules s_1^λ and s_2^λ are *linear* and given by

$$s_1^\lambda(x) = \frac{c_1}{c_1 + c_2} x + b^\lambda \qquad \text{and} \qquad s_2^\lambda(x) = \frac{c_2}{c_1 + c_2} x - b^\lambda.$$

Note that the side payment b^λ depends on λ but the proportional shares do not.

Keeping λ fixed, we next solve the decision problem, in either extensive or normal form of analysis, using the group conditional utility function u_*^λ. The resulting optimal strategy for experimentation and action will depend on λ; let's call this strategy σ_*^λ. Now associated with σ_*^λ, there is a lottery ℓ_*^λ, say, which you and your partner must partition. But you already know how to do this: If ℓ_*^λ results in payoff x, then regardless of the probability of achieving this payoff and regardless of the other payoffs and their probabilities, it is optimal to partition x by giving $s_1^\lambda(x)$ to you and $s_2^\lambda(x)$ to your partner. This partitioning rule splits the lottery ℓ_*^λ into two parts: ℓ_1^λ to you and ℓ_2^λ to your partner. Finally, you should use your own utility function u_1 to evaluate ℓ_1^λ, and then label the resulting utility number $\bar{u}_1^\lambda$; similarly, your partner will get $\bar{u}_2^\lambda$. We now know the pair $(\bar{u}_1^\lambda, \bar{u}_2^\lambda)$ is a Pareto-optimal point, but we don't know where this point $(\bar{u}_1^\lambda, \bar{u}_2^\lambda)$ will fall. It might not fall in the first quadrant. Keep in mind that you don't have Fig. 8.3 given to you. So far, all you have is a single point $(\bar{u}_1^\lambda, \bar{u}_2^\lambda)$ on the northeast boundary.

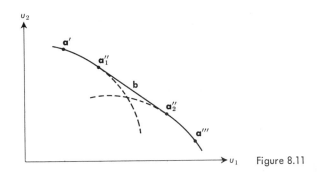

Figure 8.11

As λ moves, the optimal group (external) strategy σ_*^λ may also change, but perhaps in spurts rather than in a smooth fashion. That is, σ_*^λ might stay the same for a range of λ-values and then jump at the boundaries of the range. Furthermore, there might not be a unique σ_*^λ for some values of λ. Figure 8.11 illustrates what can possibly happen. As the first component λ_1 of λ increases from λ_1' to λ_1'', say, the optimal strategy σ_*^λ may stay fixed, and $(\bar{u}_1^\lambda, \bar{u}_2^\lambda)$ may change continuously from $\mathbf{a}'$ to $\mathbf{a}_1''$, say. In the interval λ_1'' to λ_1''', another strategy may take over and $(\bar{u}_1^\lambda, \bar{u}_2^\lambda)$ may change continuously from $\mathbf{a}_2''$ to $\mathbf{a}'''$. At λ_1'', the points $\mathbf{a}_1''$ and $\mathbf{a}_2''$ may *both* be optimal and hence the points on the line segment joining $\mathbf{a}_1''$ and $\mathbf{a}_2''$, which are achievable by randomizing between $\mathbf{a}_1''$ and $\mathbf{a}_2''$, are also on the Pareto-optimal curve. Now if point $\mathbf{b}$ turns out to be your compromise point, then you would need to use some randomized device to determine whether you and your partner should pursue the strategy for experimentation, action, and partitioning that leads to point $\mathbf{a}_1''$ or the one that leads to point $\mathbf{a}_2''$.

Let's summarize: For each λ we go through the sequence

$$\lambda \to u_*^\lambda \to \sigma_*^\lambda \to \ell_*^\lambda \to \begin{Bmatrix} \ell_1^\lambda \\ \ell_2^\lambda \end{Bmatrix} \to \begin{Bmatrix} \bar{u}_1^\lambda \\ \bar{u}_2^\lambda \end{Bmatrix}$$

and obtain a single Pareto-optimal point $(\bar{u}_1^\lambda, \bar{u}_2^\lambda)$. By varying the λ we can generate different points on the Pareto-optimal frontier. It is now up to you and your partner to decide which Pareto-optimal point to choose.

Matters would be considerably simpler if we could choose an "appropriate" λ at the outset or if u_*^λ did not depend on λ. But, alas, this happens only in very special circumstances. In general we cannot find an appropriate u_* that depends only on u_1 and u_2 and does not depend on the particular decision problem.

PART TWO: GROUP DECISIONS

10. INTRODUCTION TO PART TWO

In the ensuing sections, we shall assume that there is a group of individuals who must jointly choose a course of action. Although they form a cohesive group, they still may have different preferences for outcomes that jointly affect the group, and they may also differ in their personal probability assessments for different possible events. In Section 11, we shall consider the situation in which the individuals agree both on utilities for consequences and on conditional probability assessments for different experimental outcomes given an underlying state (say, they agree on the probability of obtaining a red ball from an urn of type θ_1). However, they disagree on their assessments of probabilities for the underlying states; for example, they disagree on an assessment for θ_1. They can either (1) compromise on a prior distribution over these states before they take their sample and then use the sample results to update their group prior distribution, or (2) each individual can use the sample results to get his very own posterior probability distribution and then all the individuals can compromise the differences in their posterior distributions to obtain a so-called group posterior distribution. Which procedure should they use? Should they compromise before or after the sample is taken?

Sections 12 and 13 consider these fundamental questions: Are the behavioral principles of transitivity and substitutability equally compelling for a group of individuals who must act together? Should the group decompose a problem and process its preferences for consequences separately and independently of its judgments about uncertain events?

11. ON COMBINING PRIOR AND POSTERIOR PROBABILITY JUDGMENTS†

Suppose two individuals 1 and 2 have a strong, binding, common interest and must jointly choose an action in an uncertain environment—they might be man and wife, for example. Suppose further that for *any* consequence c of their decision problem there is some number $\pi(c)$, such that *both* partners are indifferent between obtaining c for certain and obtaining a prize W with probability $\pi(c)$ and a prize L with complementary probability. [In the language of preceding chapters, we say that both individuals are indifferent between c and a $\pi(c)$-BRLT.] Let's assume, however, that the consequence of any one of their joint actions depends on which one of several possible events actually comes to pass and that the partners have fundamental disagreements about the judgmental probabilities appropriate to these events. Let's also assume that these partners have discussed their differing assessments with each other, and although they initially shifted ground a bit, each has finally settled down to his own viewpoint and these viewpoints differ. "Enough, enough! I've heard all your arguments already. You think what you think, but I think otherwise!"

To take a hypothetical but concrete example, suppose the two individuals are jointly given *your* basic decision problem. To make things easier, suppose they are both EMV'ers (for the amounts under consideration) but that they differ about their judgmental probability assessments for event θ_1. Let's say that 1's assessment for θ_1 is $P_1(\theta_1) = .9$, and 2's assessment for θ_1 is $P_2(\theta_1) = .3$. (It's hard to imagine how they could be this far apart after full communication, but if we're going to discuss a hole in a doughnut, we might as well imagine a doughnut with a big hole.) Finally, suppose that if 1 and 2 were forced to make a group assessment, they would agree to take $P_*(\theta_1) = (.9 + .3)/2 = .6$, in democratic fashion.

Now let's see what happens if they take a single drawing from the unidentified urn and both observe the same objective evidence. Table 8.9 exhibits

---

† This section uses results in Albert Madansky's "Externally Bayesian Groups", RM–4141–PR, The RAND Corporation, November 1964.

TABLE 8.9

a) 1's joint probabilities				b) 2's joint probabilities			
	State				State		
Outcome	θ_1	θ_2	Total	Outcome	θ_1	θ_2	Total
R	.36	.09	.45	R	.12	.63	.75
B	.54	.01	.55	B	.18	.07	.25
Total	.90	.10	(1.00)	Total	.30	.70	(1.00)

c) 1's posterior probabilities				d) 2's posterior probabilities			
	State				State		
Outcome	θ_1	θ_2	Total	Outcome	θ_1	θ_2	Total
R	.80	.20	1.00	R	.16	.84	1.00
B	.98	.02	1.00	B	.72	.28	1.00

the basic calculations needed to revise 1's and 2's probability assessments. For example, 1's joint probability of R and θ_1 is

$$P_1(R \text{ and } \theta_1) = P_1(R|\theta_1)P_1(\theta_1) = .4 \times .9 = .36,$$

and his posterior probability for θ_1 given R is

$$P_1(\theta_1|R) = \frac{P_1(R \text{ and } \theta_1)}{P_1(R)} = \frac{.36}{.45} = .80.$$

Part (c) and (d) of the table give 1's and 2's posterior probabilities for the states given the sample outcomes; hence the entries in a given row sum to unity.

Now let's see what happens if they draw a red ball: 1's assessment for θ_1 changes from .90 to .80 and 2's assessment of the same probability changes from .30 to .16. It is not so clear whether they are now closer together or further apart; it depends on your definition of closeness. If they draw a black ball B, then 1's assessment for θ_1 changes from .90 to .98 and 2's assessment changes from .30 to .72. Note the big jump in 2's assessment.

Once again in the spirit of democratic cooperation, the individuals might agree to average their revised probability judgments to obtain a group revised

TABLE 8.10

Average of 1's and 2's posterior probability tables

Outcome	State θ_1	θ_2	Total
R	.48	.52	1.00
B	.85	.15	1.00

assessment. For example, after they draw a red ball they might agree to this:

$$P_*(\theta_1|R) = \tfrac{1}{2}P_1(\theta_1|R) + \tfrac{1}{2}P_2(\theta_1|R) = \tfrac{1}{2}(.80) + \tfrac{1}{2}(.16) = .48.$$

Table 8.10 exhibits the average of 1's and 2's posterior probability tables [that is, Tables 8.9(c) and (d)].

Our two individuals could have proceeded another way. Instead of compromising or averaging between their posterior probabilities, they could have reversed the order: First they could have compromised to get a so-called group prior probability assessment and then they could have revised this group prior on the basis of the experimental outcome and thereby obtained a posterior probability assessment. Table 8.11 shows these calculations. For example, the entry .24 in the upper left-hand corner of Table 8.11(a) is obtained either from

$$P_*(R \text{ and } \theta_1) = \tfrac{1}{2}P_1(R \text{ and } \theta_1) + \tfrac{1}{2}P_2(R \text{ and } \theta_1)$$
$$= \tfrac{1}{2}(.36) + \tfrac{1}{2}(.12) = .24,$$

TABLE 8.11

a) Average of 1's and 2's joint probabilities

Outcome	State θ_1	θ_2	Total
R	.24	.36	.60
B	.36	.04	.40
Total	.60	.40	(1.00)

b) Posterior probabilities based on an average of 1's and 2's priors

Outcome	State θ_1	θ_2	Total
R	.40	.60	1.00
B	.90	.10	1.00

or from

$$P_*(R \text{ and } \theta_1) = P(R|\theta_1)P_*(\theta_1)$$
$$= P(R|\theta_1)[\tfrac{1}{2}P_1(\theta_1) + \tfrac{1}{2}P_2(\theta_1)]$$
$$= (.4)[\tfrac{1}{2}(.9) + \tfrac{1}{2}(.3)]$$
$$= .4 \times .6 = .24.$$

The entry .40 in the upper left-hand corner of Table 8.11(b) is obtained from

$$P_*(\theta_1|R) = \frac{P_*(\theta_1 \text{ and } R)}{P_*(R)} = \frac{.24}{.60} = .40.$$

Now the obvious question is whether the partners should compromise at the posterior stage and get the results described by Table 8.10, or at the prior stage and get the results described by Table 8.11(b).

TABLE 8.12

$$P_1(\theta_1) = .9$$
$$P_2(\theta_1) = .3$$
$$P_*(\theta_1) = .6$$

$$P_1(\theta_1|R) = .80$$
$$P_2(\theta_1|R) = .16$$
$$P_*(\theta_1|R) = \begin{cases} .40, \text{ prior compromise} \\ .48, \text{ posterior compromise} \end{cases}$$

$$P_1(\theta_1|B) = .98$$
$$P_2(\theta_1|B) = .72$$
$$P_*(\theta_1|B) = \begin{cases} .90, \text{ prior compromise} \\ .85, \text{ posterior compromise} \end{cases}$$

Table 8.12 brings together some of the data of Tables 8.8, 8.9, and 8.10, and we shall use it to facilitate our discussion. If the two individuals draw a red ball, then 1 will prefer the posterior compromise, since .48 is closer than .40 to .80, whereas 2 will prefer the prior compromise, since .40 is closer than .48 to .16. However, if they draw a black ball, the situation is then reversed: 1 will prefer the prior compromise, since .90 is closer than .85 to .98, whereas 2 will prefer the posterior compromise, since .85 is closer than .90 to .72.

Now I would suggest that it makes eminently good sense for the partners to agree on the prior compromise *before* learning the outcome of the experiment.

Why? Because 1 will be making a concession if red occurs [which 1 thinks has a chance $P_1(R) = .45$ and 2 thinks has a chance $P_2(R) = .75$; see Table 8.9(a)] and 2 will be making a concession if black occurs [which 2 thinks has a chance $P_2(B) = .25$ and 1 thinks has a chance $P_1(B) = .55$; see Table 8.9(b)]. *This means that before they draw, 1 believes it is more likely than not that 2 will have to make the concession, and 2 believes it is more likely than not that 1 will have to make the concession.*

We shall find some algebraic manipulation helpful at this point. Instead of using weights $\frac{1}{2}$ and $\frac{1}{2}$ for the averaging of the prior probabilities, let's say that

$$P_*(\theta_1) = \lambda_1 P_1(\theta_1) + \lambda_2 P_2(\theta_1), \qquad \text{where} \quad \begin{cases} \lambda_1 > 0, \lambda_2 > 0, \\ \lambda_1 + \lambda_2 = 1. \end{cases} \qquad (16)$$

Now if we use this as a group prior probability assessment, we find that the probability of getting an R on the first drawing is

$$\begin{aligned} P_*(R) &= P(R|\theta_1)P_*(\theta_1) + P(R|\theta_2)P_*(\theta_2) \\ &= P(R|\theta_1)[\lambda_1 P_1(\theta_1) + \lambda_2 P_2(\theta_1)] + P(R|\theta_2)[\lambda_1 P_1(\theta_2) + \lambda_2 P_2(\theta_2)] \\ &= \lambda_1[P(R|\theta_1)P_1(\theta_1) + P(R|\theta_2)P_1(\theta_2)] \\ &\qquad\qquad + \lambda_2[P(R|\theta_1)P_2(\theta_1) + P(R|\theta_2)P_2(\theta_2)] \\ &= \lambda_1 P_1(R) + \lambda_2 P_2(R). \end{aligned} \qquad (17)$$

By Bayes' Theorem, the posterior probability of θ_1 given R based on the *group* prior probability assessment is

$$\begin{aligned} P_*(\theta_1|R) &= \frac{P(R|\theta_1)P_*(\theta_1)}{P_*(R)} = \frac{P(R|\theta_1)[\lambda_1 P_1(\theta_1) + \lambda_2 P_2(\theta_1)]}{P_*(R)} \\ &= \lambda_1 \frac{P_1(R)}{P_*(R)}\left[\frac{P(R|\theta_1)P_1(\theta_1)}{P_1(R)}\right] + \lambda_2 \frac{P_2(R)}{P_*(R)}\left[\frac{P(R|\theta_1)P_2(\theta_1)}{P_2(R)}\right] \\ &= \lambda_1 \frac{P_1(R)}{P_*(R)} P_1(\theta_1|R) + \lambda_2 \frac{P_2(R)}{P_*(R)} P_2(\theta_1|R), \end{aligned} \qquad (18)$$

where the last step uses Bayes' Theorem once again. Thus we see that if we begin with the group prior probability assessment, *then the posterior probability of θ_1 given R is a weighted average of 1's and 2's posterior assessments. In notation, the respective weights are*

$$\lambda_1 P_1(R)/P_*(R) \qquad and \qquad \lambda_2 P_2(R)/P_*(R).$$

This means that if $\lambda_1 = \lambda_2 = \frac{1}{2}$, then the weights are in the proportion $P_1(R)$ to $P_2(R)$; that is, in the proportion to the chances that 1 and 2 assign to the event R.

Let's verify this result in the numerical example we have been discussing. We have

$$P_1(R) = .45, \qquad \text{from Table 8.9(a),}$$
$$P_2(R) = .75, \qquad \text{from Table 8.9(b),}$$
$$P_*(R) = \tfrac{1}{2}(.45) + \tfrac{1}{2}(.75) = .60.$$

[You could either compute $P_*(R)$ here, or take it from Table 8.11(a).] If we let $\lambda_1 = \lambda_2 = \frac{1}{2}$, (18) gives

$$P_*(\theta_1|R) = [\tfrac{1}{2}(.45/.60)](.80) + [\tfrac{1}{2}(.75/.60)](.16) = .40,$$

and this checks with the entry in Table 8.11(b). Note that if R occurs, then we weight $P_2(\theta_1|R)$ more heavily than $P_1(\theta_1|R)$, since $P_2(R) = .75$ and $P_1(R) = .45$.

Since we are assuming for the moment that both partners are EMV'ers, and since they agree on conditional probability assessments given each of the states θ_1 and θ_2, it is appropriate to examine their decision problem in the language of the normal form of analysis. Table 6.1, shows us that given 1's prior assessment $P_1(\theta_1) = .9$, the optimal strategy for experimentation and action is σ_1 (that is, to choose a_1 without experimentation); whereas, given 2's prior assessment $P_2(\theta_1) = .3$, the optimal strategy is σ_2 (that is, to choose a_2 without experimentation). If the partners agree to compromise on a prior probability and choose $P_*(\theta_1) = .6$, then it is optimal to select strategy σ_5, which prescribes taking one observation and then choosing a_2 if red and a_1 if black. Note that 1 will make the concession if R and that 2 will make the concession if B. Certainly drawing a ball is a better compromise technique than tossing a fair coin because *each partner feels that the drawing is a randomized mechanism that is biased in his favor.* In addition, we could show that if perchance they draw a red ball, then 1 would agree with 2 that they should choose a_2.

Thus we see that there are two conceptually different advantages in sampling: (1) Sampling acts as a randomization device biased in the favor of each partner, and (2) the outcome of sampling may influence one partner to change his mind sufficiently to warrant a shift in his preferred choice of an optimal terminal action.

The Bourbon-Scotch Problem Revisited

It will be instructive at this point if we take a look at another typical situation in which the members of a group wish to combine probability judgments. Suppose, for example, 1 and 2 disagree on the proportion p of doctors who consumed more scotch than bourbon last year. Suppose that after fully discussing their reasons for feeling the way they do, each individual assesses a probability distribution for p according to the techniques described in Section 3, Chapter 7, and suppose their distributions are as given in Fig. 8.12. Before they take any sample, 1's and 2's probability distributions for p are labeled $f_1^{(b)}$ and $f_2^{(b)}$, respectively. [Recall that the superscript (b) is mnemonic for "before".] Now let's assume that a random sample of 50 nonteetotaling doctors shows that 28 doctors consumed more scotch than bourbon. At this point, both 1 and 2 would revise their distributions to $f_1^{(a)}$ and $f_2^{(a)}$, respectively. [Recall that the superscript (a) is mnemonic for "after".] Besides these prior and posterior distributions, Fig. 8.12 also exhibits the scaled likelihood function kL that results from the observed sample. [Recall that to get $f_1^{(a)}$ we multiply $f_1^{(b)}$ by kL and rescale.] Since $f_1^{(b)}$ is relatively loose or *dispersed* in comparison with kL, 1's posterior distribution is close to kL. Since $f_2^{(b)}$ is more tightly distributed than $f_1^{(b)}$ in Fig. 8.12, 2's posterior distribution is not so close to kL as was the case for 1's. Note the important point, however: 1 and 2 are closer together after the sample than before because of the intercession of the likelihood function which is common to both. Furthermore, as sampling increases, the effect of kL on the posterior distributions becomes more and more pro-

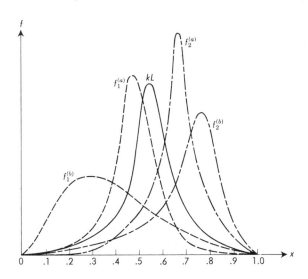

Figure 8.12

nounced, and both 1 and 2 must gradually defer to the cumulating, commonly observed, objective, sample evidence.

Now let's talk about compromises between 1's and 2's differing assessments. I have already argued that even before 1 and 2 know the results of the sample, there are strong reasons why they ought to agree to a compromise at the prior stage of analysis rather than at the posterior stage. If, for example, 1 and 2 average their prior distributions; that is, if they let

$$f_*^{(b)} = \tfrac{1}{2} f_1^{(b)} + \tfrac{1}{2} f_2^{(b)},$$

where the subscript $*$ represents a group assessment; and if they compute $f_*^{(a)}$ by multiplying kL by $f_*^{(b)}$ and rescaling, then we can manipulate normalizing factors to show that

$$f_*^{(a)} = \frac{w_1}{w_1 + w_2} f_1^{(a)} + \frac{w_2}{w_1 + w_2} f_2^{(a)}.$$

Here the weights w_1 and w_2 are not predetermined but are rather determined by the outcome of the experiment; in particular, they are the probabilities that 1 and 2 would respectively assign to the outcome that 28 doctors of the 50 consumed more scotch than bourbon and in this case w_2 is larger than w_1.

12. THE PROBLEM OF THE PANEL OF EXPERTS

Let's assume, as we often have in the past, that *you* are the decision maker and are acting for an organization. Suppose that you are quite unfamiliar with the issues of a given problem and call on a panel of experts for advice. Suppose that an analyst in your employ has already structured the problem in a decision-flow diagram and that all your experts agree on the structure of the problem but disagree on prior probabilities for uncertain states and on utility assignments for consequences. Let's also assume that these experts have talked at length amongst themselves about why each believes the way he does and that all utility and probability assessments have already been modified and remodified to take into account all the jointly perceived and available information; and still they disagree. Now it's *your* turn to decide what to do.

By this point you are hopefully a brainwashed Bayesian, so let's assume you agree with the analysis so far. The catechism says that (1) you should decompose your problem into two parts, utilities and probabilities, and (2) you should ignore considerations of probabilities when you are scaling your attitudes to obtain utilities for consequences, and you should ignore considerations of utilities when you are scaling your judgments about uncertain events to obtain probabilities. If you are to put this catechism into practice, you must somehow process the utility assessments of your experts and come up with a utility assessment of your own. Presumably, if all your experts are agreed on utilities, you would adopt their common agreement as your own. Also, presumably, you are somewhat responsive to the assignments of all your experts; if they disagree, you will not usually adopt any one particular expert's assignments without at least considering the assignments of the others. And similarly for probabilities: Your probability assignments will be a function of their probability assignments; if they agree, then so will you; and you will not allow any one of your experts to dictate to you. Once you have both the necessary utility and probability assignments, you can hand these over to your analyst and let him compute the strategy that maximizes *your* expected utility based on *your* probability assignments. Fine, so far; but controversy is about to begin!

Suppose that you must choose between alternatives a_1 and a_2, and after following the procedure just described, you come out with the conclusion that a_1 is better than a_2; in other words, you find that a_1 has a higher expected utility than a_2, given the facts that your utility curve is solely a function of your panel's utility curves and your probability measure is solely a function of your panel's probability measures. However, on further investigation you find that each of your experts, if he had used his very own utility and probability assignments, would have preferred a_2 to a_1! In other words, *all your experts agree that a_2 is better than a_1 but they disagree about the reasons for their agreement.* Would you still choose a_1 over a_2?

In such a paradoxical situation, some of you may worry about the roles of the experts, suspecting that they are trying to trick you, that they have concealed their true feelings for tactical reasons. You may hesitate to disagree with them for fear you would undermine your organization, people would quit, obstreperous coalitions would form, morale would suffer, and so on. Put all that aside; we have enough troubles as is. Imagine your experts are dedicated staff men, that you have no doubt about their sincerity, and that you are sure they would not conspire to trick you. You *know* how they feel. In these circumstances, if I were you, I should choose a_1 over a_2. I should overrule the unanimous opinion of my expert panel even though I did not have any prior feelings of my own to speak of. Most, but not all, of my colleagues with whom I have discussed this problem agree with this opinion. We are hopelessly divided, however, on some related issues that I shall raise shortly.

First, let's see how this seeming paradox could come about. Consider the following example with two states, two acts, two experts, and basic data as

TABLE 8.13

Two experts in agreement and you in disagreement

	Expert 1				Expert 2		
	Act		#1's		Act		#2's
State	a_1	a_2	probs.	State	a_1	a_2	probs.
θ_1	1	0	.2	θ_1	.5	1	.8
θ_2	.5	1	.8	θ_2	1	0	.2
Expected utility	.6	.8	(1.0)	Expected utility	.6	.8	(1.0)

Split-the-difference analysis

	Act		Your
State	a_1	a_2	probs.
θ_1	.75	.5	.5
θ_2	.75	.5	.5
Expected utility	.75	.5	(1.0)

described in Table 8.13. The first expert, for example, assigns a utility of .5 for the consequence of a_1 when state θ_2 prevails, and the second assigns a utility of 1 to this same consequence. The first assigns a .8 probability to θ_2, whereas the second assigns it .2. Suppose now in an egalitarian mood you decide to average the assessments of your experts and adopt this average as your own. Then, as Table 8.13 shows, both experts will prefer a_2 to a_1, whereas you will prefer a_1 to a_2. Now you may remark that some other way of amalgamating the two utility functions and the two probability functions might not lead to the same paradoxical result. Perhaps so; but Richard Zeckhauser has proved a mathematical theorem that states this result:

> Suppose you announce a group procedure that (1) combines utility and probability functions separately, and (2) does not single out one individual to dictate the group utility and probability assignments. *Then* you can always concoct an example such that each of your experts will agree on which act to choose but where your group procedure will lead you to a different conclusion.

Several years ago, I gave a seminar on the panel of experts and group decision problems at which John Pratt suggested that the paradox I have pointed out does not depend on having simultaneous disagreements about utilities *and* probabilities, and that a seemingly similar paradox can appear if there is only disagreement about probabilities. Pratt gave the following example. Two experts agree on utilities for consequences. The decision turns on two sources of uncertainty, however: the future value of the British pound, and whether or not a piece of equipment will fail. One expert is led to act a_2 because he thinks the value of the British pound will *rise* and quite *independently* he also thinks the piece of equipment will *fail*. The second expert is also led to act a_2 because he thinks the value of the British pound will *fall* and quite *independently* he thinks the equipment will *succeed*. In such a case, you as decision maker may want your experts to help you assess a probability distribution of your own. You may, moreover, feel certain about one thing: that your knowledge about the future value of the British pound has nothing whatsoever to do with your judgments about the piece of equipment in question. Given this, you would use your experts' opinions about the British pound to draw your own probabilistic conclusions about the British pound, and similarly you would process their information about the reliability of the equipment to arrive at your own assessment. Once you have adopted probabilities for each of the two independent contingencies, you can compute such quantities as the probability that the British pound will rise *and* the equipment will fail.

I have introduced some hypothetical numbers into Table 8.14 to illustrate these points. Table 8.14(a, b) gives the respective assessments of Experts 1 and 2. Note that because the two contingencies are assumed independent, each entry in the table is the product of its corresponding marginals. Thus, for example, Expert 1's assessment for the event (*Rise, Succeed*) is .80 × .30 = .24. In part (d), the marginal probabilities have been averaged to get the circled marginal entries and then the entries in the body of the table have been obtained by multiplying the corresponding marginals. Thus, for example, your assessment for the event (*Rise, Fail*) is

$$[(.80 + .20)/2][(.30 + .70)/2] = .50 \times .50 = .25.$$

To obtain part (c), the corresponding entries in parts (a) and (b) have been averaged. Thus, for example, the number .19 in (c) is an average of .24 and .14.

Now we come to the point of this argument. It is easy to show that if you compromise at the component level (part d), then you can easily develop a situation in which *each of your experts prefers a_2*, say, and in which *you would be led to a_1*. This anomaly cannot occur if you do the averaging at the joint level

TABLE 8.14

a) Assessments of Expert 1					b) Assessments of Expert 2			
	Rise	Fall				Rise	Fall	
Succeed	.24	.56	.80		Succeed	.14	.06	.20
Fail	.06	.14	.20		Fail	.56	.24	.80
	.30	.70	1.00			.70	.30	1.00

c) Your assessments if you average parts (a) and (b) of this table					d) Your assessments if you average marginals in parts (a) and (b) and maintain independence			
	Rise	Fall				Rise	Fall	
Succeed	.19	.31	.50		Succeed	.25	.25	(.50)
Fail	.31	.19	.50		Fail	.25	.25	(.50)
	.50	.50	1.00			(.50)	(.50)	1.00

(part c) rather than at the component level of disagreement; this follows because (c) is a simple average of (a) and (b). This fact indicates the condition of agreement: There is a consensus between you and your experts whenever your joint assessment is a weighted average of their joint assessments. Observe that if you use the assessments of (c), then you destroy independence, which you may not wish to do.

On the other hand, there is *no* weighted average of (a) and (b) that produces (d). Furthermore, we could easily show that if your joint assessments are *not* a weighted average of the joint assessments of your experts, then it is possible that although they agree on which act to choose, you will wish to act differently. This, then, is the condition of disagreement. There seems to be a conflict here between the two conditions; your alternatives seem to be to destroy the agreement on ultimate action and maintain the agreement on independence (part d), or to ignore independence and join with your experts in a consensus. What should you do?

If I were solely responsible as the decision maker, I should want to probe the opinions of my experts to assess my own utility and probability structure. I should try to keep my assessments for utilities separate from my assessments for probabilities, and I should try to exploit such common agreements as independence. Wherever possible, I should want to decompose issues to get at basic sources of agreement and disagreement. I should compromise at the primitive levels of disagreement and adopt points of common agreement as my own, so long as these common agreements were not compensating aggregates of disagreements. I should do so knowing full well that I might end up choosing an action which my experts would say is not as good as an available alternative. Throughout this discussion, of course, I am assuming that I do not have to worry about the viability of my organization, its morale, and so on.

In the next section we shall reconsider this same class of issues with a different organizational background. We shall assume that you are not ultimately responsible for the decision, but are an expert advisor to a group of decision makers, a board of directors, say, who are ultimately responsible.

13. THE GROUP DECISION PROBLEM

Our background here includes several associated individuals who must collectively decide on a course of action in a decision problem under uncertainty, and an analyst (*you*) who has structured their problem in terms of a decision-flow diagram. Let's say that there is agreement on all aspects of the problem except utility and probability assignments. Would you advise the group to behave externally as if they are a Bayesian decision-making unit? Should they thrash out a group utility function, a group probability function, and maximize expected utility?

First, let's recall a definition: We say that a group choice (an act) is Pareto-optimal (for the group) if there is no other act that puts some members of the group in a better humor without putting other members of the group in a worse one. It seems reasonable, does it not, that the group *should* choose a Pareto-optimal act? Otherwise there would be alternative acts that at least some would prefer and no one would "disprefer". Not too long ago this principle seemed to me unassailable, the one solid cornerstone in an otherwise swampy area. I am not so sure now, and I find myself in that uncomfortable position in which the more I think the more confused I become.

One can argue that the group by its very existence should have a common bond of interest. If the members disagree on fundamentals (here, on probabilities and on utilities), they ought to thrash these out independently, arrive at a compromise probability distribution and a compromise utility function, and use these in the usual Bayesian manner. In other words, the group members should consider themselves as constituting a panel of experts who advise the organizational entity; they should imagine the existence of a higher decision-making unit, the organization incarnate, so to speak, and ask what *it* should do. Just as it made sense to give up Pareto optimality in the problem of the panel of experts, it likewise seems to make sense in the group decision problem.

But now let us consider the other side, the side that favors Pareto optimality. Imagine that you have fully discussed the issues with the other members of your group and that you have acquired strong feelings of your own that a_2 is better than a_1. If all your fellow group members *agree* with you, notwithstanding the differences in the reasons why they do so, can you imagine doing otherwise than adopting a_2 over a_1? If you thought that the group for some reason might tentatively select a_1 over a_2, would it not be your responsibility as a democratic member of the group to try to undermine a_1 in favor of a_2? And how easy your job would be! "But," the critics of the Pareto-optimality criterion would retort, "would the organization be as well off? Wouldn't the organization make better decisions if the responsible parties were to thrash out their fundamental disagreements and were to build upon these compromises by maximizing expected utility?"

These issues can be dramatized as a fight between Group Bayesians and Paretians. The Group Bayesians would argue that the behavioral assumptions for individual rationality (for example, transitivity and substitutability) are equally compelling when applied to a group acting as a decision-making unit. The Paretians would argue that Pareto optimality is inviolable, and therefore the behavioral assumptions for individual rationality need to be revised when they are interpreted in a group context.

Let's look at these behavioral assumptions. To begin with, I don't think there is any argument about the Transitivity Principle. This is just as desirable for groups as for individuals, although harder to achieve. But the quarrel crystallizes when we consider the Substitution Principle. An example will help here. Suppose a two-member group must choose between a_1 and a_2. If they choose a_1, they will get an objective .55 chance at a prize W that they both consider desirable, and otherwise nothing. If they choose a_2, they will receive W if (1) a piece of equipment succeeds *and* the British pound falls in value, or (2) the equipment fails and the pound rises. Figure 8.13 exhibits these payoffs as π-BRLT's (where π gives the chance at W). Both members of the group feel these two contingencies are independent. Their probability assignments differ, however; these are the same as the ones given in Table 8.14. For example, we shall interpret the pair (.8, .2) on the *Succeed* branch in Fig. 8.13 as indicating that the first and second members respectively assign .8 and .2 probabilities to the success of the equipment. (These numbers do not necessarily have to sum to unity but I have chosen them that way to help

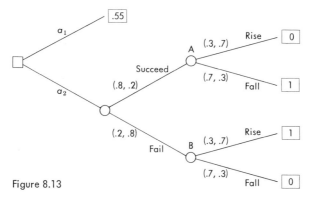

Figure 8.13

emphasize a point I shall shortly make.) Observe that member 1 would prefer a_2 because in his opinion this is equivalent to a (subjective) W-chance of $(.8 \times .7) + (.2 \times .3) = .62$. And, of course, .62 is larger than .55. Member 2 would feel the same for an analogous reason.

Now let's see what happens if the members try to compromise their differences at their basic levels of disagreement. First consider the deliberations that might take place at the last two forks of the a_2-branch. One argument goes as follows. The two members must reach an agreement at the $(a_2, \textit{Succeed})$-fork, [(A) in Fig. 8.13], where the first member thinks there is a .7 (subjective) chance at W and the second member thinks there is a .3 (subjective) chance at W. The situation has been so symmetrically designed that the obvious compromise is to *substitute* an objective .5 chance at W (in other words, a .5-BRLT) for this lottery. At the $(a_2, \textit{Fail})$-fork [(B) in Fig. 8.13], a similar situation prevails except that here the roles are reversed. Now we can work backwards. If we adopt these compromises and make these substitutions, we are led to the strategic situation presented in Fig. 8.14. Either the group can choose a_1 and get the .55-BRLT, or it can choose a_2 which, no matter what happens to the equipment, will lead to a stimulus that is equivalent, in the group's eyes, to a .5-BRLT. Obviously the group should choose a_1, in violation of Pareto optimality.

As a rebuttal to this, we might phrase a second argument in dialogue.

Member 1. Let's compromise at (A) of Fig. 8.13 by substituting a .60-BRLT.

Member 2. Why a .60-BRLT? You think the chance of W is .7 but I think it's .3. Why not substitute a .40-BRLT?

Member 1. Look, I'll tell you what. I feel more strongly about situation (A) and you feel more strongly about situation (B). I think (A) is much more likely to happen and you feel (B) is more likely.

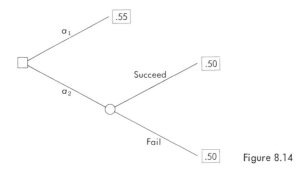

Figure 8.14

How about you giving in to me on the *Succeed* branch and I'll give in to you on the *Fail* branch?

Member 2. That's eminently reasonable. We'll substitute a .60-BRLT on the *Succeed* branch, which will please you, and a .60-BRLT on the *Fail* branch, which will please me. This lets us both have the better of the bargain. Great!

This dialogue leads to the strategic situation shown in Fig. 8.14, with the critical exceptions that .60-BRLT's have been substituted for .50-BRLT's and a_2 is now preferred to a_1, in conformity with the Pareto-optimality principle.

Let's summarize what has happened and generalize a bit, so that we can see the implications better. A group is confronted with a lottery of the form

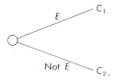

Now the group might feel that although some members prefer consequence C_1' to C_1, others feel differently, and if a group choice had to be made between C_1' and C_1 *in isolation* they would prefer C_1. Similarly they might feel the same way about C_2' and C_2. But a more complex bargain can be struck if the adherents of C_1' over C_1 believe event E is more likely than *Not E* and the adherents for C_2' over C_2 feel that *Not E* is more likely than E. In this case, each member of the group might feel happier if *both* C_1' and C_2' were respectively substituted for C_1 and C_2, even though the group would prefer C_1 to C_1' if C_2 were not in the picture, and would prefer C_2 to C_2' if C_1 were not in the picture. We can think of this procedure as a case of "internal logrolling". These considerations argue *against* the Substitution Principle for group behavior and, more importantly, *against* the Group Bayesian position as well.

I am persuaded by this argument but still I feel a bit uncomfortable. I feel that for some very cohesive groups composed of well-intentioned, responsible, idealistic members, this kind of internal logrolling is inappropriate; that somehow the group entity is more than the totality of its members.

What if the group gives up the Substitution Principle? Then we can no longer argue that the group should compromise separately on utilities and on probabilities and should maximize the joint expectation of their joint utility. However, since we are now thinking of the group merely as the totality of its members, we can proceed as we did earlier. That is, the ith individual of the group can use his own utilities and probabilities to obtain his own expected utility evaluation $\bar{u}_i(\sigma)$ for any strategy σ. If there are r members of the group, then with each strategy σ there is associated an r-tuple of evaluations $[\bar{u}_1(\sigma), \ldots, \bar{u}_i(\sigma), \ldots, \bar{u}_r(\sigma)]$, which is plotted as a point of some achievable region A. The group must then choose a "best point" in the region A. But this approach reduces the problem to the kind of problem already discussed in Section 5 under the heading *Choice of a Pareto-Optimal Point: The Bargaining Problem*. While this observation does not solve the group decision problem, it categorizes it in its proper niche.

REFERENCES ON THE GROUP DECISION PROBLEM

ARROW, KENNETH J., *Social Choice and Individual Values*, John Wiley and Sons, 1951.

———, "The Role of Securities in the Optimal Allocation of Risk Bearing", *Colloques Internationaux du Centre National de la Recherche Scientifique*, Vol. XL, 1953, pp. 41–48. Translated in the *Review of Economic Studies*, **31**(2), 86, April 1964, pp. 91–96.

BORCH, KARL, "Equilibrium in a Reinsurance Market", *Econometrica*, **30**, 3, July 1962, pp. 424–444.

BOWER, JOSEPH L., "The Role of Conflict in Economic Decision-Making Groups: Some Empirical Results", *The Quarterly Journal of Economics*, **79**, 2, May 1965, pp. 263–277.

CHRISTENSON, CHARLES, *Strategic Aspects of Competitive Bidding for Corporate Securities*, Division of Research, Harvard Business School, Boston, 1965.

EISENBERG, EDMUND, and DAVID GALE, "Consensus of Subjective Probabilities: The Pari-mutuel Method", *Annals of Mathematical Statistics*, **30**, 1, 1959, pp. 165–168.

LUCE, R. DUNCAN, and HOWARD RAIFFA, *Games and Decisions*, John Wiley and Sons, 1957, Chapter 14.

MADANSKY, ALBERT, "Externally Bayesian Groups", RM-4141-PR, The RAND Corporation, November 1964.

MARSCHAK, JACOB, "Elements for a Theory of Teams", *Management Science*, **1**, 1955, pp. 127–137.

RADNER, ROY, "Team Decision Problems", *Annals of Mathematical Statistics*, **33**, 3, September 1962, pp. 857–881.

THEIL, HENRI, "On the Symmetry Approach to the Committee Decision Problem," *Management Science*, **9**, 3, April 1963, pp. 380–393.

WILSON, ROBERT, "On the Theory of Syndicates", Working Paper No. 71R, Stanford University Graduate School of Business, July 1966. (Forthcoming in *Econometrica*.)

CHAPTER 9

THE ART
OF IMPLEMENTATION
AND A GENERAL CRITIQUE

1. INTRODUCTION

We have already described the four stages of analyzing a decision problem under uncertainty in the extensive form:

Stage 1. Exhibit the anatomy of the problem in terms of a decision-flow diagram or tree.

Stage 2. Evaluate the consequences in utility numbers.

Stage 3. Assign probabilities to the branches of chance forks.

Stage 4. Determine the optimal strategy by averaging out and folding back.

Unfortunately analyses of *real* problems are not quite so simple as artificial ones involving drawings from urns. Real problems are usually messy. In this chapter, we shall discuss the *art* rather than the *science* of analyzing real problems.

A complicated analysis does not proceed Stage 1, Stage 2, Stage 3, Stage 4, Finis! It is more of an iterative process, as we shall illustrate in Section 2. Trees that exhibit the structures of real problems have a nasty habit of getting rapidly out of hand—branches seem to proliferate everywhere, and the tree never seems to stop growing. Imagine having to assess probabilities for all those chance forks! In Section 2, we shall talk about ways to partly manage the seemingly unmanageable: how to choose a horizon close by; how to assess utilities for consequences at the tips of the tree that to some extent reflect the potential unfolding of the future; how to prune or eliminate branches as noncontenders; and how to elaborate or enrich a branch that we have described initially in rather coarse terms. Section 2 will also discuss the interplay between extensive and normal forms of analyses.

In many problems it is a gross oversimplification to summarize the consequence arising from a path through the tree in terms of a single numerical value such as money. Properly speaking, a typical consequence might be "almost adequately" described in terms of a set of scaled values. In a business context these values might be profit or loss, share of market, status of capital equipment, goodwill, experience of staff and ability to do the next job more efficiently, labor relations, prestige, and so forth. In a medical context these values might be dollars spent for doctors, for hospitalization, and for drugs; days spent in bed with symptoms A, B, or C; existence or nonexistence of complications X or Y, of death, or of contagion. Remember our task is not merely to describe consequences; if we want to employ the averaging-out-and-folding-back procedures at the fourth stage of analysis we must assign a utility value to each of these consequences. This calls for an assignment of a utility number to an array of scaled values that describes the consequence. The task is not a hopeless one, but neither is it as simple as in the problems treated in earlier chapters. This will be the subject matter of Section 3.

In Chapter 7, we discussed how one might assess a probability distribution for a single uncertain quantity. In that chapter we used as a facetious example the uncertain proportion p of doctors who consumed more scotch than bourbon in the past year. Alas, in real problems there is usually more than one uncertain quantity that plays a pivotal role in the analysis, and the decision maker and his experts are called upon to get a joint distribution of these uncertain quantities. Again, this is not hopeless, but neither is it easy. More about this in Section 4.

In Section 5, we shall briefly discuss such questions as these: Who is the decision maker? What is the role and responsibility of the analyst? How can one guard against selecting the wrong problem for analysis? How can one get the decision maker to take an active role in the analytical process? Is a decision analysis worth doing?

In Section 6 we tote up the ledger: What can be said about the methodology on the favorable side and on the unfavorable side?

2.   WHEN DOES A TREE BECOME A BUSHY MESS?

As a point of departure, let's reconsider the oil drilling problem mentioned in the introduction to these lectures and amplified a bit in the projects at the ends of Chapters 2 and 4. In this still simplified version, the wildcatter had a choice of whether or not to take seismic soundings (at a cost) and on the basis

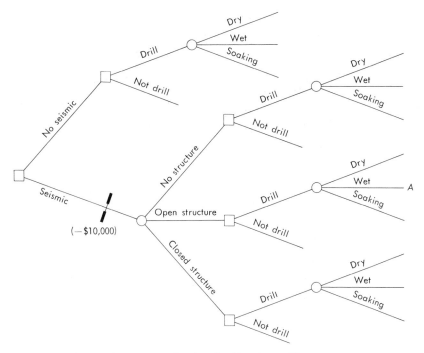

Fig. 9.1 The decision-flow diagram for the oil wildcatting problem.

of the information obtained to drill or not to drill. The decision tree is shown in Fig. 9.1.

Suppose the wildcatter looks at the path (*Seismic, Open Structure, Drill, Wet*) that leads to consequence *A*. Now at *A* he has paid out some money for seismic soundings and for drilling expenses and has obtained the information that the hole is *Wet*. How wet? Is the oil easily recoverable? How much did the drilling cost him? What will be the future prices of oil? Now that this oil well is a producer, how about sinking new development wells near this well? Given the information at *A*, how much should the wildcatter bid for the adjoining parcel of land, which is up for competitive bid? Perhaps the oil deposit will extend into that adjoining parcel, perhaps not. Should he develop this site alone or should he sell part of his rights to the *XYZ* corporation, which has great expertise in managing and developing proved wells? What part? $\frac{1}{4}$? $\frac{1}{2}$? $\frac{3}{4}$? What would he do with the money if he sold part of his rights? We could go on and on, getting more and more realistic and more and more complicated and making the analysis of the problem less and less tractable.

We can easily handle some of these considerations by adding in new branches at an existing fork. For example, instead of having a single *Wet* branch we could split it into (*Mildly wet, Just plain wet, Really wet*); and we could split *Mildly wet* into (*Mildly wet with a drilling cost of $50,000, of $60,000, . . . , of $90,000*). Similarly, instead of splitting the *Seismic* branch into only three branches, we might get more realism by splitting it into a dozen branches.

Even though we cannot conveniently accommodate certain other realistic complications we have mentioned by putting more branches into an existing fork, it is possible that we can accommodate them by inserting additional forks in the body of the tree or by adding new branching points at the tips of the tree. Thus, for example, we could put in a chance fork that describes the amount of oil, another fork that describes the economics of lifting the oil, and another that describes the price of oil next year, the year after, and so on. Life goes on after point *A* on the tree, and it is somewhat arbitrary to cut off the analysis at any specific horizon date. But the farther we look ahead and the more refined our analysis becomes, the more complex the tree becomes, and if we carry matters to an extreme the tree begins to resemble a gigantic bush. Remember the analysis requires us to assign probabilities to all chance branches and utilities to all consequences at the tips of the tree. What a brutal task!

In most realistic problems, in point of fact, one cannot possibly begin to chart out all the possible occurrences and choices far out into the foreseeable future. Compromises must be made; a touch of Art must be combined with Science.

Pruning of Branches

Here is one way in which the analyst might make his problem more manageable. The analyst first starts off with a rather crude and coarse description of the problem, with a cutoff horizon sufficiently close in. He makes crude assessments of utilities and probabilities, and on the basis of all these rather rough measures he determines whether or not he can eliminate or prune any branches at decision forks of the tree. At a decision fork there may be five choices, for example, and with a preliminary analysis it might be reasonably clear that the fourth branch, say, is a real noncontender. Before pruning branch four from the tree, the analyst might be prudent to give this branch the benefit of the doubt temporarily: He might purposely bias probability assessments and utilities in favor of branch four and see if it still remains a noncontender. If it does, the analyst should simply prune this branch. If the branch is close to the base of the tree, this could mean eliminating a sizable chunk of the tree. One might ask why the analyst included this branch in the first place, if he can eliminate it after so cursory an analysis? It is quite surprising how far a little systematic analysis goes. Actions that you initially think might be perfectly reasonable, viable, even important alternatives turn out to be ludicrous after a little systematic reflection.

Now as the analyst thins out the tree by pruning what branches he can, he can afford to take a harder look at the remainder. He refines his measurements; he embellishes certain forks by adding in more refined possibilities; he extends the horizon of his analysis. Then he prunes once more and repeats the cycle of embellishment, refinement, and horizon extension.

Use of the Normal Form

In Chapter 6, we contrasted the normal form of analysis with the extensive form. Recall that one begins normal-form analysis by listing all the conceivable strategies for experimentation and action, then evaluating each strategy conditional on each state of the world, and then averaging over these conditional evaluations by weighting the states according to their judgmental probabilities. You might have been left with the impression that this procedure is always cumbersome and involved; after all, there were 115 strategies, mostly inane ones, for the simple basic decision problem posed to you; it might have seemed to you that this procedure could never be used to analyze a real problem. This is not so. It is true that in a real problem the set S of *all* strategies might be monstrously large. However, by common sense or by some simple mathematical analysis or by both, it might be possible to find a reasonably small subset S_1 of S that is guaranteed to contain the best strategy, which the analyst is seeking. Then instead of searching through S, he needs only to search through S_1. But there are even more pragmatic approaches. The analyst may be able to isolate a really small subset S_2, say, which he feels confident from heuristic principles must contain some pretty good strategies, if not the best one, and he might be satisfied to search through S_2. True, he may not get the optimal strategy (where "optimal" ignores the cost of the analysis), but loosely speaking the best of S_2 might be optimal in a wider sense, the sense that also takes the cost and effort of analysis into account.

Sometimes it is practical to combine an extensive form of analysis with the modified kind of normal analysis we have just described. Let's consider a problem in which the effects of action taken in the present will linger on over a long period of time and in which it appears that a responsible analysis will involve a cutoff date far in the future, say 20 years. Let's suppose that a formal analysis of the entire problem in extensive form is hopelessly complex. We might compromise by choosing some horizon cutoff date, like five years out, and draw out the tree to that compromise horizon date. The trouble is that when we go to any tip A, say, of this artificially stunted tree, it is hard to assign a utility value to stimulus A because we are compelled to think what will happen after A; we are frustrated because we cannot work out the optimal path after A without getting completely bogged down. On the other hand, we might be able to assign a fairly reasonable value to A by using some nonoptimal but nevertheless reasonable procedure for evaluating the future emanating from A. For example, we might adopt a reasonable strategy of behavior for use after A, and agree on some educated guess for a value for A after simulating various future worlds. After treating all the tips of the truncated tree in a similar manner, we might then proceed to a more detailed extensive-form analysis on the truncated tree, working backwards from an epoch five years hence to the present. The point here is that although a rough-and-ready procedure may not be good enough to guide choice in the immediate future, this same procedure may be an adequate way to come to grips with the challenge of collapsing a far-off future back onto an immediate future; specifically, in this case, collapsing years 6 through 20 back onto an evaluation at the end of year 5.

Analysis without Utility Assessments

Some companies that regularly perform decision analyses of various investment problems are quite willing to assign judgmental probability distributions to all sorts of uncertain quantities, but they balk at the assignment of utilities. In such circumstances it is possible to structure a given problem as a decision-flow diagram, to assign probabilities at all chance forks, and to evaluate the monetary implications of any path through the tree. Typically, when there is a monetary flow over time, these companies use some sort of discounting principle to get a present-value monetary figure for each path through the tree. But since they do not think it appropriate to use expected monetary values and since they are reluctant to assign utilities to monetary consequences, they cannot average out and fold back in a formal manner; they prefer to revert to a modification of the normal form of analysis. In some *ad hoc*, informal manner, they choose a set of plausible strategies, say $\sigma^{(1)}, \sigma^{(2)}, \ldots, \sigma^{(10)}$—the number is not important but it is more likely to be 5 or 10 rather than 100 or 1000—and for each strategy they generate a probability distribution of possible monetary returns. For example, strategy $\sigma^{(1)}$ might give a distribution like the one shown in Fig. 9.2. The probability that $\sigma^{(1)}$ will yield a monetary return between a and b is the area under the curve between a and b. We assume that the vertical scale is such that the total area under the curve is unity. Let's refer to this curve as the *payoff density curve** of strategy $\sigma^{(1)}$.

---

* Very often this curve is generated by a process of simulation that involves a sampling of the totality of paths that could occur with $\sigma^{(1)}$.

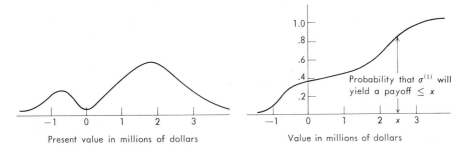

Fig. 9.2 The payoff density curve for strategy $\sigma^{(1)}$.

Fig. 9.3 The payoff cumulative curve for strategy $\sigma^{(1)}$.

Each strategy has an associated payoff density curve, and a choice among strategies boils down to a choice among their associated curves. This is the kind of problem of risky choice we considered at length in Chapter 4, and there we handled the analysis in terms of BRLT's or utilities. Sometimes we can side-step a full-blown utility analysis by observing that one curve is clearly better than the others.

In comparing two payoff density curves for a given project, it is helpful to reexpress these as cumulative curves rather than as density curves. For example, the cumulative version of the curve shown in Fig. 9.2 appears in Fig. 9.3. For any x-value on the horizontal axis, the cumulative curve gives the probability that the strategy $\sigma^{(1)}$ will result in a monetary evaluation of at most x. Note that the steep portions of the cumulative curve correspond to local maxima of the density curve. Incidentally, it is quite common for a strategy to exhibit two local maxima, as happens in Fig. 9.2: The left hump is relevant if the project has to be abandoned at a crucial juncture because the initial experience with the project is discouraging, and the right hump is relevant if the project is not abandoned.

If one payoff cumulative curve A is to the right of another payoff cumulative curve B in the sense indicated by Fig. 9.4(a), then we say that the strategy leading to A *probabilistically dominates* the strategy leading to B, and if we wish

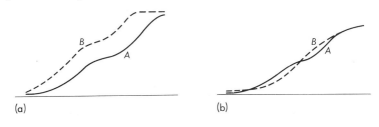

(a)   (b)

Figure 9.4

we can delete the latter strategy as a noncontender. However, if curves A and B cross in the sense indicated by Fig. 9.4(b), then we cannot summarily rule out one of the two strategies. Here one must make a more subtle analysis of this situation; it is in such circumstances as these that the theory of utility has its real payoff. If one introduces a utility-for-money curve, transforms money amounts to utility amounts, and computes expected utility values, then no matter what the utility curve looks like, strategy A in Fig. 9.4(a) will have a higher expected utility value than strategy B. It is not possible to say whether A is better than B from Fig. 9.4(b) unless one has some detailed knowledge of the decision maker's utility-for-money curve.

3. THE MULTIATTRIBUTE PROBLEM

When we introduced utility theory in Chapter 4, we considered the case in which the consequences (of acts) were as general as possible and we listed these as $C_1, C_2, \ldots, C_n$. The consequence C_i might, for example, be best described by a page (or by a book) of prose describing the full set of implications this consequence has for the decision maker. We did not assume that the consequence C_i could be scaled or characterized by one or by any number of numerical quantities. We did, however, assume that there are two reference consequences L and W such that for any consequence C_i,

1) $L \leq C_i \leq W$,

where $\leq$ is read "is less preferred than or indifferent to", and

2) there is some number $\pi(C_i)$ between 0 and 1 such that the decision maker is indifferent between getting C_i outright and getting a basic reference lottery ticket that gives W with probability $\pi(C_i)$ and L otherwise. We said precious little about how one could systematically probe one's tastes, values, and attitudes to come up with these numbers $\pi(C_1), \ldots, \pi(C_n)$.

Following the presentation of the general theory of (probabilistic) utility, we then turned to the case in which each consequence could be scaled in terms of a single numerical value, and for the sake of concreteness we focused on the case in which this value is a cash flow or monetary asset position. Letting the typical value be x, we then discussed the assessment of a utility function u as a function of the single real variable x. Instead of directly assessing a u-value for each of 1000 values $x_1, \ldots, x_{1000}$, for example, we tried to exploit the general structure of u, its smoothness, monotonicity, concavity, and decreasing risk aversion, and to make a few meaningful assessments from which the u-curve could be fitted. It is desirable to emphasize once again that the underlying units of x do not have to be money; they can be cures, or hours worked, or millions of cubic feet of gas reserves, or any other single index that captures the essence of the consequences under consideration.

In most applications it is not easy to summarize the essentials of a consequence by means of a single numerical quantity, but it is frequently possible to associate with each consequence C a sequence of numbers $[x_1(C), x_2(C), \ldots, x_r(C)]$ that for all practical purposes satisfactorily summarizes all the relevant information about C. We can interpret the number $x_i(C)$ as the *index*, *level*, or *score* of C on the ith criterion or attribute. In a business context, attribute 1 might be a cash amount, attribute 2 a share of the market, attribute 3 an index of good will, and so forth. In a medical context, attribute 1 might be cost of treatment, attribute 2 the number of days of extreme discomfort, attribute 3 the number of days for recuperation with bedrest, attribute 4 the probability of a relapse after the cutoff date of the analysis, and so forth. In another context, $x_i(C)$ might refer to individual i's personal evaluation of consequence C and an administrator or a benevolent dictator might wish to consider evaluations of others in his own utility function. In still another context, x_i might denote the net cash flow in period i; then the set of numbers would depict the cash flow, or perhaps the consumption flow, over time.

We shall now develop some techniques that can help a decision maker think systematically about assessing a utility function over an r-tuple of numbers $(x_1, \ldots, x_r)$. Keep in mind that if x' and x'' are two such r-tuples (hereafter called "points"), then not only is it true that u must reflect ordinal preferences (that is, the better the r-tuple, the higher its associated utility number), but it is also true that the utility of the lottery that gives a p_i chance at $x^{(i)}$, where $x^{(i)}$ is short for $[x_1(C_i), \ldots, x_r(C_i)]$, must be

$$p_1 u(x^{(1)}) + p_2 u(x^{(2)}) + \cdots + p_n u(x^{(n)}).$$

It will be easier if we generalize from the case of a single numerical value to a pair of numerical values and then go on to the case of r numerical values. To avoid subscripts in this section, we shall let the typical point be (x, y) instead of (x_1, x_2). For concreteness' sake, let us also assume that preferences are to the northeast in the xy-plane; that is, that both x and y represent values of desirable commodities.

Constant Substitution

Suppose the isopreference curves in the xy-plane are parallel straight lines, as in Fig. 9.5. In this case there is some substitution rate λ, say, such that a

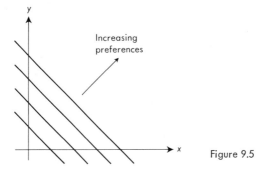

Figure 9.5

decrement of a unit of y is equivalent to an increment of λ units of x. Hence the point (x, y) is indifferent to the point $(x + \lambda y, 0)$. [Alternatively we could say that (x, y) is indifferent to $(0, y + x/\lambda)$.] Thus we can summarize the (x, y)-point by the single numerical value $x + \lambda y$.

Now let's consider the lottery in Fig. 9.6, where one obtains C_i with probability p_i, and assume that we can summarize C_i by the pair (x_i, y_i). By the Substitution Principle we can replace (x_i, y_i) by $(x_i + \lambda y_i, 0)$, and by convention let us agree to abbreviate $(x_i + \lambda y_i, 0)$ as $x_i + \lambda y_i$, keeping in mind that the suppressed second component is zero. Finally we can assess a utility index u_i for the single value $x_i + \lambda y_i$. As an example, let (x, y) be the amounts of cash that flow in periods 1 and 2, respectively. A decision maker may decide that he is indifferent between (x, y) and $(x + \lambda y, 0)$ or $(0, y + x/\lambda)$, perhaps because he can reinvest the money from period 1 to produce more money tomorrow, or because he finds consumption today sweeter than consumption tomorrow. Here we can think of λ as the (subjective) effective discount rate. It is now a matter of convenience whether we choose the discounted value $x + \lambda y$ or the accumulated value $y + x/\lambda$ as the basic numerical index.

In this example it seems natural to push one of the two components to zero. However, it may be more meaningful in some circumstances to choose a value

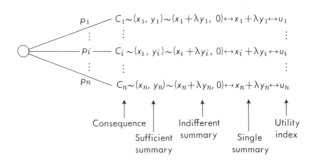

Figure 9.6

y^*, say, and use the result that

(x_i, y_i) is indifferent to (x_i^*, y^*) for all i,

where

$$x_i^* = x_i + \lambda(y_i - y^*).$$

Now when we consider putting a utility value on the scalar quantity x_i^* (for $i = 1, \ldots n$), we must keep in mind that the second component has the constant value y^* for each of the n consequences.

Variable Substitution

In general, isopreference curves in the xy-plane are not parallel straight lines. The substitution rate between a unit of y and x generally depends on the levels of both x and y. If we have an indifference map (and this is a big *if*) (see Fig. 9.7), then we can proceed almost as before. We could first choose a value y^*, say; second, for each (x_i, y_i)-pair, we could find the point on the same indifference curve of the form (x_i^*, y^*) where the second component is the same for all i; third, we could proceed to consider the single numerical quantity x_i^*; and finally, keeping the value of y^* in mind, we could associate a utility with each of the x_i^*.

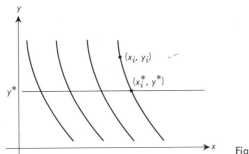

Figure 9.7

If we have a "reasonable" number of different (x_i, y_i) to consider, we may choose not to get the full indifference map. Indeed, all we want to get is the point (x_i^*, y^*) that is (subjectively) indifferent to the point (x_i, y_i). A judicious choice of y^* will often make these subjective indifference assessments easier to work with. Sometimes it is easiest to choose y^* as the minimum or maximum of the y_i; at other times we might choose the y^* as some natural focal point near the median of the y_i. Of course, we could have chosen an x^* instead of y^* and scaled (x_i, y_i) into (x^*, y_i^*). One must be sensibly imaginative in choosing the most convenient reduction procedure.

We can easily and most helpfully generalize the technique described in this section. A firm may be primarily interested in profitability, for example, but usually it must entertain a host of other considerations as well: orderly labor relations, its public image to stockholders and to peer groups, share of the market, nonmonetary selfish interests of the management elite, and so forth. We might find that we can choose a "base state" y^* that describes a typical profile of these second-order characteristics. Now we can readily think of consequence C_i as giving rise to an evaluation (x_i, y_i), where y_i is a conglomerate stimulus that describes everything except monetary direct profits. The trick of the game is now to find the particular value x_i^* such that (x_i, y_i) is indifferent to (x_i^*, y^*), where once again the second component does not depend on i. If y_i is less desirable than y^*, then we are asking this question: "Imagine you are at (x_i, y_i); exactly how much would you be willing to decrease x_i, if y_i were to be changed to the base state y^*?" Certainly this question should not be answered by a snap judgment; the answer may require considerable soul searching and the analysis may involve a good deal of data gathering and number pushing. However, once we have scaled (x_i, y_i) in terms of (x_i^*, y^*), we can proceed as before.

Examples from Medical Treatment

Recent years have seen several exploratory decision analyses of medical treatment problems, ranging from the treatment of the common sore throat to surgical treatments of duodenal ulcers.† None of these analyses was meant to be definitive. In each case the analysts ignored certain branches of the decision tree because they would only have complicated matters and would not have contributed to an understanding of the methodological issues that arise with this approach. The probability assignments at chance forks were only roughly

---

† Dr. J. Polissar, after receiving his M.D. degree, continued working for a Ph.D. degree in Operations Research at Harvard. As part of a course he wrote a term paper called "Treatment of the Common Sore Throat". Ronald Rubel, a doctoral student of mine at the Harvard Business School, considerably amplified Polissar's treatment and completed a thesis called "Decision Analysis in Medical Diagnosis and Treatment". Rubel worked on the problem of renal hypertension as well. Mr. Lewinnek, a senior medical student at Harvard, delivered a paper at the Boylston Society on the surgical treatment of duodenal ulcers and asymptomatic gallstones. Dr. R. Greenes, another M.D. who is studying for his Ph.D., wrote a paper for me called "Diagnosis and Treatment of a Gastric Ulcer". (Rubel's thesis can be obtained through interlibrary loans, but the other papers are not available for distribution.)

assessed, and these numbers were not meant to be taken very seriously. In pilot studies of this kind, however, these inadequacies are not serious stumbling blocks; one could easily draw more comprehensive trees that would capture the essence of the problem, and convene a panel of experts to study published statistical results and assess responsible probabilities at chance forks. In each of these studies, the weakest link in the chain of the analysis turned out to be the treatment of the utility structure. I should now like to look at this problem more closely.

One might effectively summarize a typical consequence at the end of a branch in any one of these studies by a 7-tuple $(x_1, x_2, \ldots, x_7)$, where

x_1 = amount of money spent for treatment, drugs, and so forth,

x_2 = number of days in bed with a *high* index of discomfort,

x_3 = number of days in bed with a *medium* index of discomfort,

x_4 = number of days in bed with a *low* index of discomfort,

$$x_5 = \begin{cases} 1, \\ 0, \end{cases} \text{if complication } A \begin{cases} \text{occurs,} \\ \text{does not occur,} \end{cases}$$

$$x_6 = \begin{cases} 1, \\ 0, \end{cases} \text{if complication } B \begin{cases} \text{occurs,} \\ \text{does not occur,} \end{cases}$$

$$x_7 = \begin{cases} 1, \\ 0, \end{cases} \text{if complication } C \begin{cases} \text{occurs,} \\ \text{does not occur.} \end{cases}$$

In the sore-throat case, complication A might be death by shock caused by a reaction to a penicillin injection, B might be rheumatic fever, C might be glomerulonephritis (a *very* serious kidney disorder). The task is to assess a utility function over the 7-tuple $x = (x_1, \ldots, x_7)$.

It will simplify the presentation if we put all the awesome complications at the end of the tree. Therefore let's group together all points with a common (x_1, x_2, x_3, x_4)-history; these points are

$(x_1, x_2, x_3, x_4, 0, 0, 0),$

$(x_1, x_2, x_3, x_4, 1, 0, 0),$

$(x_1, x_2, x_3, x_4, 0, 1, 0),$

$(x_1, x_2, x_3, x_4, 0, 0, 1).$

(We are assuming that there are no double or triple complications.) These are displayed on branches of the chance fork Z in Fig. 9.8. We summarize the

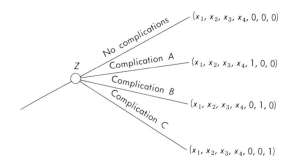

Figure 9.8

entire chance move at Z by the generalized 7-tuple

$$(x_1, x_2, x_3, x_4, p_A, p_B, p_C),$$

where p_A, p_B, and p_C are the conditional probabilities of the awesome complications A, B, and C, respectively, at that particular fork of the tree. It is reasonable to make these assumptions:

1) The trade-offs between x_1, x_2, x_3, and x_4 do not depend on the particular values of p_A, p_B, and p_C.

2) The trade-offs between p_A, p_B, and p_C do not depend on the particular values of x_1, x_2, x_3, and x_4.

In other words, the index sets $\{1, 2, 3, 4\}$ and $\{5, 6, 7\}$ are externally independent in the sense that the trade-offs between components of one set do not depend on the values in the other set.

Now let's think hard about the 4-tuple (x_1, x_2, x_3, x_4) and try to summarize this 4-tuple in terms of a single numerical index, let's say in terms of equivalent days in bed with medium discomfort (a discomfort level described by $100°$ fever, headache, general weakness, slight nausea, and little specific pain). We could go through three successive reductions:

$$(x_1, x_2, x_3, x_4) \rightarrow (x_1, 0, x_3', x_4) \rightarrow (x_1, 0, x_3'', 0) \rightarrow (0, 0, x_3''', 0).$$

For example, for the first reduction we must ask, "Keeping x_1 and x_4 fixed, if x_2 is reduced to zero, how should we change x_3 so that the modified 4-tuple is indifferent† to the original 4-tuple?" These successive reductions are not easy to do, but nevertheless it is possible to think about them in a responsible, systematic, and meaningful way. Once we have made these reductions, we can summarize the resulting special 4-tuple, with three zeroes, by the single

---

† The value of x_3' might, of course, depend on the particular values of x_1 and x_4 as well as on x_2.

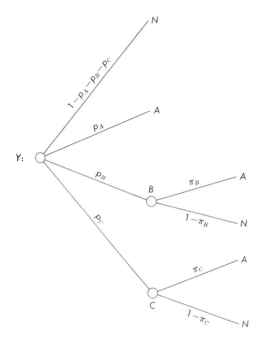

Figure 9.9

numerical value x_3''. For convenience, let's set the other components x_1, x_2, and x_4 equal to zero and drop the subscript and primes from x_3'', and simply let x represent the pseudoequivalent days in bed with medium discomfort.

Now let's think hard about the 3-tuple (p_A, p_B, p_C) and try to summarize this 3-tuple in terms of a single numerical value, let's say in terms of a pseudo-equivalent probability of death. Let N represent *No complications* and assume that our preferences go

$$A \prec B \prec C \prec N.$$

The stimulus (p_A, p_B, p_C) represents the chance fork Y in Fig. 9.9. Now for consequences B and C let us substitute equilibrating lotteries having A and N as reference payoffs. Suppose that if the patient had complication B he would just be willing to risk a π_B-chance at A to get a $(1 - \pi_B)$-chance at N. Similarly for C replacing B. For these assessments the stimulus (p_A, p_B, p_C) would be indifferent to a

$$(p_A + \pi_B p_B + \pi_C p_C)\text{-chance}$$

at A and a zero chance at B or C; see Fig. 9.9. In symbols,

$$(p_A, p_B, p_C) \sim (p_A + \pi_B p_B + \pi_C p_C, 0, 0).$$

We now can summarize this last special 3-tuple, with two zeros, by the single numerical value

$$y = p_A + \pi_B p_B + \pi_C p_C.$$

For convenience, let's set the probabilities of complication B and C equal to zero and interpret the remaining y as the pseudoequivalent probability of complication A.

We have now reduced the 7-tuple $(x_1, \ldots, x_7)$ to the pair (x, y), where x is the pseudoequivalent days in bed and y is the pseudoequivalent probability of complication A. Now comes the hardest part—not that the other assessments were easy: How can we assess a utility function on (x, y)-pairs?

Slight Digression. There are those who would argue that there is no change in x that could compensate for an increase in y. After all, a few days more or less in bed does not mean very much when we are comparing it with a change in the probability of death. Those who feel this way suggest that (x, y)-pairs should be ranked only by the y-component and that the x-component should be taken into consideration only if there are ties on the y-component. I don't think this is correct, and to argue my point I should go to an extreme case: Would you spend a year in bed to decrease your chance of death from .000008 to .000007? If so, then just increase the time in bed and add a few more zeros to the probabilities until you switch.

The problem of finding substitution rates between x and y leads us to such questions as "How many additional days in bed would you be willing to spend to reduce the probability of death from .001, say, to zero?" Or, if the first component refers to monetary assets, the question might be "What proportion of your present assets are you willing to exchange to reduce the probability of death from .001, say, to zero?" These are difficult questions to answer— some would say they are impossible to answer responsibly—and it would be nice if we somehow could skirt the issue. We could try to do this by a *sensitivity* analysis, which might go as follows. Suppose that the isopreference curves in the xy-plane are parallel straight lines. (If they are not, then we still might be able to straighten out the curves by transforming the x-coordinate appropriately; but this gets us into intricacies beyond the level of these elementary lectures.) Let λ be defined as the substitution rate between x and y; that is, for any Δ, let

$$(x + \lambda\Delta, y - \Delta) \sim (x, y).$$

Instead of trying to determine λ, we might keep this troublesome quantity in algebraic form for a while and determine a conditional strategy such as this: If λ is in the interval from zero to λ_1, then strategy σ' is best; if λ is in the interval from λ_1 to λ_2, then σ'' is best; if λ is greater than λ_2, then σ''' is best. Perhaps this would suffice to solve the problem. Another tack is to investigate how individuals actually behave in such situations and to ascribe a value to λ based on their revealed preferences. How much are people willing to pay for seat belts, for safer tires, for fire protection, and so forth? I am skeptical about this approach, partly because the data usually come from people who have not done any informed analyses; if they were to do so, their aggregate behavior might change drastically. Most of my economist colleagues, however, do not agree with me.

Schelling has treated these vexing measurement issues extensively and I take leave of this subject by referring you to his detailed treatment.* His intriguing paper also provides a guide to the further literature on the "value of a life".

During this argument you have perhaps wondered about who is supposed to be the decision maker in these medical problems. Is it the doctor or the patient? I should think that in most situations the decision maker is the doctor, but ideally the doctor should still be responsive to the fundamental preferences of his patient. Now I certainly don't suggest asking a miserable, feverish, apprehensive patient who has a severely inflamed sore throat whether he would rather stay in bed for an extra couple of days to reduce the chance of rheumatic fever from .007 to .006. That would be silly indeed. However, it might not be unreasonable for medical researchers to investigate how a sample of individuals feel about certain critical trade-offs. Then, on the basis of these sampled responses and on a detailed decision analysis of a given medical problem, these researchers might convey their qualitative findings to the general practitioner in articles, lectures, textbooks, and so forth.

REFERENCES ON THE MULTIATTRIBUTE PROBLEM

ACKOFF, R. L., in collaboration with S. K. Gupta and J. S. Minas, *Scientific Method: Optimizing Applied Research Decisions*, Wiley, 1962, Chapters 2 and 3.

FISHBURN, PETER C., "Independence in Utility Theory with Whole Product Sets", *Operations Research*, Jan.–Feb., 1965.

MILLER, J. R., III, "The Assessment of Worth: A Systematic Procedure and Its Experimental Validation", doctoral dissertation, M.I.T., June, 1966.

---

* Schelling, Thomas, "The Life You Save May Be Your Own", in Samuel B. Chase, Jr., (Ed.), *Problems in Public Expenditure Analysis*, Brookings Institution, 1968.

4.   ASSESSMENTS OF SEVERAL UNCERTAIN QUANTITIES

In Chapter 7, we considered one special procedure for assessing a probability distribution for a single uncertain quantity. The particular uncertain quantity we chose for illustrative purposes was the proportion p of doctors who consume more scotch than bourbon. There are other procedures for assessing probability distributions, and although it might be interesting to engage in a technical empirical discussion of the comparative merits of these procedures, for the sake of brevity we shall forego this luxury. However, in this section we must consider a fairly typical situation where the decision maker and his experts are called on to get a joint probability assessment of several uncertain quantities.

An Example Involving Several Uncertain Quantities

As a concrete example, consider a large chemical company that has done basic research on a new synthetic leather product. Imagine that the really basic physics, chemistry, and engineering of the new process are reasonably well understood and that the investigation has passed from the basic or pure research stage to the so-called development stage. If all goes according to plan, the company will commercialize some new synthetic leather products anywhere from one to three years hence. The management must decide a whole range of issues: product types, production procedures, marketing channels, patent rights, plant capacities, factory and warehouse locations, pricing, advertising and promotion, test markets, organizational control, and so on. The problem may involve many uncertain quantities running the gamut from the uncertain costs of raw materials to the uncertain demand for a specific product. The purchaser of raw materials might know a great deal about the future uncertain prices of these raw materials, but he may know next to nothing about the uncertain demand for a particular product marketed at a particular price and given level of promotional activity. To make matters even more complicated, the uncertain acquisition costs of raw materials may be related to the uncertain final demand because both may depend to some extent on the general level of business activity.

Let's be even more concrete and suppose that there are 30 uncertain quantities that play some role in the deliberations. Not all these uncertain quantities are of equal importance—some are critical, others less so; some are wildly uncertain, others almost certain. Suppose that a preliminary sensitivity analysis shows that 15 of these uncertain quantities are of second-order importance. To make the problem more manageable, the analyst might for the time being decide to treat these uncertain quantities *as if* they were certain and assign some rough figure to each. In a later and more sophisticated iteration of the analysis, he would scrutinize some of these uncertain quantities more closely and give them a rough probabilistic treatment. Of the remaining 15 uncertainties which he does not dispense with in such a cavalier manner, there may be five that are relatively independent of the rest and for which he can easily assess their probability distributions using readily available, historical, relative-frequency data. He is now down to ten uncertainties still needing consideration. Suppose that he can assess another five by conducting standard statistical experiments and surveys. To be sure, there is a question of how much experimenting or sampling he should do and this can be answered rigorously only in the context of the action problem. However, analysts necessarily make all sorts of compromises in messy problems, so let's assume that somehow or other, by some scheme of rough-and-ready calculations, he has devised and carried out a statistical design for information gathering that allows him to make the relevant assessments. I might mention that these statistical experiments are often done in stages, with revision and refinement, and the results needn't be so arbitrary as you might think.

Now let's consider the five remaining uncertain quantities. Although one may find some objective data that bear on these uncertainties, these data may be only tangentially related. Furthermore, the analyst may suspect that the data so gathered will be seriously biased; or perhaps the only relevant experiments are much too time-consuming or too costly to be feasible. The point, in short, is that we shall assume that for the five remaining uncertain quantities there is no objective way out. True, there is information, but it just is not quite the right kind to enable the analysts to assess objectively probability distributions for these remaining uncertain quantities. Still, *if decisions have to be made* and if these uncertain quantities are critical, it may be desirable to elicit subjectively assessed probability distributions from the decision makers and their experts. This procedure calls on the human mind, so to speak, to synthesize disparate pieces of objective data and to codify these in articulated judgments. Of course these judgments may be wrong, but what is the alternative? A few remarks about subjective assessments of probability distributions for several uncertain quantities are now in order.

Independence of Uncertain Quantities

Let $\tilde{x}$ and $\tilde{y}$ be two uncertain quantities,* where $\tilde{x}$, for example is the marginal cost of producing part XYZ at a projected volume of 1000 items per day,

---

* A tilde $\sim$ above a letter designates that the quantity represented by the letter is uncertain.

not taking into account raw materials acquisitions, and $\tilde{y}$ is the proportion of distributors who initially agree to carry consumer product PQ. The uncertain quantities $\tilde{x}$ and $\tilde{y}$ are judgmentally independent if knowledge of one does not change judgments about the other. For measurement purposes, this is a happy state of affairs; if $\tilde{x}$ and $\tilde{y}$ are judgmentally independent, then the analyst can assess the distribution of $\tilde{x}$ without worrying about $\tilde{y}$, and the distribution of $\tilde{y}$ without worrying about $\tilde{x}$. Furthermore, in this case, the production manager could assess $\tilde{x}$ and the marketing manager could assess $\tilde{y}$. With independence, it is easy to decompose the joint evaluation into two noninteracting evaluations; and it is this type of decomposition that makes messy problems tractable.

Independence of Subsets of Uncertain Quantities

Suppose that we have five uncertain quantities $\tilde{x}_1$, $\tilde{x}_2$, $\tilde{x}_3$, $\tilde{x}_4$, and $\tilde{x}_5$ and that we are in the unfortunate but realistic position in which knowledge of any four may affect the analyst's judgments about the fifth. Then we cannot say that these uncertain quantities are judgmentally independent. However, there are cruder possible decompositions. For example, it may be possible to partition the five uncertain quantities into two groups $\{\tilde{x}_1, \tilde{x}_2, \tilde{x}_3\}$ and $\{\tilde{x}_4, \tilde{x}_5\}$ such that full knowledge of the values of the uncertain quantities in one group does not affect the judgments about the uncertain quantities in the other. Here we can say that the two groups are judgmentally independent, and we can decompose the overall assessment problem into two simpler noninteracting assessment problems.

Transformations to Achieve Independence

Suppose the analysis calls for the assessment of a judgmental distribution of $\tilde{x}_1$ and $\tilde{x}_2$ where these uncertain quantities are not judgmentally independent. As an example, suppose $\tilde{x}_1$ and $\tilde{x}_2$ are next period's uncertain sales in two adjoining sales areas. The marketing expert might be able to think comfortably about two related uncertain quantities that he feels are judgmentally independent. Thus, for instance, he might feel that the average sales $(\tilde{x}_1 + \tilde{x}_2)/2$ and the difference between sales $(\tilde{x}_2 - \tilde{x}_1)$ are judgmentally independent. (Instead of considering $\tilde{x}_2 - \tilde{x}_1$, he might prefer to think of

$$\frac{\tilde{x}_2 - \tilde{x}_1}{(\tilde{x}_1 + \tilde{x}_2)/2},$$

which is the difference expressed as a proportion of the average sales.) If the analyst has the assessed distributions of these two judgmentally independent, new, auxiliary uncertain quantities, he can get the joint distribution of $\tilde{x}_1$ and

$\bar{x}_2$ by following a simple technical procedure. Unfortunately, we don't have time for details in these lectures. We can generalize and say that it is sometimes possible to circumvent the problem of judgmental dependence by concocting meaningful, auxiliary, mathematically related quantities that are judgmentally independent. This is one of the tricks of the trade.

Indirect Assessments

My last remark raises another point, one that we have touched on repeatedly throughout these lectures but one that we should emphasize once again. If the decision analysis calls for assessments of $\bar{x}_1, \ldots, \bar{x}_5$, say, this does not necessarily imply that we must assess these uncertain quantities directly. It might be more appropriate to assess other quantities that are algebraically related to the quantities of basic interest and to employ mathematical techniques to generate the distributions we need. This point is similar to one we have already discussed, when we had to assess probabilities for chance forks on the e_1-branch of your basic decision problem. Recall that at the second fork you had to assess the probablity of red, $P(R)$, and then the posterior probability of θ_1 given R, $P(\theta_1|R)$, at the fourth fork. Your information was such that you were actually given $P(R|\theta_1)$ and $P(R|\theta_2)$. If you then assessed a probability $P(\theta_1)$ for θ_1 (in the version in Chapter 5 this requires a judgmental assessment), it was then routine for you to *calculate* the needed values of $P(R)$ and $P(\theta_1|R)$. The important point to observe is that we often must manipulate the uncertain quantities in our problems to exploit the natural information we already have.

Explanatory Variables

Suppose a gasoline company wants to assess a distribution for the uncertain amount $\bar{x}$ of gasoline that will be pumped in the first year at a new gasoline station located next to a superhighway that has just opened for general traffic. Some local representative of the company could assess a distribution for $\bar{x}$ directly, but it might be more appropriate to get this assessment via an indirect route. One of the critical factors determining the amount of gasoline to be pumped is the uncertain density $\bar{y}$ of traffic that will flow over the new road. Instead of thinking informally about $\bar{y}$ when assigning a distribution to $\bar{x}$, the company might find it more satisfying to formalize this procedure. They could first conduct a study to determine a distribution for $\bar{y}$ and then establish the bridge to $\bar{x}$ by assessing the conditional distribution of $\bar{x}$, given different assumed values for $\bar{y}$. Again, this is not the place to go into details, but we clearly can think of $\bar{y}$ under such circumstances as an *explanatory* variable that helps to explicate $\bar{x}$.

The company's local representative, then, who could have directly assessed $\tilde{x}$, may not be the appropriate person to assess $\tilde{y}$. In fact it may be desirable to get an outside consulting firm to build a model of traffic flow that would help the company assess a distribution for $\tilde{y}$. In this case, incidentally, the consulting firm would be able to fulfill its obligation without getting confidential information from its client. Furthermore, unlike the company's representative, the consulting firm would not be liable to a conflict of interest. The representative might either consciously or unconsciously bias his responses to favor higher x-values, to make the deal appear more favorable. Or he might bias his responses downwards so that he will have an easy target rate to beat. He could still bias his responses if he is asked to assess conditional distributions of $\tilde{x}$ for different assumed values of $\tilde{y}$ but now he does not have so much freedom to fool himself or his superior.

Note. I personally was involved in a study dealing with the introduction of a new product into a Latin-American country. The assessments were made considerably more meaningful by introducing the uncertain inflation rate $\tilde{y}$ as an explanatory variable. An economics professor and some of his graduate students were then employed to build an econometric model to obtain a responsible assessment of $\tilde{y}$. Experts within the company then assessed the distribution of an $\tilde{x}$-variable for different values of $\tilde{y}$.

Conditional Independence

Let's suppose that the uncertain quantities $\tilde{x}_1, \tilde{x}_2, \ldots, \tilde{x}_5$ are judgmentally dependent because each depends to a varying degree on an underlying, explanatory, uncertain quantity $\tilde{y}$, e.g., the quarter's business activity. However, let it be true that the uncertain quantities $\tilde{x}_1, \ldots, \tilde{x}_5$ are judgmentally independent, conditional on $\tilde{y}$'s taking any specific assumed value, y_0 say. We now can go to five separate experts and have each of them assess the distribution of that uncertain quantity $\tilde{x}$ with which he is most familiar, conditional on $\tilde{y}$ taking on the value y_0, the value y_1, the value y_2, and so on. Next we can get an entirely different expert to assess the distribution of the explanatory uncertain quantity $\tilde{y}$. Of course it goes without saying (but I'll say it anyway) that some of these experts may be a single individual wearing different hats.

Hierarchical Structures

Another generalization will carry us a step further toward a hierarchical system of explanation. The uncertain quantities $\tilde{x}_1, \ldots, \tilde{x}_5$ may be judgmentally dependent, and try as we might we may not be able to introduce a known meaningful explanatory uncertain quantity $\tilde{y}$ that renders the various $\tilde{x}$ independent. We may, however, be able to introduce *two* explanatory variables $\tilde{y}_1$ and $\tilde{y}_2$ (for example, business activity and new housing starts) that do this job: If we assume values for $\tilde{y}_1$ and $\tilde{y}_2$, then we can view the uncertain quantities $\tilde{x}_1, \ldots, \tilde{x}_5$ as judgmentally, conditionally independent and thereby assess them. Next we must turn our attention to the joint assessment of $\tilde{y}_1$ and $\tilde{y}_2$. If these are independent, fine; if not, we may find algebraic combinations that are independent, or perhaps we can be ingenious enough to introduce a new meaningful explanatory variable $\tilde{z}$ that renders $\tilde{y}_1$ and $\tilde{y}_2$ conditionally independent. And so it goes. A little science and a bag of tricks.

One might use hierarchical techniques to select an investment portfolio. An investment analyst would want to assess the joint distribution of the market prices of various securities at the end of an investment period (say six months), and this should include any appreciation in the value of the stocks as well as dividends. On the basis of this joint assessment he would select the portfolio that is "best", in the sense of maximizing expected utility. There are so many available securities that direct assessment of their joint distribution is not feasible.

Let the uncertain value of the ith investment (per dollar invested) be $\tilde{x}_i$. (Typically the range of i can go into the hundreds or thousands.) It is possible for an analyst to use common sense or statistical analysis to group stocks into homogeneous classes, such as the railroads, the airlines, electrical utilities, and so on. For the jth homogeneous class, the analyst can concoct an index $\tilde{y}_j$ that describes the overall performance of stocks in this class. (Typically j might range up to twenty or thirty.) Given knowledge of $\tilde{y}_j$, he might reasonably assume that the uncertain future prices of the stocks that comprise the jth homogeneous category are conditionally independent. Now in assessing the joint distribution of the $\tilde{y}_j$, it may be worthwhile for him to take another step. Knowledge of a few summary indices such as next period's GNP, unemployment rate, bank mortgage rates, and so on may serve to make the $\tilde{y}_j$ conditionally independent. Let's denote the typical economic index by $\tilde{z}_k$, where k runs up to five or six, say. If the analyst decides to use these summary indices, then he is faced with assessing a joint distribution for these $\tilde{z}_k$. Perhaps he can go still another stage in the hierarchical assessment, or perhaps at this point it might be better for him to resort to a general dynamic econometric model that can provide the joint assessments of the $\tilde{z}_k$.

A Disclaimer

I do not mean these rather scattered remarks about assessments of several uncertain quantities to be in any way comprehensive; I mean them rather to serve as an appetizer or as a peek into a largely unexplored world that desperately needs some intensive cultivation. It is not difficult to give examples that highlight different pitfalls one may naively fall into, but once again this would force us to consider technical details that are more appropriately left to a more comprehensive treatment of uncertainty analysis.

5.   GETTING STARTED ON A DECISION ANALYSIS

It is often remarked that the most important part of a decision analysis comes in the first stage, where one considers the qualitative anatomy of the problem. "Not so," one of my colleagues remarked, "the creative stage is the one before that, the stage in which the decision maker decides he has a problem and decides to consider it in earnest." So far in these lectures, we have always assumed that there is an identifiable decision maker who has an identifiable problem. There are a host of intriguing questions that precede this stage of development, and in this section we shall consider such questions as these: Who is the decision maker? What is the role and responsibility of a decision analyst? How does one avoid choosing the wrong problem? How can one get the decision maker emotionally, intellectually, and administratively "involved" in a decision analysis? Is the cost of an analysis worth the benefits? How shall management decide whether they ought to adopt decision analysis? I wish I had a good set of answers for these questions. Perhaps the best I can do is offer a few rather disconnected comments to make you sensitive to some of the issues.

Who Is the Decision Maker?

Suppose Mr. Smith holds a place in the hierarchy of management of a large corporation and the corporation calls an analyst in to help him with a specific problem. Smith wants to know what *he* should do. So as far as the consulting analyst is concerned, Smith is the decision maker—the analyst must use Smith's values and judgments and the analyst must solve Smith's problem. Of course, Smith's values and judgments might derive from the expertise of others. Now Smith is not the corporation, and Smith's motivations may not be in agreement with those of his immediate superior or of the corporation president, the board of directors, the totality of stockholders, or of the society at large. An analysis of the same problem from the perspective of Smith's superior, say, might be quite different; and not only might the assessments of probabilities and utilities be different, but the structure of the decision tree might also be different. Still, Smith is the decision maker. In analyzing his problem it might be appropriate to bring into consideration the motivation and feelings of others; but then again it might *not* be.

To take a slightly different tack, let us suppose that Mr. Smith does not *decide* on action but *recommends* action to be taken by Mr. Jones. The analyst, however, is working for Smith and not Jones, and let's add that Jones can't be bothered with details. Here Smith and his analyst must be concerned not only with what Smith thinks but also with what Jones is likely to do, and the analyst might be wise to carry out an uncertainty analysis of Jones' reaction to Smith's specific recommendations. In addition, the analyst must help Smith assess preferences for consequences that are a composite of what Smith recommends, what Jones is likely to do, and what actually happens. They may have to incorporate uncertainties about political realities as chance moves in Smith's problem. Of course, all this is more easily said than done.

As a third case, suppose that Smith asks an analyst to study a company problem and suppose that Smith does not think of himself as the decision maker—in fact, no one seems to want to take ultimate responsibility. Here the identity of the decision maker is in limbo. In some mysterious way a decision will eventually be made, and *after* everybody learns how it has turned out the identity of the decision maker will suddenly come to the surface. In such a situation the analyst himself may be the "fall guy" if his recommended strategy turns out to be a poor choice after the fact; and equally, the analyst may not gather any glory even if his strategy turns out well.

We have assumed throughout that the analyst helps organize and structure the decision maker's thought process, elicits judgmental information from him and from his delegated experts, checks the internal inconsistencies of judgmental inputs, assists the decision maker in bringing these judgments together into a coherent whole, and finally processes this information and identifies a best strategy for action. Nowhere in these functions is the analyst supposed to inject his own personal views or biases. Of course, this demarcation of the role of the analyst is not always so clear-cut. In some circumstances, for example, the decision maker may ask his analyst to incorporate his own judgments. More importantly than this, however, the analyst can influence the outcome in a myriad of subtle ways: by what he chooses to incorporate in the analysis, how he phrases questions, the grimaces he makes in dialogue with an expert, the tone of voice he uses in an oral presentation, and the issues he may conceal behind a barrage of mathematical mumbo-jumbo. Indeed, in some circumstances it turns out that the analyst is the real decision maker and the alleged decision maker is the front man. It is therefore crucial for management to comprehend and intimately involve itself in the process of analysis.

A last point is that an analyst may find himself in violent disagreement with the preference structure of his client. He may also think that it's better for society if certain misguided individuals are inefficient rather than efficient in their behavior. Hence the analyst sometimes faces a vexing moral problem: Should he or should he not work for that immoral Mr. Smith?

Where Smith is a paragon of virtue and the analyst shares a common sense of moral values with him, things are perhaps easier. Still, if Smith insists on a critical assessment that the analyst finds really absurd, the analyst is once again in a difficult position. Should he use Smith's judgments? Or should he dissociate himself from Smith lest he be party to an action which might reflect unfavorably on his professional reputation? If the analyst cannot opt out, should he try to influence the results by the type of analysis he makes? Let me duck this question and merely remark that this is a grey area in which moralistic sermons tend to be a bit too simplistic.

Analyzing the Right Problem

In my first operations research problem, I fell into the trap of working on a wrong problem.* I was given a free hand to investigate how a department store could become more efficient in its sales effort. I very quickly became interested in bringing order out of the chaos that was a daily affair in the women's blouse subdepartment. On one counter, in particular, blouses were strewn about everywhere and the poor shopper was beside herself trying to locate her size. She wasted precious minutes because of the inefficiency of management. How easy it would be to arrange the merchandise neatly, and inaugurate a simple inventory replenishment scheme that would cut down the service times and make an orderly queue possible! After writing what I considered a masterful analysis of the problem I was invited to visit the store at opening time to see how the chaotic melange developed over time. Just before opening time, after the employees had got the entire stock neatly arranged and checked styles and sizes very carefully, they took the blouses out of their boxes, threw them on the counter, and very methodically mixed them up. Things were so inefficiently arranged that half an hour after opening there was

---

* One of the most popular paradigms in the theory of mathematics describes the case in which a researcher has either to accept or reject a so-called null hypothesis. In a first course in statistics the student learns that he must constantly balance between making an error of the first kind (that is, rejecting the null hypothesis when it is true) and an error of the second kind (that is, accepting the null hypothesis when it is false). I believe it was John Tukey who suggested that practitioners all too often make errors of a third kind: solving the wrong problem. I should like to nominate a candidate for the error of the fourth kind: solving the right problem too late.

a crowd of women milling about the counter, and this crowd, like a magnet, lured other bargain hunters into the melee. I learned. Now I make other mistakes.

In large hierarchical organizations there is often a tremendous organizational gap between the analyst and the decision maker. More than one analyst has made a complete study of the wrong problem because of lack of feedback between the decision maker and the analyst. Usually the analyst's work will not have been entirely wasted, but a precise answer to the wrong question is not nearly so desirable as an incomplete answer to the right one. In some circumstances, also, the analyst may isolate the real problem only to find that the decision maker is not sophisticated enough to recognize it, or to find that the decision maker is no longer emotionally involved in the problem and will not meet the analyst halfway. The communications gap must be closed if an effective relationship is to be established between decision maker and analyst. At each stage of an analysis it is critical that one check and recheck to see that the analyst is working on the problem that the decision maker wants him to work on.

In the initial stages of an investigation, the analyst should acquaint himself with the general qualitative nature of the problem. To gain some reasonable perspective and sensitivity for a problem area, he might then write out a few plausible scenarios: "If we do this and this occurs, and then if we do this, and . . ." He might construct a few "nonsurprise" scenarios, and then some on the pessimistic side and some on the optimistic side. Still in the initial phase, he might construct some fairly crude decision trees, put in ballpark guesses for some of the uncertain quantities that are not very important, indicate the sources of objective data that bear on the uncertainty at each chance fork, list the experts who perhaps know something about the uncertainties at the various forks, and record any apparent conflicts of interest that might distort these experts' judgments. He might write out descriptions of the consequences and implications that certain paths through the decision tree would have for the company, its competitors, and society in general. (We can associate each of these more detailed scenarios with a particular path through a decision-flow diagram.) At the end of this initial phase and before he assigns any hard numbers, before he probes experts for their judgments, before he begins to worry the decision maker with critical tradeoffs or substitution rates between diverse attributes, before he gives dollar values to intangibles, before he investigates attitude towards risk, and before he makes any tentative analyses of the crude decision tree, he and the decision maker ought to review the analysis thus far to see that it is addressed to the *real* problem.

The Involvement of the Decision Maker and the Need for Documentation

Management and the analyst should use this preliminary qualitative investigation as a communication vehicle, to get on the same wavelength, as it were. (One company I have consulted for insists on written documentation of this introductory qualitative report.) If a broad, qualitative, comprehensive description of the problem area is available, then it is easier for the decision maker and his analyst to jointly choose the facets of the problem they wish to incorporate in a more formal quantitative analysis, and to set priorities for the analysis of different subproblems. After they have completed the formal analysis, they can then investigate informally whether certain qualitative considerations that they omitted from the formal quantitative analysis tend to reinforce or to weaken the general conclusions. Documentation is important at each stage of analysis because it serves to facilitate the communication process, to crytallize agreements, to invite constructive criticism from impartial outsiders, and not least of all to train others in the necessary techniques and to record the development of the analysis for the use of other managers and analysts who may be involved with the same problem at a later date.

Finally, a critical ingredient that determines whether or not management will ever implement an analysis is the quality of the involvement of the decision maker in the analytical *process*. Of course, this involvement can be overdone. It can become too demanding.

Is It Worth the Effort?

People often ask, "How do you know whether or not it is worth the effort to make a formal analysis of a decision problem? Is this a decision problem itself? Can you do a decision analysis of whether it is worth doing a decision analysis?" I don't know anyone who can give definitive answers to these questions, and I suspect one runs into a messy and explosive infinite regression if he tries to incorporate considerations of these questions into the formal structure of a decision-theoretic model. Nevertheless we can make some common-sense remarks: If the problem involves millions of dollars, you probably cannot go too far wrong if you spend a few pennies, comparatively speaking, on systematic review and analysis. At the other obvious extreme, it takes a peculiar mentality to justify hiring an expensive consultant to handle a nonrepetitive situation in which the monetary issues are paramount and in which the monetary gains of analysis cannot possibly pay the consultant's fees.

The situation is a lot trickier in repetitive situations. It might be quite expensive to analyze the first one of a series of similar problems, but after that, subsequent analyses might be routine and comparatively inexpensive to perform. These issues are also intimately related to other issues we have already discussed in this chapter. Consider, for example, a situation in which a decision maker has three alternative branches to choose amongst at the very start of a decision-flow diagram. Suppose he has formally investigated two of these branches, and the question under review is whether it is worthwhile to formally analyze the third branch. The analyst may believe that in a formal analysis the third alternative will prove to be worse than the best of the other two alternatives, but he may think that even if he is wrong, the possible merits of the third alternative cannot be large enough to warrant the expense of the analysis. In this case, surely, he should merely prune this third branch, unless, of course, he can gain some insight into the evaluation of the third branch by a cruder and less costly mode of analysis. Is it worthwhile analyzing this? Maybe yes, maybe no; it depends. It's better, I believe, to keep such considerations outside the formal theory and handle them in a pragmatic, informal manner.

The Decision to Adopt Decision Analysis

As a member of a business school faculty, I am occasionally asked to lecture on decision analysis to top executives of large corporations. Invariably these executives ask if I can cite some success stories and some stories of failures. A few years ago I was rather hard pressed to furnish them with meaningful sketches but my repertoire has grown with the growing number of companies that are now adopting these techniques. After a while, one of the executives is sure to ask, "How should I decide whether or not this is some fad that will do more harm than good? I'm not worried about the costs of analysis—that's the least. However, I *am* worried about getting sucked into making a really stupid error. Would decision analysis, or whatever you call it, have prevented Ford from making their terrible mistake with the Edsel? Could you analyze whether or not I should give orders to adopt these techniques in my company?"

It is tempting to say that our method couldn't have cost any more. Seriously, however, one clearly cannot answer a question like this in very definitive terms. What is called for is a bit of weaseling. At one lecture I gave, an executive in the audience gave a good answer to a question very similar to the one above, and since that time I have often quoted his remarks with a few modifications of my own. He said, "My company feels these ideas are too new and too radical to use today on really big decisions. But these ideas are too promising to ignore altogether. We are encouraging our management to experiment with them and to actually carry out decisions based on these analyses for selected medium-sized problems in some departments where middle management feels that it makes sense to do so. We are keeping tabs on these developments. At the same time, we are monitoring some really important decisions on paper, insofar as that is possible, to see what decisions our management comes up with using our old seat-of-the-pants techniques and what suggested strategies come out of these more formal procedures. As yet, we don't allow the formal procedures to contaminate our intuitive analyses of major problems, but after a decision has been made we sometimes like to compare notes with those fellows who have been formally analyzing the problem on the side. When they're way off they complain they are not privy to the counsel of the top people, but when they're right they sometimes can raise some embarrassing questions. I think we'll adopt these techniques for some big problems in the future. Which ones these are will largely be determined by our internal politics and personalities, and by the luck of the draw." I think this is a good answer; perhaps a bit weak, but I suppose anything more requires a great deal more detail of specific circumstances.

You can't get around it, though: So long as men engage in big activities they will occasionally make costly mistakes. We can hope to reduce these costs and their frequency, and increase the benefits of the sucesses.

6. PROS AND CONS OF DECISION ANALYSIS

The systematic approach of decision analysis has its merits and demerits, and vivid testimony appears on both sides of the ledger. Also, what is a merit to some is a demerit to others. Someone might wax eloquent and say, "Decision analysis is great because it encourages the introduction of subjective judgments and preferences into the formal analysis." But others might retort, "That's a disadvantage, as I see it. Managers can now legitimatize their prejudices and misconceptions." It is true that dwelling on potential pitfalls and citing stupid abuses can undermine almost any list of favorable features, and on the other hand there are those who can see the brighter side of any sordid picture, who can even see the "civilizing" effects of war. Be this as it may, here are some of my rough evaluations on my score card. Obviously, of course, my tally comes out in favor of decision analysis; otherwise I should never have had the ambition and motive to give these lectures.

The Favorable Side

☐ The methodology of decision analysis encourages the decision maker to scrutinize his problem as an organic whole. The systematic approach forces him to come to quantitative grips with the interactions between various facets of his problem.

☐ The systematic approach helps communication. It allows each expert to give testimony about his area of expertise in an unambiguous quantitative manner, testimony that can be incorporated in the overall analysis.

☐ Systematic examination of the value of information in a decision context helps suggest the gathering, compilation, and organization of data from new sources.

☐ Analysis distinguishes the decision maker's preferences for consequences, including his attitudes towards risky situations, from his judgments about uncertainties.

☐ Analysis serves as a stimulus for the decision maker and his staff to think hard, at the time when it counts, about new, viable, alternative actions.

☐ A hard analysis helps the decision maker emphasize the point that the decision has not been made on frivolous grounds; he can use it to communicate the rationale of his adopted strategy and rally support for it. Analysis helps put the arguments of an opposing point of view in perspective. "Yes, these factors are cogent but we incorporated them in our analysis and found that they were outweighed by consideration of this, this, and this." By the same token, if the factors have not been included, this is immediately laid bare.

☐ The methodology of decision analysis is useful as a mediating device in situations in which the advisors to a decision maker disagree about an appropriate course of action, provided that the advisors are men of goodwill who want to get at the heart of the matter and are not concerned with dysfunctional polemics. By decomposing the problem into its basic parts, they can quickly focus on those issues on which they have fundamental disagreements. Even though these advisors might not be able to agree on a course of action, they might be able to agree on the qualitative structure of the problem, or perhaps on the evaluation of consequences, or on the assessments of probabilities. Hopefully they might even agree on *why* they disagree. If they disagree on assessments of probabilities, are they all privy to a common pool of information? Can they agree that certain data gathering, sampling, and experimentation will furnish objective information that will bring them closer together? This process of deliberation need not necessarily culminate in sweet agreement (indeed, it may heighten differences), but it surely will sharpen the specificity and sophistication of their arguments and may engage them and the decision maker in the kind of constructive dialogue that will bring them all to grips with the complex issues of his problem.

☐ Systematic analysis provides a framework for contingency planning and for the continuing evaluation of new facts that is necessary as the dynamics of a problem unfold. Not only does it suggest which alternative action should be chosen presently, but it suggests what could happen in the future and prepares a rationale for ensuing action. It provides a framework for continuous reevaluation of a decision problem that has a distant time horizon. The documentation of an analysis can serve as a briefing report for a new decision maker or staff man who is assigned to a problem area at a time when the denouement is still in progress. This documentation can also provide a dated record of expert testimony that can be used for calibration purposes; for example, "Jones' record in the past is better than Smith's, so perhaps Jones should have more influence now, all other things being equal." (Of course, this type of calibration might find divisive uses in an organization, and prudent executives should balance the benefits against the liabilities.)

The Unfavorable Side

☐ In hearings before a subcommittee of the Committee on Appropriations, House of Representatives, Eighty-ninth Congress (second session), Admiral Rickover unmercifully criticized the narrow advocates of cost-effectiveness studies. Since his statements are eminently quotable and apply with equal vigor to the methodology of decision analysis, let us start off the testimony on the unfavorable side of the ledger by seeing what he has to say.

"On a cost-effectiveness basis the colonists would not have revolted against King George III, nor would John Paul Jones have engaged the Serapis with the Bonhomme Richard, an inferior ship. The Greeks at Thermopylae and at Salamis would not have stood up to the Persians had they had cost-effectiveness to advise them, or had these cost-effectiveness people been in charge. . .

"Since the calculations are extensive and complex, the experienced people in positions of management responsibility do not have the time or the detailed understanding to review them. Judgment as to the weight that should be given to various factors in the analysis is left to the analyst himself instead of to the judgment of people who have experience in the field that is being analyzed. . .

"The basis for using cost-effectiveness studies as the rationale on which to make a decision is the assumption that the important factors can be expressed in numerical form and that a correct judgment of the situation can then be calculated mathematically. But for most complex situations this is an unrealistic assumption. Frankly, I have no more faith in the ability of the social scientists to quantify military effectiveness than I do in numerologists to calculate the future. . .

"Considerations which cannot be quantified are necessarily left out of the calculation. . .

"In my opinion the ability of the social scientists to calculate numerical values for military effectiveness is even less than our ability to calculate a numerical basis for many of the engineering decisions we are forced to base on judgment, experience, and intuition. To make the correct engineering decisions requires extensive knowledge and experience in engineering. Mathematical ability alone will not suffice. . ."

[Who knows how much informal cost-effectiveness analysis the colonists, or John Paul Jones, or the Greeks actually did? Perhaps formalizing their analyses might have led them to other choices, less desirable ones after the fact; and perhaps not. But what does this prove? Historians can provide us with loads of examples on the other side, examples of actions that were undertaken for highly emotional or mystical reasons or on the basis of wishful thinking, that have resulted in disastrous consequences which any reasonable, systematic analysis could have foreseen. Would Napoleon have tried to carry out his grand scheme of conquering Russia if he had given full weight to the Russian climate and geography? Still I believe Admiral Rickover is quite correct to caution against relinquishing control of a military study to analysts (social scientists or mathematicians) who are not themselves men of experience in military matters. Certainly a poor analysis can be far worse than no analysis at all. I suppose I differ with the Admiral about the extent to which it is possible to quantify intangibles. After all, if he prefers one bundle of intangibles to another bundle of intangibles, as indeed he seems to do, he has started already on the road to quantification.]

☐   The spirit of decision analysis is divide and conquer: Decompose a complex problem into simpler problems, get one's thinking straight in these simpler problems, paste these analyses together with a logical glue, and come out with a program for action for the complex problem. Experts are not asked complicated, fuzzy questions, but crystal clear, unambiguous, elemental, hypothetical questions. The trouble is that *these basic questions are the most difficult to answer*, and many decision makers shudder at the idea of thinking about these starkly simple, hypothetical situations. Indeed, in some circumstances it would be political suicide for an administrator to disclose how he would choose in a classically simple situation. Often he needs to take refuge in the complexity and fuzziness of real-life situations. It is true that one can often impute basic values and judgments to a decision maker on the basis of his revealed choices in complicated situations, but one can never be quite sure whether he chose A because of consideration of X or Y, or Z.

▢ Decision analysis requires the explicit articulation of a thought process. A decision maker may be able to grapple unconsciously with a myriad of interconnected considerations, but if he is forced to give a verbal description of his thought processes, it may appear that he is much more restricted in the complexity of his analysis than he really is in practice. The human brain can be a magnificent synthesizer of disparate pieces of nebulous information, and often formal techniques and procedures thwart and inhibit this mysterious mechanism from operating efficiently.

▢ Many critics of formalized, systematic analysis suspect that the breed of individuals who elect to go into this sort of work lack "heart"; that they are so concerned with putting numbers on everything that they bias a study in a direction that leaves out many human and artistic qualities and that analysis therefore inhibits creativity. "Everything is reduced to dollar signs or lives saved. But what about the quality of life? Sure, you say that this could be scaled and incorporated into the analysis, but do you do it? No. The methodology you espouse seems to narrow the focus and the 'hard' tends to drive out the 'soft', even though the 'soft' might be far more important in the long run. You seem always to feature those aspects of the problem that are readily amenable to analysis and to ignore like the plague those intangibles that really count."

[I don't disagree fully with this accusation. Much more attention should be given to "quality of life", and measurement techniques should be developed to (statistically) harden the "soft." It is heartening to note the rising interest of some of our governmental representatives and academics in the development of a series of social indicators* designed to measure quality of life.]

7. ONE LAST REMARK

Even if you don't analyze your decision problem by the methodology described in these lectures, you still must act. What will you do? In my personal opinion, one part of the justification for adopting the methodology of decision analysis is that the underlying behavioral assumptions are appealing; a second part of the justification is that this methodology is an operational mode of analysis (at least for many problems, and the class is widening); and the final part of the justification is, "What would you do otherwise?"

---

* See (1) Bauer, Raymond A. (Ed), *Social Indicators*, The M.I.T. Press, 1966, and (2) "Social Goals and Indicators for American Society", *The Annals* (of the American Academy of Political and Social Science), Volume I (May 1967) and Volume II (September 1967).

CHAPTER 10

FURTHER PERSPECTIVES,
AND A GUIDE
TO THE LITERATURE

1. SUBJECTIVE PROBABILITY: HISTORICAL PERSPECTIVES

Man's concern with probabilities goes back to the earliest of times. Gambling is an obvious example—backgammon boards were buried with the Pharaohs, and perhaps even the cavemen tossed a bone to decide minor matters. It was Gerolamo Cardano (1501–1576)* who first formalized the notion of probability in gambling; but when he did so he worked from a base of folklore, an aggregate of the many secrets about proper odds that had been handed down from one gambler to another. Cardano, and literally millions of people before and after him who have been interested in the pursuit of gambling, have defined the probability of an event, such as obtaining a seven in the roll of two dice, as the ratio of the number of favorable outcomes to the total number of possible equally likely outcomes. If someone had argued that since there is a total of eleven possibilities for the sum of two dice and since only one of these ways produces a seven, the chance of rolling a seven is therefore $\frac{1}{11}$, the practical gambler would simply have said (as he might still say), "You will go broke." Even a sixteenth-century gambler, for example, who did not have the benefit of any formal theory, knew from his own experience, or from what he had heard from others, that if you make a long series of trials you will roll a seven roughly one-sixth of the time. He would have

---

* An English translation of Cardano's *The Book on Games of Chance* appears in Ore, Oystein, *Cardano, the Gambling Scholar*, Princeton University Press, 1953.

felt quite secure in his opinion. Cardano put the point in more analytical fashion: He considered that since there are 36 possible ways for two distinguishable dice to fall, and since six of these 36 ways produce a seven, the probability of producing a seven must be $\frac{6}{36}$, or $\frac{1}{6}$. We might note that the reason it is appropriate to use the number 36 as the denominator in this fraction is because each of the 36 outcomes is equally likely to occur. It is *not* appropriate to use the number 11 for the denominator, because it is not true that each of the eleven possible sums is equally likely to occur.

Although early writers used the analytical definition of probability as a ratio of favorable cases to the total number of equally likely cases, the empirical-frequency interpretation of probability remained in the background as a useful check on the appropriateness of the "equally likely" designation. This frequency interpretation helped to clarify such questions as "What is the probability of a seven in a roll of a pair of deformed dice?" Although it wasn't until 1837 that Denis Poisson formally defined probability as a limit of a long-run relative frequency, I am sure that gamblers long before the time of Poisson (and before Cardano for that matter) quoted odds based on frequency of occurrence in a limited number of trials. So long as one deals with repetitive phenomena of a standardized variety such as occur in games of chance, in actuarial science, in genetics, and in statistical mechanics, the relative-frequency point of view and the classical view, equating probability to the ratio of favorable to total cases, are adequate. True, certain critical philosophical issues are bothersome: What does one mean by "outcomes are equally likely in an objective sense"? What is the empirical meaning of "It is *almost* a certainty that a relative frequency will approach a limit in the long run"? Several great mathematicians have in fact attempted to clean up these fine points, unsuccessfully so far as I am concerned. At any rate, these philosophical issues did not inhibit the constructive application of the theory of probability.

In his *Ars Conjectandi* (1713), James Bernoulli enunciated an alternative to the objectivistic view that probability is a physical concept such as a limiting relative frequency or a ratio of physically described possibilities. He suggested that probability is a "degree of confidence"—later writers use degree of "belief"—that an individual attaches to an uncertain event, and that this degree depends on his knowledge and can vary from individual to individual. There are at least two associated views that I ought to mention here. Pierre Simon de Laplace, in *A Philosophical Essay on Probabilities**, stated that probability is but the "expression of man's ignorance" and that the probability calculus is

---

* English translation of the fifth (1825) edition of Laplace's treatise, Truscott and Emory, Dover, 1952.

relevant to "the most important questions of life" and not just to repetitive games of chance. And Augustus De Morgan in his *Formal Logic* (1847) argued that "By degree of probability we really mean, or ought to mean, degree of belief . . ."

Let's now jump to the twentieth century, first to the works of Jeffreys and Keynes and then to those of Ramsey. In the period preceding the 1920s, one finds that although philosophers, who are naturally more concerned with logical foundations than with specific applications, maintained an interest in the Laplace-De Morgan interpretation of probability as a "degree of belief", statisticians and others who used probability theory concentrated exclusively on either the classical or the relative-frequency interpretation of probability. An impressive triumvirate at Cambridge University challenged this division of interest. In his *A Treatise on Probability* (Macmillan, 1921), John M. Keynes took the position that a probability expresses the *rational* degree of belief that should hold logically between a set of propositions (taken as given hypotheses) and another proposition (taken as the conclusion). Jeffreys adopted a similar point of view, which he best expressed in his *Theory of Probability* (third edition, Oxford, 1961). The first edition of Jeffrey's work appeared in 1939 and some writers describe Jeffreys as a follower of Keynes. However, in the preface to his third edition Jeffreys wrote:

> Without wishing to disparage Keynes, I must point out that the first two papers by [Dorothy] Wrinch and me in the *Philosophical Magazine* of 1919 and 1921 preceded the publication of Keynes' book. What resemblance there is between the present theory and that of Keynes is due to the fact that Broad, Keynes, and my collaborator had all attended the lectures of N. E. Johnson. Keynes' distinctive contribution was the assumption that probabilities are only partially ordered [implying that not all degrees of belief are numerically measurable]; this contradicts my Axiom 1 . . . Keynes himself withdrew his assumption in his biographical essay on F. P. Ramsey [in *Essays in Biography*, Macmillan, 1933].*

Frank Plumpton Ramsey was the first, so far as I am aware, to express an operational theory of action based on the dual, intertwining notions of judgmental probability and utility. In his essay "Truth and Probability" (1926)†, Ramsey adopted what is now termed the subjective or decision-theoretic point of view. To Ramsey, probability is *not* the expression of a logical, rational, or necessary degree of belief, the view held by Keynes and Jeffreys, but rather

---

* Reprinted by permission of the Clarendon Press, Oxford.
† This paper is reprinted in *Studies in Subjective Probability*, a series of papers edited by Kyberg and Smokler, published by Wiley, 1964.

an expression of a subjective degree of belief interpreted as operationally meaningful in terms of willingness to act or of overt betting behavior. Ramsey died four years later, in 1930, at the tragically early age of 26. Besides his essay on probability, Ramsey is recognized today for his pathbreaking contributions to the theory of optimal economic growth and the problem of decidability in mathematical logic.

A second essay in the Kyberg-Smokler *Studies* that deserves to be mentioned in a short synopsis of historical developments is Bruno De Finetti's "Foresight: Its Logical Laws, Its Subjective Sources", originally published in 1937. De Finetti, like Ramsey and also Borel (see Kyberg-Smokler), assesses a person's degree of belief by examining his overt betting behavior. By insisting on the assumption that a series of bets be internally consistent or coherent, in the sense that a shrewd operator cannot make a sure profit or "book" regardless of which uncertain event occurs, De Finetti demonstrates that a person's degrees of belief—his subjective probability assignments, if you will—must satisfy the usual laws of probability. In his contribution to the Kyberg-Smokler *Studies*, De Finetti appended this footnote as an afterthought to his 1937 paper.*

> Such a formulation could better, like Ramsey's, deal with expected *utilities*; I did not know of Ramsey's work before 1937, but I was aware of the difficulty of money bets. I preferred to get around it by considering sufficiently small stakes, rather than build up a complex theory to deal with it.

Von Neumann and Morgenstern developed the modern probabilistic theory of utility in their second edition of *Theory of Games and Economic Behavior*, published in 1947. These authors, however, deal exclusively with probabilities of the canonical variety;† that is, with drawings from an urn where each elemental outcome is deemed "equally likely". Evidently they also were not aware of the published work of Ramsey. For further historical remarks about the tortuous development of utility theory, from the correspondence of Daniel Bernoulli and Gabriel Cramer in 1731 through Alfred Marshall, Frank Ramsey, and von Neumann and Morgenstern, see William Fellner's *Probability and Profit* (Irwin, 1965), especially Chapter 3, "Postulates underlying modern theories of utility and probability".

Even this sketchy historical account of the subjectivist point of view in decision theory would be incomplete if I did not mention the influence of the

---

* Reprinted with permission of Wiley.

† In a footnote on p. 19, however, the authors state that if one objects to the frequency interpretation of probability, then probability and utility can be axiomatized together.

eminent mathematical statistician, Abraham Wald. Continuing in the tradition of the Neyman-Pearson school of statistics, Wald formulated the basic problem of statistics as a *problem of action*. You will find the most complete account of his work in his *Statistical Decision Functions* (Wiley, 1950). (I must warn you that this is an advanced mathematical monograph.) The problem Wald poses is an abstract embellishment of the basic problem posed to *you* in Chapters 5, 6, and 7. He analyzed the general problem in terms of a normal-form analysis (see Chapter 6), and the problem as he states it boils down to selecting a best strategy for statistical experimentation and action when the true state of the world is unknown. If we denote the typical strategy by σ and the typical possible state by θ, in conformity with our notation in Chapter 6, then by mathematical analysis we can compute (or derive) an expression $v(\sigma|\theta)$ that gives the "expected worth" of σ *if θ happens to be the true state.* (Wald works with "loss" rather than "worth", but this is a minor difference.) Wald assumed that for any given state θ it is appropriate to use *expected v-units* as a summary measure. In other words, without explicitly stating it, he assumed that the utility function over the v-scale is linear, or else the v-scale is in terms of utilities to begin with.

Wald was primarily concerned with characterizing those strategies for experimentation and action which are *admissible* or *efficient* for wide classes of prototypical statistical problems. If you refer back to Fig. 6.2 and the case of two possible θ-values θ_1 and θ_2, you will remember that a strategy is admissible if its evaluation falls on the northeast boundary of the joint evaluation set; or, in other words, a strategy is admissible if there does *not* exist another strategy with at least as good or better conditional v-evaluation for each possible state of the world and a better one for some state. Although Wald's accomplishments were truly impressive, statistical practitioners were left in a quandary because Wald's decision theory did not single out a best strategy but a family of admissible strategies, and in many important statistical problems this family is embarrassingly rich in possibilities. The practitioner wanted to know where to go from where Wald left off. How should he choose a course of action from the set of admissible contenders? The feeling of Wald and some of his associates was that while this is an important problem, it is really not a problem of mathematical statistics; they felt that there just is no scientifically objective way to make this final choice: It is a matter of judgment.

Well, science deplores voids, and practitioners searched after further guiding principles. In the early 1950s there was a rash of proposals suggesting how a decision maker should objectively choose a best strategy from the admissible class. No sooner did someone suggest a guiding principle of choice, however, than someone else offered a simple concrete example showing that this principle was counterintuitive in some circumstances and therefore the proposed principle could not serve as the long-sought key. Instead of applying specific proposed decision principles to carefully selected decision problems, thereby determining whether or not each principle complied with intuitive notions of "reasonableness", several investigators in the early 1950s inverted the procedure: They specified certain compelling desiderata that any "reasonable" principle ought to fulfill and then investigated the compatibility and the logical implications of these desiderata. You will find a fairly full account of these developments in Chapter 13 of *Games and Decisions* (Wiley, 1957) by Luce and myself.*

2.   AN OVERVIEW OF STATISTICS†

First let me say a few words about branches 0, 1, and 2 in Fig. 10.1. Note that branch 0 stands apart from the rest. The parts of statistics that are included under branches 1 and 2 are primarily concerned with such questions as "What experiments should be performed and what conclusions should be reported about a population on the basis of a sample of that population?" In contrast to this orientation, branch 0 deals with analysis of masses of data that essentially can be thought of as constituting the population itself. Here the statistician is not concerned with drawing inferences from a part to the whole, but rather with bringing order to a seeming chaos. His mission is to glean fundamental insights about the data; to explore relationships that help structure and thereby "explain" the data. In other words, he "reports without inference". To do this he must work the body of data over, "massage" it, as it were; and after he comes to understand what the data seem to say he must report the results in such a way that the data are self-explanatory. For further information, see the article by Frederick Mosteller and John W. Tukey, "Data Analysis, Including Statistics," in the (Revised) *Handbook of Social Psychology*, edited by Gardner Lindzey and Elliott Aronson, to appear in 1968 (Addison-Wesley).

---

* I, for one, adopted the subjectivist, Bayesian platform (use of subjective probabilities and utilities) gradually and begrudgingly in the early 1950s. It's not easy to give up an identification with "scientific objectivity". At that time I was influenced mostly by Cowles Commission preprints of papers by H. Chernoff, H. Rubin, J. Marshak, K. Arrow, and L. J. Savage. But my intellectual conversion from the objectivistic to the subjectivistic school did not carry any emotional convictions until I began working with Robert Schlaifer on concrete decision problems in business.

† This section takes its organization from the taxonomic display in Fig. 10.1. Comments about the display are headed by numbers that agree with those on the figure.

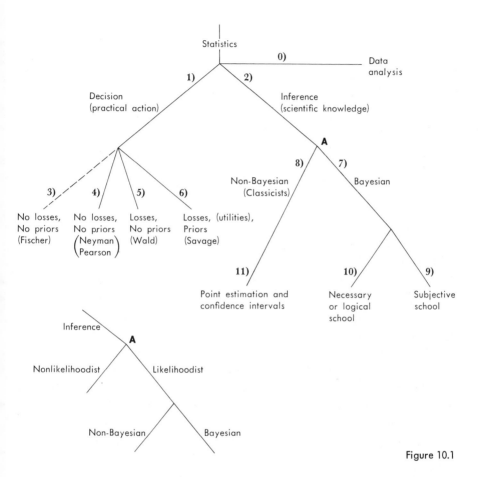

Figure 10.1

Now let's examine the rest of the taxonomy of Fig. 10.1. As we discuss the different schools of statistical thought, it will be helpful if we keep this example in mind. Suppose we are interested in the unknown proportion $\tilde{p}$ of individuals in a target population who will successfully complete a given task after they are exposed to a new indoctrination and training program. Let us assume that we know the proportion of successful completions using an old, well-established training process is .25. On the basis of a small sample of subjects trained with the new process, what can we say about the unknown new proportion $\tilde{p}$ and about its comparison with the old proportion .25?

1), 2) Statistical problems can usually be assigned to one of two major groups: problems of *decision* and of *inference*. I say "usually", because it may be difficult to decide in a given instance whether the problem falls in one category or another. Wallis and Roberts say that

> the purposes for which statistical data are collected can be grouped into two broad categories which may be described loosely as *practical action* and *scientific knowledge* . . . For statistics the important difference between the two purposes is that in practical action the alternatives being considered can be listed and, in principle at least, the consequences of taking each can be evaluated for each possible set of subsequent developments; whereas scientific knowledge may be employed by persons unknown and for decisions not anticipated by the scientist.*

The words "practical" and "scientific" are unfortunately loaded with connotations of value judgments and therefore I prefer to use "decision" instead of "practical action" and "inference" instead of "scientific knowledge". The pure theoretical physicist, for example, is often faced with practical action (or decision) problems in his quest for "truth", and the businessman may wish to conduct a consumer survey for general "scientific knowledge".

3) I have decomposed the decision category into four schools and labeled each with the name of its principal advocate. In the diagram I have used a broken rather than a solid line to indicate the Fisherian school since R. A. Fisher† and most of his disciples would feel uncomfortable indeed if they were categorized in the decision camp. I chose to include Fisher in this category since there is an aspect of his work that should be discussed in any reasonably systematic account of the decision branch. The following interchange between a critic and an enthusiastic researcher typifies the Fisherian philosophy on testing hypotheses, and I think it illustrates the aspect I have in mind.

Critic.   Of course, you would like to conclude that the new proportion is greater than .25, but you really should be more restrained in your enthusiasm. After all, if the true new proportion were indeed .25, the same as the old proportion, then there would still be eight chances in 100 that you would get an experimental sample even more favorable to your case than the one you did in fact obtain.

---

* Wallis and Roberts, *Statistics: A New Approach*, The Free Press, 1956, p. 4. Reprinted with permission.

† Most statisticians consider Sir Ronald A. Fisher (1890–1962) as *the* most important figure in the development of the theory of statistical inference. His most widely read book is *Statistical Methods for Research Workers*, Oliver and Boyd, Edinburgh, 1st edition, 1925, 12th edition, 1954.

Researcher.   But I am not at all discouraged by the experimental results and here you want to cast doubts on my efforts.

Critic.   Not at all. But it is good scientific discipline to play devil's advocate with oneself and not to include in the body of respected scientific conclusions results that may be wrong and that are only partially corroborated by experimental findings. I can reasonably say that you could have obtained your experimental results by chance *even if the true new proportion were less than .25.* I am not suggesting that your conjecture is wrong, but rather that you should suspend judgment until you get enough hard experimental data that you cannot explain, beyond a reasonable level of doubt, except by concluding that your conjecture is correct.

This type of analysis makes no explicit formal use of quantitative losses associated with various possible errors and it does not assign probabilities to states such as $\tilde{p} \geq .25$. It is primarily concerned with the probability of rejecting a null hypothesis, such as $\tilde{p} \leq .25$, if the null hypothesis happens to be true.

4) Neyman and Pearson[*] have argued explicitly that the acceptance or rejection of a hypothesis is an *action* problem. In deciding which strategy of experimentation and action he should adopt, the researcher should first evaluate the error characteristic of each strategy under consideration. This error characteristic indicates the probability that the strategy will result in an error for each possible underlying state of reality. Thus strategy σ_A might have an error characteristic such as the one shown in Fig. 10.2. The horizontal axis represents the domain of possibilities for the true new proportion $\tilde{p}$; the vertical axis gives the probability that strategy σ_A will lead to a wrong action or an error, conditional on the true new proportion's being any particular point on the horizontal axis. Figure 10.2 shows us that if we use σ_A, then there is a .03 chance of making an error if the true proportion is .15, a .10 chance of making an error if the true proportion is slightly below .25, and a .13 chance of making an error if the true proportion is .50. Ideally, of course, the researcher would like to adopt a strategy where the probability of making an error is low for each and every possible value of $\tilde{p}$. The rub is that for a given level of experi-

---

[*] Neyman and Pearson, "On the Use and Interpretation of Certain Test Criteria for Purposes of Statistical Inference", *Biometrika*, **20A**, Part I, 175–240, and Part II, 263–294. See also Neyman's delightful book, *First Course in Probability and Statistics*, Henry Holt, 1950.

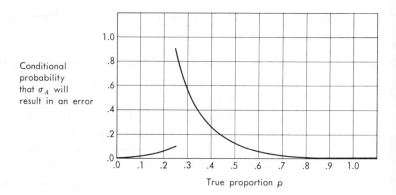

Fig. 10.2 The error characteristic of strategy σ_A.

mentation one can get better error control on one side of the critical value .25 only at the expense of getting worse error control on the other side. It is usually possible to get uniformly better error control by increasing the experimental sample.

Neyman and Pearson have also argued that we must keep in mind the entire error characteristic as well as the cost of experimentation when we evaluate the merits of any strategy. They did not spell out just how we should go about keeping these factors in mind, but presumably this should depend on the particular problem, on the relative seriousness of different types of errors, and on the researcher's guesses as to where the true proportion may lie. All probability statements are conditional statements about sample outcomes, given assumed values of $\tilde{p}$. *Never* does one assign probabilities to events about $\tilde{p}$, given sample results.

5) Wald, following in the Neyman-Pearson tradition of treating certain classes of statistical problems as *action* problems, went one important step further than Neyman and Pearson. He incorporated such concepts as cost, loss, profit, value, and worth of consequences in the very formulation of a general statistical decision problem. He did not scale these economic factors in terms of utility values, but he did assume implicitly that it was appropriate only to consider expected values of these economic factors. Also Wald did *not* assign probabilities to the underlying states of nature. In our illustrative example, he would not have assigned probabilities to the possible values of the true new proportion. He would only have used probabilities of the following kind: If the true new proportion is .30, then the probability of getting at least 20 successes in a sample of 50 experimental subjects is .085.

The previous section contains further comments about Wald's approach. You can also find a very readable treatment in a book by Chernoff and Moses.*

6) The Savage† School extends Wald's results by formally introducing both subjective utilities for consequences and probabilities for states of the world. This has been the approach I have taken in these lectures, and no more need be said.

7), 8) Let's turn once again to the *Inference* branch of our breakdown of statistics. Here, you will recall, we are concerned with such questions as "What does the experimental data say? What have we learned? What should we now think?"

The subjectivist or Bayesian wants to phrase his answers to such questions in terms of a probability distribution, describing his degrees of belief about the unknown true state. In our illustrative example, he might report as follows: "On the basis of my formerly held beliefs (described before) and of the specific sample outcomes, I now believe there is a .92 chance that $\tilde{p}$ is greater than .25, a .5 chance that $\tilde{p}$ is greater than .40, a .25 chance that $\tilde{p}$ is greater than .58, and a .05 chance that $\tilde{p}$ is greater than .72. For further details about my prior and posterior distribution of $\tilde{p}$, see Figs. X and Y."

The objectivist or non-Bayesian, sometimes called "classicist" or "sampling theorist", refuses to make probability statements about the population parameter. So far as he is concerned, the true proportion $\tilde{p}$ is either greater than .25 or not, and he chooses not to get involved in the subjective betting game in which one tries to formalize psychological attitudes. He only admits probabilities that can be interpreted from a relative-frequency point of view.

9), 10) Is there a *logically correct* degree of belief that one should hold about a particular statement, given a body of evidence? For example, suppose there is no available evidence about an unknown proportion $\tilde{p}$, other than the fact that a random sample of 50 subjects resulted in 20 successes. In these circumstances, is there a logically correct degree of belief that one should hold about the statement "$\tilde{p}$ lies in the interval from .25 to .35"? Keynes thought there is

---

* In *Elementary Decision Theory* (Wiley, 1959), Chernoff and Moses introduce statistics as the science of decision making under uncertainty. On page ix they say, "Our greatest debt is to Sir Ronald A. Fisher, Jerzy Neyman, Egon S. Pearson, John von Neumann, and [particularly to] Abraham Wald." The authors elucidate in great detail the various viewpoints of these eminent scholars.

† L. J. Savage, *The Foundations of Statistics*, Wiley, 1950.

and Ramsey thought there isn't. But Keynes, in his biographical* comments about Ramsey, had second thoughts, and finally he seemed to side with Ramsey. Jeffreys thought Keynes made a terrible error when he was swayed by Ramsey. Among statisticians, Jeffreys would be acclaimed as the foremost advocate of the Necessary or Logical School. Savage, on p. 3 of *The Foundations of Statistics* †, sums up the necessarist position very succinctly:

> *Necessary* views hold that probability measures the extent to which one set of propositions, out of logical necessity and apart from human opinion, confirms the truth of another. They are generally regarded by their holders as extensions of logic, which tells when one set of propositions necessitates the truth of another.

Subjective views hold that probability measures one's degrees of belief as evidenced by one's betting or action behavior, and that there is nothing "necessary" about one's degree of belief. Of course, however, it does demand coherence or consistency in one's beliefs.

In Chapter 7, I indicated that to obtain the posterior density function of a population parameter ($\tilde{p}$, in our illustrative example), we must multiply the prior density by the likelihood function and rescale or normalize so that probabilities sum to unity. The likelihood function gives the conditional probability of the sample findings for each possible value of the state parameter. For our example, therefore, if the sample results in the outcome $\{S, S, F\}$, where S is success and F is failure, then the likelihood function, as a function of the true new proportion p, is

$$L(p) = p^2(1 - p).$$

The likelihood function is objective, based on relative frequencies. The prior density, on the other hand, represents the degree of belief one has about the population parameter *prior* to observing the experimental results.

The split between the necessarists and the subjectivists gains operational significance when we discuss whether there is a "scientifically objective" prior distribution that appropriately captures the state of "no prior information". The necessarists think there is a logically appropriate prior distribution and their posteriors build up in a formal manner on this prior. The subjectivists disagree. They feel the necessarists' suggestions for "informationless" prior

---

* Keynes, John Maynard, *Essays in Biography*, "F. P. Ramsey, 1903–1930", Rupert Hart Davis, London, 1933, 1951, pp. 239–252.

† Reprinted with permission of Wiley.

distributions are *ad hoc* and do not stand up to careful scrutiny; they feel the necessarists are seeking a scientifically objective basis for inference which will forever remain elusive.

If you want to delve further into this philosophical controversy, I suggest you consult the masters. In particular, read Chapter 4 of Savage's *Foundations of Statistics* and both the first and last chapter of Jeffreys' *Theory of Probability*.

11) The non-Bayesian or classicist chooses not to make probability statements about the unknown proportion p. He is interested, however, in reporting what the experimental data seem to say about p. His standard procedure is to give a point estimate of p and a standard error for this estimator, or to give a confidence interval for p. For example, suppose a sample of 25 subjects results in 14 successful completions. The classicist might report as follows:

a) An unbiased estimate of p is $\frac{14}{25}$ or .64. This means that if a very large number (say one million) independent samples of size 25 were taken, then the method of estimation is such that the average of the resulting one million estimated values would be approximately p. Furthermore, these one million estimated values would scatter according to a bell-shaped (normal) distribution about the true p, with a standard deviation of $\sqrt{p(1-p)}/25$. Therefore for p-values near .6 this standard deviation is about .1. Be sure to keep this variability in mind when you interpret the point estimate of .64.

b) On the basis of the sample, I assert that p lies in the interval .42 to .83 with *confidence* .95. By this I mean that I have in mind a procedure that associates with each sample an interval of p-values, a procedure that has the property that given a large number of independent samples, 95% of the associated intervals will contain the true underlying p. And furthermore, the particular sample that actually has been observed happens to have associated with it the interval .42 to .83.

Both statements (a) and (b) are frequentist statements that very delicately avoid assigning probabilities to the unknown true proportion. In particular, the statement about the confidence interval does not mean that you should give 95-to-5 odds that p lies in the interval .42 to .83; if you have a great deal of judgmental information about p before the experiment, then both statements (a) and (b) *are still perfectly legitimate statements to make* but they may not be strictly relevant for betting purposes. Also observe that in confidence-interval theory you must first select the confidence level and procedure and then the vagaries of the sample will generate a particular interval. You can*not* legitimately reverse the procedure—that is, you cannot choose an interval such as .50 to .75, say, and then ask on the basis of the sample what confidence you can place on this interval. Unfortunately, unsuspecting practitioners often interpret confidence intervals as posterior probability statements, and sometimes their interpretations may be misleading.

The *A*-fork. The fork labeled *A* in Fig. 10.1, the one that follows the *Inference* branch and splits into the Bayesian and non-Bayesian categories, can be further decomposed in a manner shown in the figure. There are many orthodox statisticians who are not willing to adopt all the arguments leading to the Bayesian point of view, but who are nevertheless swayed by the reasonableness of the so-called *Likelihood Principle*. This principle asserts that any information about an experiment and its outcome over and above the likelihood function is irrelevant for inferences or decisions about the population parameter. Bayesians, of course, agree with this principle. For example, if a medical researcher is concerned with the unknown proportion $\tilde{p}$ of patients who will recover from a new surgical operation, and if he has performed this operation on three patients with outcomes $\{S, S, F\}$, then the likelihood function is

$$L(p) = p^2(1 - p),$$

and it is irrelevant whether the experiment called for exactly three patients, or whether the surgeon experimented until he got his first failure, or whether he operated until he was summoned away to perform some other administrative duty. In each case the likelihood function is the same, and the likelihood principle states that the conclusions inferred from these experimental results shall be the same in all three cases.

Many basic statistical methods do not satisfy the Likelihood Principle. For example, tests of significance, confidence interval estimation, and unbiased point estimation violate this principle. Statisticians who are not swayed by the reasonableness of the Likelihood Principle feel that the experimental frame of reference cannot and should not be ignored; they particularly feel that it is needed to supply conditional probability assessments for other possible sample outcomes, which, in fact, have not occurred.

Bayesian inference and decision methods, as I have said, satisfy the Likelihood Principle. To get the posterior distribution of a parameter, the Bayesian multiplies his prior by the likelihood function and rescales. In posterior analysis he is never concerned with what might have happened but actually didn't.

Statisticians are particularly concerned about the implications of the Likelihood Principle for the sequential analysis of decision problems and for problems of *optional stopping*. Suppose a medical researcher wants to convince others that the cure rate of a new treatment is higher than of an old treatment.

If he experiments with the new treatment and reports part of the data that is favorable to his case, he is guilty of the cardinal sin of optional *selection* of data. No one would condone this. But what if he samples with no plan in mind other than to amass data until he builds up a favorable case for himself? He selects the stopping point for experimenting and then reports *all* the cases in his analysis, but he does not report why he stopped experimenting. Is this legitimate? Is it acceptable scientific practice? The likelihoodists, who include the Bayesians, think it is legitimate, and think that the optional stopping procedure is irrelevant to the analysis of the data. Nonlikelihoodists object violently. They argue that significance levels, confidence intervals, and so on must reflect the experimental frame of reference, and when he analyzes the evidential meaning of the data the statistician must bear in mind the biases of the experimenter who optionally selects his sample size to improve his point. The likelihoodists retort that since significance levels, confidence levels, and unbiased estimates depend on the stopping procedure and not just on the likelihood function of the observed sample, this is just one more argument against the appropriateness of using these classical procedures. The argument is joined.

The Likelihood Principle is a consequence of the behavioral axioms or assumptions leading to the Bayesian point of view. There is another basic principle, due to Birnbaum,* that helps elucidate the differences between the Bayesians and non-Bayesians. Birnbaum's *Principle of Conditionality* implies the Likelihood Principle but does not necessarily lead to the full Bayesian viewpoint. Before I define this principle, let me first describe a simple situation that illustrates how it may apply.

Suppose there are two tests, both imperfect, that a physician can use to ascertain whether Mrs. A is pregnant: a frog test and a bunny test. In a rather cavalier manner, the physician decides to toss a coin to determine which test to use—heads, he will use the frog test, and tails, he will use the bunny test. When he tosses the coin, it comes up heads, and the physician accordingly applies the frog test to Mrs. A and analyzes the results. "Wait," an enthusiastic assistant interjects, "don't draw any inferences or conclusions yet! I have just determined that the coin that was tossed is biased." Does this make any difference? Should knowledge about the bias of the coin influence the physician's evaluation of the evidence from the frog test? The Principle of Conditionality would say, "No".

---

* Allan Birnbaum, "Foundations of Statistical Inference", *Journal of American Statistical Association*, **57**, 1962, 269–305.

Principle of Conditionality. Suppose there are several experiments, each of which bears some information about an unknown state parameter $\tilde{\theta}$. Suppose we choose a particular experiment by a randomized device (that has nothing to do with $\tilde{\theta}$) and observe the outcome. Then the evidential meaning of the particular outcome of this randomly chosen experiment shall *not* depend on the probabilities of the randomized device leading to this experiment.

We repeat that the Principle of Conditionality implies (and is implied by) the Likelihood Principle. The argument I used in Chapter 4 in connection with the Allais paradox (see Fig. 4.21) is very similar to the Principle of Conditionality.

Further Reading

In London, in the summer of 1959, members of the Joint Statistics Seminar of Birkbeck and Imperial Colleges held a two-day conference on the foundations of statistical inference. The conference was divided into three parts. First, Professor L. S. Savage delivered a paper titled "Subjective Probability and Statistical Practice". In the second part, five other prominent statisticians gave short prepared papers putting forward alternate views on the foundations of statistical inference. The third part consisted of a spirited, informal discussion by the distinguished participants of the seminar. Thanks to the efforts of G. A. Barnard and D. R. Cox, the entire proceedings of that conference have been organized, edited, and published in a small 100-page monograph entitled *The Foundations of Statistical Inference*, by L. J. Savage and other contributors, Methuen and Company, John Wiley and Sons, 1962.

3. GAME THEORY, GAMESMANSHIP, GAMING, AND DECISION THEORY

Let's consider a problem in which we (you and I) must decide on a course of action in a situation in which one of our several uncertainties is the particular course of action some other actor, Smith, say, will choose to follow. If we choose action w_i and Smith chooses action s_j, then the consequence will depend on the chosen pair (w_i, s_j) and perhaps as well on particular values that other states of the world assume—rainfall, extent of oil deposits, and so on. Let us label all uncertainties other than our uncertainty about Smith's choice with the symbol n, as a mnemonic for "nature". So far as we are concerned, $\tilde{s}$ and $\tilde{n}$ are both unknown.* In this situation, we should presumably review all our information pertaining to $\tilde{n}$ and then assess a probability distribution for it

---

* Recall that a tilde $\sim$ over a letter indicates that the quantities represented by that letter are unknown.

by some technique or other. But what should we do about $\tilde{s}$? This is the problem I should like to consider now.

First, let's suppose that Smith is not even aware that we exist, that so far as he is concerned our w-choice has no discernible implication for him. In this case, I submit that we ought to treat $\tilde{s}$ just as we have treated $\tilde{n}$. We should use whatever information we have available to assess a distribution for $\tilde{s}$. This distribution is a systematic codification of our judgments about how we think he will behave. As part of our investigation we might put ourselves in Smith's position and analyze how we think he ought to behave, or how we should behave if we were he; but this bit of *prescriptive* research is designed only to help us with our probabilistic predictions of his actual behavior. Alternatively we might simulate Smith's problem in a laboratory and employ different people to play Smith's role; this would sharpen our ability to predict his behavior. That is, we might make a *descriptive* analysis of Smith's behavior preparatory to making a *prescriptive* analysis of our own behavior.

As we have stated it, this problem has none of the flavor of real problems that are treated in the theory of games, where one easily gets hopelessly enmeshed in interacting, reflexive arguments. It does not require us to think about what Smith was thinking about our thinking of Smith's thinking of our . . . Now let's examine the other extreme case. Suppose now that not only is Smith aware of our existence but also that our w-choice will materially affect his welfare. In addition, let's suppose that our interests and Smith's are irreconcilable: His preferences are strictly opposed to ours, and what is good for him is bad for us and vice versa. There is no point in getting together with him to discuss our joint welfare because there *is* no joint welfare; we are engaged in a duel in which there is no room for compromise. The late eminent mathematician John von Neumann provided a solution to this dilemma. As early as 1926, he proved the now famous minimax theorem* which suggests a rational mode of behavior for each of the players, that is, for Smith and for us. The theorem proves the existence of a set of strategies S^0 for Smith and W^0 for "we" such that

1) if Smith chooses any strategy in S^0, we cannot do any better than to choose a strategy in W^0;

2) if we choose any strategy in W^0, Smith cannot do any better than to choose a strategy in S^0;

---

* The classical work in the theory of games is von Neumann and Morgenstern, *Theory of Games and Economic Behavior*, Princeton University Press, Princeton, N. J., 1st edition, 1944, 2nd edition, 1947.

3) there is a so-called utility value u^0 of the game such that if we choose any strategy in W^0 we guarantee ourselves an expected utility of at *least* u^0 (regardless of what Smith does), and if Smith chooses any strategy in S^0 he guarantees that we will get an expected utility of at *most* u^0 (regardless of what we do).

If we believe that Smith is aware of this theorem, if we know that he can actually find strategies in S^0, and if we believe he will act according to the theorem, then we ought to assess a judgmental probability of unity to the event that his choice will fall in S^0; and when we analyze our prescriptive problem from the point of view we have taken in these lectures (that of maximizing expected utility), our best choice will be to select a strategy from W^0. Thus the strategic structure of the problem helps generate for us, in an objective fashion, an appropriate probability distribution for Smith's choice. The same goes for Smith when he looks at us. Furthermore, the theory is self-fulfilling in the sense that if we guess that Smith is thinking this way, then nothing suggests that we ought to act contrarily to the way Smith thinks we shall.

When we depart from this extreme case in which there are two players with strictly opposing interests, game theory has very little advice to offer us. True, it does establish a relevant vocabulary and a pattern of thinking, but it is silent when it comes to telling us precisely how *we*, as one of the players of the game, should go about analyzing our problem. One difficulty is that the theory attempts to be neutrally prescriptive, to give advice simultaneously to each player of the game, and it cannot accomplish this except in a small subset of strategic conflict situations. In the next few paragraphs I should like to sketch out different approaches to two-party conflicts. The question I wish to approach is "What should we demand of a theory?"

I think I know what to say about the desiderata of a decision theory that is to be used when one party is working against an indifferent environment (for example, a decision maker planning against machine breakdowns, or against other individuals whose actions are *not* basically related to his own problem). In one-party games, one might be interested in a theory of *descriptive* behavior—how people make decisions, how they rationalize their choices of action, how they learn, and so on; or one might be interested, as I have been in these lectures, in a theory of *prescriptive* behavior—how one *ought* to behave in complex situations to be consistent with some basic preferences, judgments, and principles of so-called rational behavior.

As we have seen, when we turn from one-player games to two-player games, the simple dichotomy of descriptive versus prescriptive becomes much fuzzier. In the *jointly descriptive* case, we should like to report empirical behavior in actual conflict situations. We should like to give a taxonomy of the concepts and motivations that are considered in actual practice, to rationalize observed behavior, to predict behavior by informal or formal techniques, to test hypotheses about behavior both in actual conflicts and in simulated conflict situations in the laboratory, and to contrast negotiating behavior in different areas—in labor-management differences, in duopoly situations, in tariff negotiations, in arms control, in civil disputes, in mergers, and so on. We might also wish to draw cultural contrasts in behavior between children and adults, men and women, different countries, different tribes, different races, and so on. Our reports might describe bargaining and negotiation as a dynamic process aimed at stabilizing convergent expectations, and we might attempt to explain why, in some situations, negotiations so alter the aspiration levels of the players that a zone of agreement comes into being while in other situations, negotiations lead to a hardening of interests that precipitates a showdown of sheer power. Our possible agenda is almost endless.

The classical theory of games takes a *jointly prescriptive* approach. It attempts to give advice to each individual in the conflict situation. While the theory provides profound insights into the limited class of game situations in which there are just two players with strictly opposing preferences for outcomes, it does not provide clear-cut guidance for action in the vast class of other game situations. Thus, for example, in two-person games in which the players are not irreconcilably opposed to each other and in which there are no communications barriers between the players (the case that is most relevant for arms control and labor-management conflicts), von Neumann's theory suggests that the players *should* jointly negotiate to eliminate all joint actions that are jointly dominated; that is, they shouldn't settle for a given outcome when there is an alternative outcome that both prefer, and each should demand from the negotiations at least as much as he can secure unilaterally. Which particular outcome the players ought to choose the theory does not specify, but rather says that this choice *descriptively* depends on the bargaining and negotiation behaviors of the players. Von Neumann and Morgenstern did not formalize or mathematize the strategic elements involved in this bargaining process.

One could tackle the problems of bargaining and negotiation from an *externally prescriptive* point of view. In *Games and Decisions* Luce and I have made the following observation.*

Let us suppose that the players of a specific cooperative game have restricted their attention to the negotiation set and that they are bitterly

---

* Reprinted with permission of Wiley.

bargaining over which point to select. The harder each bargains, the more he will probably get—except, of course, if he is forced to carry out a threat! This is the rub about cooperative games. It is well known that in such situations so-called "rational" people (and countries) frequently have failed to reach an agreement, and the threats have had to be carried out, to their mutual discomfort. For these reasons players are often willing to submit their conflict to an arbiter, an impartial outsider who will resolve the conflict by suggesting a solution.

We may suppose that the arbiter sincerely envisages his mission to be "fairness" to both players; however, there are not, as yet, any simple and obvious criteria of "fairness", so, in effect, he is being asked to express a part of his ethical standards when resolving the game. The arbiter can be assumed to want to suggest a solution which will seem "reasonable", both because he is sincere and because he may wish to be hired for such tasks in the future. Thus, for example, he would be mistaken to suggest a solution having an obvious alternative which is preferred by both players. Or suppose there are two different conflict situations and that everyone agrees player 1 is strategically better off in the first than the second; then the arbiter should not give player 1 less in the first than the second. In short, an arbiter will (or should) try to satisfy some consistency requirements. In addition, as with most adjudicators, he will be anxious to defend his suggested solutions with some fairly good rationalization. All of this means that he should be prepared to formulate and to defend the basic principles which lie behind his suggested compromises—they should not be completely arbitrary!

We then went on to describe compelling desiderata for so-called "fair arbitration" and to investigate their compatibility, their logical implications, and how they help resolve particular simple problems.

The spirit of these lectures suggests that it is most appropriate to consider conflict situations from a *one-sided prescriptive* point of view. How should *we* behave in light of our understanding of how our adversary might in fact behave? We want to build up a descriptive model of his behavior so that we may responsibly assess a probability distribution for his choices to help us determine what we ought to do. The difficulty is that we must allow for the possibility that he is thinking in a similar manner; he might guess at the type of analysis we might make to help himself decide what we might do and what he therefore ought to do. This level of his thinking will of course upset our original assessment of what he is likely to do. Such complications are very common in the business world, and they are devilish to analyze. They appear in advertising, promotion (for example, credit card distribution), pricing, bidding on contracts, introduction of new products, T.V. programming, and so on. In one circumstance, however, we may be lucky, because the more realistic and complex a problem becomes, the more difficult it is to engage in this kind of iterative, destabilizing reflection. In some situations we might be able to assess a distribution of our adversary's actions by studying the history of his performance or by studying the behavior of persons designated to play the role of our adversary in simulated laboratory games.

The analysis of one-sided prescriptive behavior in bargaining and negotiation is a fertile field. No one will ever have the last word; however, Tom Schelling has done a masterful job in probing this area in *The Strategy of Conflict*, Harvard University Press, 1960. He discusses such fascinating topics in gamesmanship as how you can make a threat credible by committing your honor, or by using internal pressure groups, or by delegating authority to someone who is known to have little flexibility for action; how you can signal your intentions to your adversary without a face-to-face confrontation; how you can store up credit by appearing to give in on minor points that you have disingenuously advertised as major concessions; how you can rationally exploit an irrational posture (i.e., play the role of a "madman"); how to complicate the issues of negotiation so that you can back down on a threat gracefully and without loss of face; when you ought to take a hard line and when a soft line; and when you ought to submit a conflict for mediation or arbitration. If you read Schelling's book and enjoy it, don't stop there. He has been prolific since that time, and his more recent writings both amplify and apply in diverse contexts the exciting ideas developed in his 1960 book.

In the last decade, several professional business schools have instituted courses of instruction in which students are required to play the roles of corporation executives in a simulated competitive environment. Some schools have gone so far as to tie the student's grade in the course to the status of his company in the game. Indeed, the story has it that one business school is thinking of demanding several years of industrial experience as a prerequisite for admittance, as a guarantee that the student is qualified to play an effective role in its business game. The business gaming models now in use have evolved from early designs that involved control of five possible decisions to designs that require up to 300 decisions for each of several corporations in a simulated industrial area. These later designs are based on complex models of the environment, and they require efficient handling of massive amounts of data which can be effectively controlled only by modern digital computers. As it is used in most business schools, the primary aim of simulation gaming is to develop a student's managerial skills through his experience with an active, dynamic, evolutionary situation in which he must make decisions and live with these decisions. Instructors repeatedly emphasize the point that while the student must pay attention to details of pricing, production scheduling, advertising, personnel development, plant capacity, capital accumulation, and so on, he must also pay close attention to the coherency and balance of these separate areas to make sure that he is treating the business as an integrated unit.

Although a complex simulation game represents a type of problem that conceptually falls within the realm of game theory, it is not clear how the theory can be used to guide the actions of one of the players. I believe, however, that this is a challenge that should be taken up in earnest by decision analysts, who after all purport to help decision makers in an uncertain environment. A simulation game can serve not only as a laboratory to develop skills of the general manager but as a generator of challenging problems that can help motivate and guide the development of relevant techniques for decision analysis. I am aware that some work has been done in this area, but not enough!

A few pages back I remarked that it is frustratingly difficult to assign probabilities to our adversaries' potential choices in competitive, interacting decision problems, especially if they are thinking about what we are thinking about what they are thinking, and so on. In such circumstances it might be appropriate to simulate the actual problem, let experts take the roles of our adversaries, play the simulated game several times (perhaps with different players), and use the experience of this laboratory game as another source of information that we can exploit to generate probability distributions for the choices our adversaries might make. Of course, we better have some justified faith that our experts understand the general motivations of our adversaries, or we can really delude ourselves. (When I use the word "adversary" here, I don't necessarily mean that we are in strict conflict; there may be a joint set of actions that we and our adversaries can take that will lead to commonly satisfactory returns to all.)

If we develop a simulated model of a real problem area that evolves dynamically over time, not only can we use it to guide our present actions, but, equally importantly, we can follow the denouement of the problem in real time; the implication is that at any stage we can use the model, the actual choices made in the past, and the pattern of information currently known to analyze what our present best choice should be and to anticipate problems that we may face in the future.

For further reading in game theory, I suggest the paperback volume edited by Martin Shubik, *Game Theory and Related Approaches to Social Behavior*, Wiley, 1964. At the end of the volume there is an extensive "Bibliography with some comments", which also includes references to more complete bibliographies. For further discussion of gaming, I recommend James L. McKenney, *Simulation Gaming for Management Development*, Division of Research, Harvard Business School, 1967; Martin Shubik, "A Business Game for Teaching and Research Purposes", IBM RC–731, Yorktown Heights, N.Y., 1963; J. P. Young, *A Survey of Historical Developments in War Games*, Operations Research Office, Johns Hopkins University, 1960.

4. OPERATIONS RESEARCH, SYSTEMS ANALYSIS, AND DECISION ANALYSIS

Formal, analytical techniques were extensively used to analyze military problems for the first time in those desperate days in World War II when England was facing her greatest crisis. Groups of scientists, including physicists, biologists, statisticians and mathematicians, were organized in *operations analysis* teams to help solve critical strategical and tactical problems. As an outgrowth of these activities a discipline was born, called "Operations Analysis", or, as the British prefer to call it, "Operational Analysis". As the discipline developed, the names designed to capture the subtle nuances of each particular domain of activity in the field grew in number. We now have Operations Research, Management Science, Decision Science, Cost-Benefit Analysis, Cost-Effectiveness Analysis; Planning, Programming, and Budgeting; Optimal Allocation; Decision and Control; and finally, Systems Analysis. I don't want to get bogged down here in an attempt to straighten out these labels. Probably any attempt of the kind would only cause further proliferation of names and hence further confusion.* But I would be remiss if I failed to indicate that some individuals will deplore my constant use of the term "decision analysis" in these lectures. They may feel that I have been concentrating on a rather small segment of a discipline known as Systems Analysis. Perhaps so; but my main concern in these lectures is the development of methods, techniques, and *attitudes* that will help a decision maker to choose wisely in an uncertain environment. True, systems analysts are also concerned with many of the things I have been talking about, but there is something grandiose about the term "systems" that would give a misleading impression of my intentions in these lectures.

---

* John Tukey calls IT "the field-of-many-names-sometimes-called-operations research".

I think a few more general remarks about these terms will not go astray. E. S. Quade, in a presentation to the Electronic Industries Association Symposium on *Systems Analysis in Decision Making*, in June 1966, said, "Broadly speaking, any orderly analytic study designed to help a decision maker identify a preferred course of action from among possible alternatives might be termed a systems analysis." In this sense, perhaps, I have been talking about "systems analysis" throughout these lectures.

As commonly used at RAND, "Systems Analysis" describes decision analyses of very complex problems that are rather loosely specified. "Operations Research" is reserved for those decision analyses of a more limited character in which the structure and goals of the problem are rather well-defined. Of course, there is no hard line of demarcation between the two. Thus Operations Research would comprise such problems as control of inventories, choice of the number of counters to serve a queue, inspection plans for quality control, scheduling of production, and allocation of specific scarce resources to maximize profit or minimize cost; whereas Systems Analysis would comprise such problems as determination of our strategic posture for deterrence, allocation of resources for space exploration, and development of a program to aid the poor, increase education of the disadvantaged, and decrease urban blight. The Operations Research literature includes many articles that illustrate how we can abstract a class of real-world problems in terms of a mathematical model, and then, as we specialize, generalize, and analogize, how we can squeeze the model to produce interesting mathematical results, whether or not they are of practical, operational interest. Articles written by systems analysts, on the other hand, tend to be much less mathematical; they are often merely accounts of how systematic, common-sense reasoning has helped structure a complex morass.

In their writings, most operations researchers and systems analysts stress the importance of using judgment in the selection of the model and the variables to be included in the analysis. They are also fond of pointing out that decision makers must use their judgment in interpreting the output of a model and that before they act, decision makers must think clearly about those intangibles, subjective feelings, and hunches that the model does not include. Schematically speaking (see Fig. 10.3), there is a judgmental gap between the output of the model and the real world. This judgmental gap may be so wide that the analysis does not pass the threshold of relevance; the analysis may fall short of furnishing meaningful insights into the problem, and hence the analysis may be (and all too often is) ignored. Analysts naturally prefer not to wind up in this frustrating position, and therefore they tend to be selective about the problems they choose to consider.   By and large, most operations researchers prefer to work on problems that are repetitive in nature and that do not require subjective inputs.   Those one-of-a-kind strategic problems, the analyses of which must be based to a large extent on the opinions and judgments of experts, have received only scant treatment in the literature of Operations Research, for this very reason.

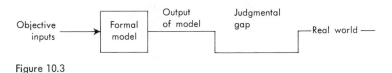

Figure 10.3

In these lectures I have indicated how a decision maker's preferences for consequences, attitudes towards risk, and judgments about uncertain events can be scaled in terms of subjective utilities and probabilities and how these can be incorporated into a formal analysis.   By these means it may be possible in some circumstances to reduce the judgmental gap and to bring the output of the model closer to the demands of the real-world problem; the model will then have more of a chance to pass the test of relevance.   We should also be aware that an analyst's methodological orientation and biases materially influence *which* types of problems he chooses to concentrate on.

Many operations researchers and systems analysts agree with my appraisal, but they add that important decision makers have not in the past and will not in the future engage in the kind of soul-searching demanded by the approach taken in these lectures.   "Imagine," they might say, "getting the President, a cabinet minister, or a general to bare his true feelings on hypothetical questions!"   Well, perhaps some of the decision maker's trusted advisors could play this role.   At any rate, I agree that a lot of teaching and learning has to be done; and even if these are done well, I acknowledge that their critical comment will still apply, but hopefully less acutely.

For a more detailed digest of the Systems Analysis point of view, see the compilation of RAND papers, *Analysis for Military Decisions*, edited by E. S. Quade, Rand McNally/North-Holland, 1964.   Although most of these papers draw their illustrations from military aspects of national security, the philosophical and methodological approach is relevant for planning and analysis in many nonmilitary fields.   The papers point out, in balanced fashion, both the effectiveness and the weaknesses of Systems Analysis.

5.   SKETCHY GUIDE TO THE LITERATURE

I know no better way to introduce you to the literature of the subject area of these lectures than to refer you to

Fellner, William, *Probability and Profit: A Study of Economic Behavior along Bayesian Lines*, Richard D. Irwin, Inc., 1965, 239 pp.

In the last chapter of his book, Fellner gives bibliographical commentaries ranging from a few lines to a couple of pages on fifty-two well-chosen titles. In addition, he indicates which of these titles include extensive bibliographies of their own. I see no point in repeating here what Fellner does so well.

In the remainder of this section I should like to add a few titles that have special relevance to our subject which have appeared since the publication of Fellner's book or which appeared before the publication date but were somehow overlooked.

Aoki, Masanao, *Optimization of Stochastic Systems*, Academic Press, 1967, pp. 354.

> The theory of optimal (feedback) control has received a lot of attention in the last two decades from control engineers and applied mathematicians (e.g. Pontryagin and his associates), and more recently from mathematical economists interested in economic growth. (See for example, Karl Shell (Ed.), *Essays on the Theory of Optimal Economic Growth*, M.I.T. Press, 1967, 299 pp.) The present book discusses the theory of optimal control when perfect information is not available. It uses the Bayesian approach throughout. The book is an outgrowth of class notes for a graduate-level seminar on optimization of stochastic systems. The book contains 143 references in its bibliography, mostly from the fields of control engineering, statistical decision theory, and dynamic programming.

Becker, Gordon M., and Charles G. McClintock, "Value: Behavioral Decision Theory," *Annual Review of Psychology*, 1967.

> An interpretive and critical review of the literature on models of choice behavior, both prescriptive and descriptive. The authors cite 207 titles. This review brings up to date the review article by Ward Edwards, "Behavioral Decision Theory," *Annual Review of Psychology*, 1961, pp. 275–284.

Edwards, W., *Bibliography: Decision Making*, Engineering Psychology Group, University of Michigan, Ann Arbor, Michigan, 1964, 41 pp.

Hadley, G., *Introduction to Probability and Statistical Decision Theory*, Holden-Day, 1967, 580 pp.

The author emphasizes the Bayesian approach to statistical decision theory, based on the use of prior probabilities and utilities, although he also gives consideration to statistical methods that do not make use of prior probabilities. The text is written in a mathematical style but most of the book can be read without a calculus prerequisite.

Pratt, John W., Howard Raiffa, and Robert O. Schlaifer, *Introduction to Statistical Decision Theory* (*preliminary edition*), McGraw-Hill, 1965.

A Bayesian introduction to mathematical analysis of the problems that arise when the consequence of action depends on the uncertain state of the world and the decision maker either has obtained or can obtain additional information about the state of the world by sampling or experimentation. Starting from basic behavioral assumptions, the authors argue that the decision maker should maximize expected utility based on a subjective probability distribution. The book discusses at length binomial and normal sampling, both univariate and multivariate. It uses the calculus throughout and matrix algebra in the latter part of the book, which deals with multivariate normal distribution, stratified sampling, portfolio analysis, and regression theory.

The book includes many of the results found in a less palatable form in Raiffa and Schlaifer, *Applied Statistical Decision Theory*, Harvard Business School, 1961.

Schlaifer, Robert O., *Analysis of Decisions under Uncertainty* (*preliminary edition*), McGraw-Hill, 1967.

An introduction to logical analysis of problems of decision under uncertainty that arise in the practice of business administration. Schlaifer and I adopt the same approach: The decision maker structures his problem in terms of a decision-flow diagram, assesses utilities (or "preferences", in Schlaifer's terminology) and judgmental probabilities, and maximizes expected utility. His book goes less deeply into the foundations of the subject than mine, and he chooses not to get embroiled in controversial topics. However, he shows in great detail how one can structure apparently realistic problems and how one can elicit responsible judgmental inputs from the decision maker. His book is much more of a how-to-do-it text, replete with exercises, than my own. The book was written to be used as a text for a course given to all students in the first year of a two-year Master of Business Administration program at Harvard. Therefore, although Schlaifer occasionally gets involved in some long and tightly reasoned logical arguments, he does not use mathematics beyond high school algebra. Nevertheless, the book can be rewarding reading for those who have far greater mathematical skills.

Schlaifer's earlier texts, *Probability and Statistics for Business Decisions* (1959) and *Introduction to Statistics for Business Decisions* (1961), both McGraw-Hill, are much narrower in focus than his present one. The earlier texts deal mainly with problems of *statistical* sampling and are not concerned with the vast class of business decision problems where formal experimentation plays only a minor role.

INDEX

THE DATA OF YOUR BASIC PROBLEM

Actions a_1: Guess the urn is of type θ_1,
            a_2: Guess the urn is of type θ_2,
            a_3: Refuse to play.

States The unidentified urn may be of type θ_1 (state θ_1) or of type θ_2 (state θ_2). In Chapters 1 to 4 you know that there are 800 urns of type θ_1 and 200 of type θ_2. The contents of the urn are as shown below (but remember that the urns are opaque!).

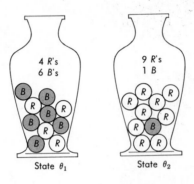

State θ_1 State θ_2

Payoffs

| | Act | | | Probability |
State	a_1	a_2	a_3	of state
θ_1	40	−5	0	.80
θ_2	−20	100	0	.20

Experiments e_0: no observations, at cost $0.00,
            e_1: a single observation, at cost $8.00,
            e_2: a pair of observations, at cost $12.00,
            e_s: a single observation at $9.00 with a privilege of another observation at $4.50. You also have the option of replacing the first ball.